BETWEEN FEMINISM
AND LABOR

BETWEEN FEMINISM
AND LABOR

The Significance of the Comparable
Worth Movement

LINDA M. BLUM

UNIVERSITY OF CALIFORNIA PRESS
BERKELEY   LOS ANGELES   OXFORD

University of California Press
Berkeley and Los Angeles, California

University of California Press, Ltd.
Oxford, England

© 1991 by
The Regents of the University of California

Library of Congress Cataloging-in-Publication Data

Blum, Linda M.
    Between feminism and labor : the significance of the
comparable worth movement / Linda M. Blum.
        p.   cm.
    Includes index.
    Includes bibliographical references.
    ISBN 0-520-07032-1 (alk. paper).—ISBN 0-520-07259-6
(pbk. : alk. paper)
    1. Pay equity—California—Case studies. 2. Pay equity—
United States. 3. Feminism—United States. I. Title.
HD6061.2.U62C23   1990
331.2'153'0973—dc20   90-37561
                                                                      CIP

Printed in the United States of America
9 8 7 6 5 4 3 2 1

The paper used in this publication meets the minimum
requirements of American National Standard for Information
Sciences—Permanence of Paper for Printed Library
Materials, ANSI Z39.48-1984. ∞

For Roger, and our son, Saul

Contents

Acknowledgments

Like many such efforts, this research began as a part of my graduate work in sociology at the University of California, Berkeley, developing into a doctoral dissertation and finally a book. Along the way I have benefited from the response and involvement of many people. I am most grateful to Michael Burawoy, my thesis advisor, whose intelligence, inspiration, and support throughout the dissertation and my entire graduate career were invaluable; without his heartening response to my first-term paper on sociological theory, I might never have continued. I also thank Arlie Hochschild, who acknowledged with much enthusiasm my earliest efforts at becoming a feminist sociologist and offered consistently supportive readings of the thesis later on. Michael Reich, the third member of my thesis committee, gave helpful commentary, many useful references, and provided, in his political economy seminar, a smart and sympathetic audience. My dear friends Louise Jezierski and Brian Powers, together with the other members of Michael Burawoy's dissertation seminars (1984–1986), also provided an important sounding board for my first attempts at drafting the thesis. But I am especially indebted to Vicki Smith for the generous emotional and intellectual support she gave throughout the dissertation stage.

Excerpts from this work were summarized in an essay in *Gender & Society,* to which Paula England, Judith Lorber, Barbara Reskin, and Ronnie Steinberg all gave thought-provoking readings. Development from dissertation to book writing was also spurred by the response of my good colleagues in the Department of Sociology at Ann Arbor, with special thanks to Howard Kimeldorf and Jeff Paige.

Others who read portions of the manuscript and offered help include Peggy Kahn, Polly Phipps, and Abby Stewart.

Rachel Kahn-Hut, Ruth Milkman, Barbara Nelson, and Judy Stacey each provided extensive, detailed, and instructive criticism of the entire manuscript. Their guidance has been indispensable.

I thank all sixty of my respondents, and especially acknowledge the contributions of Bill Callahan, Diana Doughtie, Mike Ferrero, Lee Finney, and Joan Godard.

Finally, my deepest appreciation and admiration goes to my husband, Roger Tobin, who in addition to offering unending love and moral support (as well as ever-patient tolerance of my kvetching) has thoughtfully edited nearly every draft of these chapters.

This research was partially supported by a University of California Regents Fellowship and a Woodrow Wilson Foundation Dissertation Award in Women's Studies.

One

Justice You Can Bank On

Recently the *New York Times* ran a front-page series entitled "Women's Lives: A Scorecard of Change," which began: "A quarter-century after the start of the women's rights movement, American women say that despite their gains, it is still a man's world" (Belkin 1989). What provokes such comments is no doubt obvious to the readers of this book: while women have made significant gains in the past twenty-five years, they are far from achieving equality in either the home or the workplace. As is well known, more than half of all women now work in the paid labor force and, like men, can expect to remain employed most of their adult lives. Yet most occupations remain sex-segregated, and most women continue to hold low-status, female-typed, dead-end jobs, earning much lower wages than men. The tenacity of these facts has led to a reconsideration of the agenda and strategies of the feminist movement. It has also created strong interest in a new set of strategies, the most significant of which may be comparable worth.[1]

Comparable worth, or pay equity, is a strategy to raise wages for women's sex-segregated occupations.[2] The different jobs that men

1. The title of this chapter, "Justice You Can Bank On," is the slogan of the National Committee on Pay Equity (NCPE).
2. Reskin (1987) and Evans and Nelson (1989) prefer the term *comparable worth* as connoting specifically the reevaluation of the worth of women's work. In contrast, others favor the term *pay equity* to emphasize continuity with the already-legitimated equal pay principle (Newman, cited in Hamilton 1986) and to evoke basic notions of fairness. Although the significance of language in politics is undeniable, in this case most analysts use the two terms interchangeably (e.g., Acker 1989, 229 n1; *Ms.* 1988; Thomas 1986, 278); therefore, I too use both terms.

1

and women perform can be compared in terms of requisite levels
of skill, effort, responsibility, and working conditions; therefore,
according to comparable worth arguments, pay for women's jobs
should be comparable to that for equivalently ranked male jobs. Although this line of reasoning is somewhat awkward and unwieldy
(as my difficulty in succintly explaining it demonstrates), comparable worth has emerged in the past decade as a useful tool to assist
low-paid women nationwide, mainly in public-sector employment,
through both collective bargaining and legislation. By latest count
all but five states and over 1,700 localities (including cities, counties, and school districts) have adopted pay equity policies or are in
the process of doing so (NCPE 1989d). Comparable worth has also
emerged internationally as a useful approach for working women in
several different countries (ILO 1986; NCPE 1988a). However,
while the practical benefits that pay equity has brought to low-paid
women are of obvious importance, my interest goes beyond these
benefits to the long-range impact on class and gender politics.

Comparable worth, as Joan Acker (1989) has brilliantly argued,
challenges the way gender is incorporated into the class structure.
Its central premise—that women are as valuable as men and are
equally entitled to a just "living wage," regardless of the value
the market places on their work—contests the ideological underpinnings of the existing, unjust system. I believe the ultimate success of this challenge will hinge on the ability to transform both
political discourse and the consciousness of employed women in
radical ways. In this book I explore such radical possibilities by examining the potential of comparable worth to mobilize or politicize
low-paid women.

The major actors in the comparable worth effort are the two
organized movements that might be expected to effect such a mobilization: the labor movement, which provides the major voice articulating subordinate class interests; and the feminist movement,
which provides the major voice articulating women's gender interests. I argue in this chapter that both are in need of renewed moral
purpose and an expanded constituency and, moreover, that both
have largely failed to mobilize low-paid women. This failure stems
in large part from labor's historical focus on class to the exclusion of
gender, and feminism's focus on gender to the exclusion of class.
Much of the radical potential of comparable worth lies in its ability

to broaden the discourse of both movements, to promote active alliances between the two, and to help push each movement in more progressive directions. But before I turn to this discussion of the labor and feminist movements, I will briefly outline the organization of the book.

In subsequent chapters I analyze the origins, the promise, and the possible limitations of the comparable worth movement. My primary focus is on two local efforts in Northern California.[3] The first case, presented in Chapter 3, is that of the city of San Jose. Often held up as exemplary, this effort involved a prolonged period of agitation and culminated in a dramatic and successful strike—the first ever for comparable worth. The second case, discussed in Chapter 4, is that of Contra Costa County, California. This case lacked the notoriety and the single dramatic confrontation of the San Jose effort, but here too, activists succeeded in mobilizing low-paid women. Because both cases represent grass-roots movements, they are not representative of all pay equity efforts; for my purposes, however, grass-roots cases illuminate the potential of comparable worth to transform consciousness and mobilize women in a way that studies of top-down or elite-controlled efforts cannot (Acker 1989; Evans and Nelson 1989; Steinberg 1987a).

But such studies prompt another question that threads through my analysis: To what extent does comparable worth face an inherent danger of becoming a top-down reform, losing the grass-roots emphasis I observed? Because many scientific and technical questions are involved in comparing men's and women's jobs and gauging the extent of female undervaluation, comparable worth may be framed largely as a bureaucratic reform to be administered by managerial experts and outside consultants. If such technocratic control were to be the general outcome, the issue would lose much of its potential to take on a politicized, social movement character or to mobilize low-paid women.

I also address several related themes in this book. Comparable worth, for all its radical potential, is a movement built on liberal foundations; it emerged—both nationally and in my case studies—

3. A variety of methods were used to conduct these case studies. Principally, I conducted in-depth interviews with participants and examined archival and documentary materials. In addition, I attended conferences as a participant-observer and collected secondary literature. Details are provided in Appendices B and C.

from the earlier liberal strategies of the feminist movement, notably affirmative action. This national context is taken up in Chapter 2, where I show that although affirmative action only marginally affected employment patterns, it had a substantial impact on political discourse, laying the basis for the more far-reaching comparable worth claim. I also show how the convergence of class and gender politics in the comparable worth movement emerged from a long history of class divisiveness within women's movements.

Following the case studies in Chapters 3 and 4, the second half of the book explores the implications, limitations, and possibilities of the comparable worth movement. Chapter 5 takes up one problematic aspect of comparable worth. In contrast to affirmative action, which directly attacks the gender-based boundary lines in the workplace, comparable worth leaves them in place, and may even reinforce them. Simply put, whereas affirmative action aims to move women into men's work, comparable worth aims to raise the value of women's work. In this chapter, then, I ask whether women may have a legitimate interest in maintaining such boundary lines.

In Chapter 6 I consider the limitations of comparable worth as a progressive strategy. The movement contains several contradictory tendencies, stemming from its liberal underpinnings, which can compromise its radical possibilities. These include the tendencies to universalize its appeal across both class and gender lines, to reify the legitimacy of occupational hierarchies, and to enhance managerial control.

Finally, in Chapter 7 I return to the central question of this work: What is the potential of comparable worth to politicize women and contribute to the development of a broader progressive movement?

Background: The Argument for Comparable Worth

The rationale for comparable worth stems from the widely accepted tenet of "equal pay for equal work": that men and women with the same jobs should receive the same pay. Because few women have the same jobs as men, however, this popular principle does little to advance women's interests. Comparable worth advocates argue that the principle should be extended, as objective measures show that women's jobs are underpaid compared with the equivalent male jobs. Much of the gap in earnings between men's and women's jobs therefore constitutes sex discrimination, which, according to proponents, should be illegal. It is not my purpose to document this claim. Numerous studies by economists find that a sizable portion of the wage gap cannot be explained by human capital differences, such as amount of education or experience; nor can it be explained by job characteristics, other than the percentage of female occupants (Treiman and Hartmann 1981). Women's lower earnings, according to comparable worth arguments, represent the institutionalization of past discriminatory practices and contradict any notion of the "free" market or the laws of supply and demand. Proponents thus argue that market rates should be disregarded, women's jobs reevaluated on the basis of nondiscriminatory criteria, and preferential wage adjustments assigned to bring those jobs to the level of equivalent male-dominated jobs.

The call for the reevaluation of women's work is not new. The notion that wage scales in sex-segregated jobs should be set by a standard of "equal pay for jobs of equivalent value" or, as Phyllis Schlafly is fond of saying, "equal pay for UNequal work," was implicit in the earliest calls for "equal pay for equal work." In 1908, for example, when women of the Bookkeepers and Accountants Union Local 1 of New York adopted that slogan, they compared themselves to higher-paid male hod carriers (Feldberg 1980, 57). A comparable value standard was first explicitly advocated during World War II, by a small number of women trade unionists concerned with the women in wartime factory jobs. After the war, with most women pushed back into full-time homemaking or traditional sex-typed jobs, norms of sex segregation took on renewed intensity, and the labor movement lost much of its New Deal–era strength. The notion of comparable worth wages for women lay dormant (Milkman 1987a; Steinberg, 1984b). As we will see in the next chapter, only in the last fifteen years, in the context of the "second wave" feminist movement and equal employment opportunity policies, has the idea been reintroduced.

Comparable worth can also be used to address racial segregation and wage discrimination in the labor market. Initially, however, race was not often raised in pay equity cases; it was not, in fact, raised in either of the two cases I focus on in this book. I can only speculate as to why this has been true in general, and must apologize for my own lack of analysis of this problem in my case studies. In some instances, race may have been overlooked simply because a low proportion of the concerned workers were members of a minority group (for example in Oregon, as Acker [1989, 13] suggests). In other cases, the lack of attention has perhaps been due not only to implicit racism, but also to a lack of cooperation among unions, feminists, and minority groups. Academic proponents of comparable worth, however, have worked to incorporate race as a part of the issue, as well as to show the confluence of interests between low-paid white women and men and women of color. Malveaux (1985–1986), for example, has demonstrated that minority workers are highly concentrated in female-dominated jobs and so are likely to benefit from pay equity. In addition, some of the larger, more recent state cases, such as New York and New Jersey, have included race in pay equity studies and policies (NCPE 1987).

The pay equity issue, because it contests the low wages and job denigration of the "pink-collar ghetto" (that is, of female-typed, female-dominated jobs), articulates the class and gender interests of low-paid women, both white and nonwhite (and, to some extent, of minority men). It speaks to groups as of yet poorly integrated into either the labor movement or the feminist movement. It is thus no surprise that both movements have embraced the pay equity issue. But as I will show, there are significant differences between the interests expressed by comparable worth and those posed by the labor and feminist movements. These differences may ultimately have important effects on both movements.

The Labor Movement

Historically, the record of the organized labor movement in representing working women has been poor. It has included the exclusion of women from male unions and male occupations, and a lack of support for organizing those employed in female occupations. Such tactics have reinforced the sex segregation of the work force and the marginalization of women workers (Foner 1980; Kessler-Harris 1982). To a considerable extent, these practices persist, but in recent years the labor movement has turned increasingly to women workers to shore up its position in the face of new economic realities. The labor movement's endorsement of comparable worth represents a part of this new turn. The issue was first formally endorsed by the American Federation of Labor and Congress of Industrial Organizations (AFL-CIO) executive board in 1979, but it was more enthusiastically embraced in subsequent years as an official part of labor's "New Agenda" (Bureau of National Affairs 1981, 129–132; Portman, Grune, and Johnson 1984; Shinoff, 1985).

Labor's New Agenda

As the smokestack industries of the Rust Belt continue to decline under increased world competition, the traditional constituency of organized labor declines with them. The white male workers of the capital-intensive, durable-goods manufacturing industries such as auto and steel have been the backbone of the American labor movement, yet their numbers are falling. In the reconfigured American economy, whether we identify it as postindustrial, post-capitalist, or advanced capitalist, the service sector has become the major area of job growth (Bluestone and Harrison 1982; Noble 1985a; Rothschild 1981), and the new jobs tend to be female sex-typed and to pay low wages (Hacker 1985; Kuhn and Bluestone 1987; Needleman 1986). Clerical work, which is extremely female dominated,[4] has become the single largest census occupational category, employing approximately 20 percent of the labor force (Cain 1985) and fully one-third of all working women (Bianchi and Spain 1983). The lower white-collar work force, which includes clerical workers, may be seen as constituting the "new" working class of the postindustrial era (Oppenheimer 1985). It may seem surprising to regard these as working-class jobs, since they are classified as white collar, occur in relatively "clean" settings, and often require educational levels that blue-collar jobs do not. Such jobs certainly do not, however, offer middle-class incomes, status, or opportunities for advancement.[5]

4. Slightly over 80 percent of clerical workers are women, but when several anomalous jobs are removed from the larger occupational category (such as mail carriers and postal and shipping clerks,) the figure may be as high as 90–95 percent female (Malveaux 1982).

5. Structural theories of social class have debated women's location. Giddens (1973) and Poulantzas (1975), most notably, have emphasized the distinction between mental and manual labor, and thus locate most female occupations in the middle classes. In contrast, Braverman (1974), Glenn and Feldberg (1977), and

Other white-collar groups involved in comparable worth are members of the traditional female professions. Nurses, social workers, librarians, and teachers may be thought of as middle class owing to their requisite college degrees and self-identification as professionals, but to occupational sociologists they are only semiprofessionals, lacking the theoretical knowledge, autonomy, authority, and status of the male professions (Etzioni 1969). Some class theorists consider the semiprofessions an upper layer of the "new working class," paralleling the position of the skilled blue-collar segment within the traditional working class (although their earnings are considerably lower) and thus a potentially organizable group (Oppenheimer 1985, 9–19).[6]

In the past the union movement demonstrated little interest in organizing white-collar women, casting them as "unorganizable" because they did not easily identify with labor. There was some truth to this stereotype: women remained primarily identified as homemakers, saw their jobs as temporary, and may have felt superior to blue-collar workers. As late as the 1950s and 1960s, unions lost elections in shops with large numbers of women clericals (Oppenheimer 1985, 165). Yet managerial strategies that exacerbate gender differences to ensure a docile, low-paid work force bear much of the blame, for management shapes a paternalistic structure and an "intimacy" within the office in which union organizing is branded as personal disloyalty. Furthermore, the sexism of the male labor movement itself turned the stereotype of

---

others (e.g., Wright 1982, esp. 128) argue that the deskilling of office work has made the mental/manual distinction meaningless. In response to this debate, West (1978, 235) aptly observed: "Women occupy the most disputed terrain of the class structure."

Since a primary purpose of this book is to discern the political role of low-paid women, I adopt the class categorization articulated or implied by participants themselves. Clearly, the major purpose of most class theorizing is to discern what political role particular classes and class fractions may play. However, as many analysts point out (e.g., Acker 1989; Thompson 1963), this cannot be determined simply by structural location but must be examined in the context of concrete movements and political conflicts.

6. The semiprofessions are also vulnerable to deskilling processes (Oppenheimer 1985, 143–155), and this vulnerability, in addition to low earnings, flat career trajectories, and female sex typing, creates the close alliance of interests between clerical and professional women demonstrated in the comparable worth movement.

women's antiunionism into a self-fulfilling prophecy. Even progressive organizers like those of the CIO in the 1930s tended to assume it was a woman's "nature" to be a loyal "office wife" (Strom 1985; also Feldberg 1980; Foner 1980; Kessler-Harris 1982; Lynch 1986; Nussbaum 1980).

Even as women formed an increasing proportion of the labor force, the sexist practices of the union movement remained entrenched (Moore and Marsis 1983b). Between 1954 and 1977, 75 percent of resources for organizing efforts went toward the goods-producing sectors, whereas 90 percent of the new jobs—the jobs bringing women into the labor force—were in the service sector (cited in Baden 1986, 244). The lack of resources for organizing women represented one aspect of the AFL-CIO's generally conservative stance. Labor leaders continually emphasized their own interests, the interests of white, male, skilled workers, over those of other segments of the working class. In 1972, for example, George Meany, AFL-CIO president, commented: "Why should we worry about organizing groups of people who do not want to be organized?" (cited in Edsall 1984, 151). Only in the past decade, with the decline of the traditional industrial sector, has organized labor turned its attention to such other groups in hopes of shoring up the movement.

Gaining a foothold in the pink-collar sector became a goal of several unions in the 1980s. The Teamsters increased their female membership greatly; they are now second only to the National Education Association in the number of women members (Milkman 1985). The United Auto Workers (UAW) elevated its pink-collar organizing branch, District 65, from an affiliate to a full-fledged department in order to "lead a campaign to enlist white-collar workers across the nation" (Prial 1987 B3). Service Employees International Union, along with the women's organization 9 to 5, established District 925, which, like the UAW's District 65, aims to organize in the pink-collar ghetto (Baden 1986; Milkman 1985; Needleman 1988). Also, though with only mixed success, the AFL-CIO has directed major resources toward a multiunion organizing effort at Blue Cross/Blue Shield, one of the nation's largest health insurance companies and a huge employer of clerical labor (Noble 1986a; Serrin 1986).

Even prior to these efforts, the gender composition of labor union membership had been shifting; indeed, by mid-decade some observers claimed we were witnessing the "feminization" of the union movement (Milkman 1985, 304).[7] In fact, the growth in female white-collar union membership has represented the largest increase in unionization in the last fifteen years (Freeman and Leonard 1985). Much of this unionization has occurred in the public sector, where the demand for female labor between 1950 and 1970 rose dramatically with the growth in state employment;[8] within public-sector unions, women make up nearly half the membership (Freeman and Leonard 1985). Yet, as several feminist analysts point out, these new union members were not recruited as "women," or with particular sensitivity to gender issues. Rather, they were brought in as specific occupational groups in which women happened to predominate, as labor moved to organize the public sector, first in education, then in the health services, and finally among clericals and social service agencies (Bell 1985; Milkman 1985; Moore and Marsis 1983b). The emergence of feminist issues such as comparable worth has been primarily an unintended consequence of this shift in membership within the larger context created by the women's movement.

Nevertheless, as a result of the "feminization" of membership, some unions are making sincere commitments to address women's concerns and are becoming leaders in shaping labor's new agenda. Baden (1986) studied fifteen national unions, each having a minimum of 100,000 female members, and found that at least five had committed significant organizational resources to women's con-

7. From only 18 percent of all union members in 1960, by 1980 women were 30 percent of labor group adherents (Needleman 1986, 228); and by 1984 women were 33.7 percent of total union membership, the highest proportion ever (*Monthly Labor Review* 1985, 29).

8. After civil service reforms allowing collective bargaining by public-sector employees were implemented in the 1960s, organized labor began to carve out this new base (Oppenheimer 1985, 167–169). While only 15.8 percent of white-collar workers in general are currently unionized, in the public sector nearly 40 percent of employees are union members. Furthermore, while in the private sector women are less than half as likely as men to belong to a union (less than 10 percent, compared to just over 20 percent), in the public sector women and men are unionized in roughly equivalent proportions (38.1 percent and 39.2 percent, respectively). As a proportion of total union membership, women in private-sector unions account for just under one-third (Freeman and Leonard 1985).

cerns, with public-sector unions being among the best. The American Federation of State, County, and Municipal Employees (AFSCME), for example, with over 400,000 women members, has been a leader in comparable worth efforts (AFSCME 1983). Baden also found that the number of women in leadership positions, while still low, had been increasing through the 1980s.

Although formidable obstacles remain to the full incorporation of women into the labor movement, several analysts see a far greater potential gain from "feminization" than just the addition of new members. They see the possibility for a much-needed revitalization of the movement as women's concerns and greater family orientation may provide a catalyst for humanizing the workplace and the internal structure of unions. Lynch (1986), for example, contends that the most decisive factor in successful organizing is the attention to interpersonal dynamics, to building individual recognition, trust, and openness between workers and union leaders— all features of more "feminine" styles. Similarly, Needleman (1986, 1988) argues that women's more collective, participative styles of communication are needed, as much by male as by female members, if the union movement is to be revived. Both hope that the full inclusion of women can initiate a new "social unionism," reminiscent of the militancy surrounding the great CIO industry organizing drives of the 1930s (see Dionne 1987).[9]

Many years of eroding popular support for labor (Edsall 1984) have culminated recently in the frontal attack of the Reagan administration and the Bush administration's "gentler" rhetoric of international competitiveness. The union movement now has good reason to seek a revitalized moral basis, in addition to new membership. Women's concerns and family issues may well provide part of this new moral grounding. At a minimum, issues of gender equity like comparable worth strengthen the labor movement because they cannot be dismissed strictly on economic grounds; at the same time, such issues begin to honor women's distinct experiences.

---

9. "Social unionism" describes a more militant labor movement, with both a broader social agenda and a broader base of working-class membership than the conservative "business unionism" of the AFL (Aronowitz 1973).

The Discourse of Class Politics

The changing discourse of the "family wage" has provided both the principal moral grounding for the labor movement's economic demands and the ideological basis for its exclusion of women. This discourse asserts the right of every worker to a "living wage" sufficient to maintain a family, that is, enough that one's dependents need not seek paid employment. It also expresses the complex and changing character of class and gender relations over the history of capitalist development. In this sense, while the family wage ideal has represented women's dependence on a "manly wage" for much of the twentieth century, today the same ideal provides the moral vocabulary for the struggle against female dependence, as represented by comparable worth.

Analysts have debated the interests that led to the dominance of the "manly wage," male breadwinner ideal. Some argue that working men were interested chiefly in maintaining their traditional gender privilege, both at home and in the workplace (e.g., Hartmann 1979). Others differ, contending that the "manly wage" discourse invoked gender categories primarily to defend the interests of the working-class family during the brutal laissez-faire era; in other words, the ideal was aimed not so much at female subordination as at class unity in the face of highly exploitive conditions (Humphries 1977; May 1982, 1985). Nonetheless, most agree that by the twentieth century the interests of dominant classes had led to the cultural entrenchment of the male-breadwinner/female-dependent family ideal. For newly monopolized industries, the "manly wage" provided the justification for using (white) men as a higher-paid, disciplined primary labor force while using women as "a uniquely flexible reserve army" (Folbre 1987, 501), thus maintaining labor peace by maintaining the hierarchical division of the working class.[10]

Unfortunately, the organized labor movement, at least the "prestige" unions of the American Federation of Labor, colluded with the major industrial capitalists in this process. The pragmatic unionists of the AFL—primarily white male skilled workers—acted to pre-

10. Also, the ideology appealed to the progressive middle-class reformers of the early twentieth century. Preserving the traditional family promised the maintenance of social order and American values in the face of mass immigration (May 1982, 1985).

serve their advantage, with respect not only to women but also to ethnic and African-American men. The discourse of the male breadwinner invoked by organized labor thus became a defense of the higher wages of white men. And so an ideal that had symbolized class opposition came to legitimate women's exclusion from both the primary labor force and the labor movement (Aronowitz 1973; May 1982, 1985).

The pragmatic "business unionism" of the AFL, which sacrificed the larger vision of a united working-class movement, remained the predominant stance of organized labor even after the merger with the more militant CIO in the 1940s. The postwar era has been characterized by the further erosion of labor's moral force. In fact, the AFL-CIO leadership has often used managerial discourse, basing demands on productivity and profits as much as on nonmarket, moral criteria like the family wage (Aronowitz 1973; Edsall 1984). Meanwhile, the male breadwinner ideal has continued to reinforce labor as an essentially male movement (Baden 1986).

Today, although the male-breadwinner/female-homemaker family is becoming an anomaly, the ideology persists. Acker (1988, 484) argues that female dependence has become "enshrined" in American culture, institutionalized not only in the economy but in family law and state welfare policy as well. In fact, as late as the 1960s the Department of Labor still referred to the marked rise in women's labor force participation as temporary (Needleman 1986, 208). Well into the 1970s many unionists clung to the goal of a family wage for male members while still treating women as marginal workers (Milkman 1985, 307; Moore and Marsis 1983b). Even in the 1980s when two-paycheck families became the rule, many unions remained ambivalent about such issues as day care, which make it easier for mothers to work (Bell 1985).

Comparable worth arguments can be seen as an attempt to reshape and revitalize the family wage ideal, extending it to include women breadwinners. Like the earlier version of the family wage, comparable worth is framed as a moral demand for a "living wage" based explicitly on social justice, as opposed to a "market wage" based on the amoral principle of supply and demand. Issues like comparable worth may thus help the labor movement recover the "moral high ground" as the defender of working men and women, which it has lost in the current era (Roback 1986,

13). Given the poor health of the movement, with plant closures, offshore production, declining membership, and concession bargaining, the limited success of comparable worth is one of labor's few hopeful developments.

However, comparable worth also represents an attack on the gender arrangements inscribed in the male breadwinner ideal to which labor has clung. Arguments for pay equity attack the assumption that men have a more fundamental or "natural" right to paid labor, and to higher earnings, than women. They also challenge the corollary set of assumptions about women's dependence: that women do not belong in the work force, that they need no more than "pin money," and that their jobs do not require skills or make contributions on the order of men's jobs. Finally, pay equity arguments implicitly challenge the normative legacy of the family wage: the deeply held belief that women's participation in paid labor is detrimental to family life and the social good (May 1985, 17). As a result, the endorsement of comparable worth by the traditionally male union movement may prove significant in mobilizing women and redefining the terms of strategies and debates for the future.

The Feminist Movement

Like the labor movement, the contemporary feminist movement is in need of both increased participation and a renewed sense of moral purpose. According to the the *New York Times* assessment that began this chapter, fully two-thirds of women agree that there should be a strong women's movement, yet only one-quarter feel they have personally benefited from it; and after a decade of right-wing backlash, the movement itself is described as fragmented over tactics and strategies (Dionne 1989). I suggest that because comparable worth builds on and extends multiple strands of feminist discourse, it may help overcome such fragmentation. It also may help strengthen the movement, by speaking to those who have not directly benefited from past strategies.

Class

While contemporary feminism contains many voices, most analysts agree that the dominant one has been that of "pragmatic" liberalism as expressed by the movement's core organizations (such groups as the National Organization for Women, the National Women's Political Caucus, and the Women's Equity Action League) (Carden 1974, 1978; Eisenstein 1981; Gelb and Palley 1987). This mainstream has often overlooked the centrality of class and class structure in determining women's experiences. Although concern for poor and minority women has been consistently present, liberal feminism has tended to universalize the interests of its central membership of white, highly educated women (see, e.g., Carden 1974, 117, 147; Carden 1978). Its notion of the labor market has emphasized enhanced opportunities for individual mobility—for example, through affirmative action policies—rather than any transformation of the class structure (e.g., Gelb and Palley 1987; Hole and Levine 1971). In contrast, other strands of feminism (including socialist, radical, and other Left strands) stress a vision of class transformation that is decidedly egalitarian. If affirmative action exemplifies the mainstream vision of the labor market, comparable worth, even with its liberal underpinnings, may move toward a more radical vision of class transformation.

Although Left feminist discourse treats class and gender as separate forms or systems of power relations, the two are considered "mutually reinforcing" or "mutually dependent." Because class processes and class exploitation are built on the exacerbation of preexisting differences (of gender, race, and ethnicity), a socialist or radically egalitarian transformation of economic relations is considered a necessary, though insufficient, condition for full gender equality (e.g., Eisenstein 1979; Kuhn and Wolpe 1978; Mitchell 1971; Rubin 1975).[11]

Comparable worth is in some respects compatible with this radically egalitarian agenda, although in other respects it is troubling. As Steinberg (1986, 124) comments, comparable worth certainly "will not bring socialism to the doorways of American business." Yet the policy does raise critical challenges to the ideology of the market and the wage relationship, questioning the assumption that existing wage hierarchies are determined by abstract forces and are

11. Radical feminism differs by the degree to which it views women's oppression as more fundamental and transhistorical than class exploitation, but it also generally agrees that an egalitarian transformation or end to class exploitation is a necessary condition for women's liberation (e.g., Firestone 1970). Also see Alcoff's discussion of cultural feminism (1988).

somehow "natural" (Amott and Matthaei 1988; Feldberg 1984; Steinberg 1986, 1987b). Furthermore, by recognizing that women's low wages are a systemic feature of the economy, not somehow deviant or epiphenomenal, comparable worth acknowledges the interrelation of class and gender in determining assignment to the secondary labor force (Amott and Matthaei 1984; Cerullo and Feldberg 1984; Freeman 1984; Hartmann 1985).

Still, comparable worth is problematic when considered from an egalitarian perspective. In stating that comparable worth challenges the ideology of the marketplace, I oversimplify somewhat. Certainly the notion of the market in our era is consistent with some degree of state intervention, and in this sense comparable worth stands squarely on its liberal foundation. Furthermore, comparable worth does not dispense with the belief that the reward structure should be based on skill and human capital differentials (e.g., Bergmann 1987, 47), and it has therefore been accused of reinforcing the liberal notion of a meritocratic labor market (Brenner 1987). While the comparable worth movement has redistributive goals that might be considered fairly dramatic, it is true that it does not argue for equality per se (Feldberg 1984).

Because of these shortcomings, some Left feminists voice concern and criticism. They suggest that comparable worth may disproportionately benefit educated women, and that it may become a disguised form of credentialism (Cerullo and Feldberg 1984; J. Rosenberg 1984). In fact, many comparable worth cases, including those I studied, involve members of the traditional female professions who feel an affinity to the idea of pay equity at least in part because it valorizes their credentials (Amott and Matthaei 1988). The policy may also hurt less skilled workers, in that it may undermine their struggles for decent earnings by legitimizing large merit-based differentials between occupations (Brenner 1987; Feldberg 1984).

Comparable worth does depart less from a liberal vision of the labor market than I and many others would prefer.[12] However, there is another side to the issue. By demonstrating that the value

12. Some Left advocates report hearing such complaints (Freeman 1984; Malveaux 1985; Steinberg 1986). Hartmann (1985), for example, reports on a Left conference in which comparable worth was only "grudgingly supported," and Feldberg and Cerullo (1984, 3) are explicit about their own initial problems with the concept (also Feldberg 1984, 328).

of work can be an object of struggle, comparable worth reveals that
the recognition of skill is itself an inherently political process (see,
e.g., Feldberg 1984; Steinberg 1987b). In other words, acknowl-
edging the connection between skill and gender may open the
wage relationship to greater scrutiny, revealing that what society
deems valuable is in fact part of a field of social conflict, determined
not by intrinsic value, "natural" merit, or abstract market forces but
by power relations. This discovery places comparable worth substantially beyond the meritocratic view of the labor market.

I suggest that comparable worth has a radical thrust even with
its hierarchical assumptions. Comparisons of male and female jobs
show that men earn substantially higher pay at *all* skill levels; thus,
equity policies can substantially benefit women at the bottom of
the occupational hierarchy even if the proponents' original intent is
to benefit educated professionals. Those who already have benefited include entry-level clerks, food service workers, and office
building cleaners (Amott and Matthaei 1988, 113; also Steinberg
1986). Moreover, the vast clerical work force represents a group of
potential beneficiaries and participants that dwarfs the relatively
small number of professionals. Clerical work is not only the largest
female-dominated occupation, but also, with the routinization and
growth of office work and its rock-bottom pay scales, an occupation
greatly in need of mobilization if feminist goals are to be achieved.
To the extent that comparable worth promotes such collective action, then, it moves beyond its own liberal underpinnings to a
more radical vision of class transformation.

Gender

As the strands of feminist discourse differ in their visions of class
transformation, they differ also in their visions of gender transformation. The notion of androgyny—the idea that polarized gender
roles should be transcended and biological sex differences made irrelevant to the social world and the division of labor—may have
represented the predominant feminist vision of gender transformation in the past (e.g., Fergusen 1974; Heilbrun 1973), where it
translated into policy objectives of strict equal treatment. But, as
Eisenstein (1988) has argued, in concrete terms this meant treating
women like men, and as divergent strands of feminism have come
increasingly to agree on the importance of valorizing women's dis-

tinct experiences, the androgyny ideal has met with both theoretical
and political criticism. If affirmative action represents the earlier,
androgynous vision, comparable worth may represent an alternative that valorizes gender difference.

Analysts who prefer androgynous remedies for gender inequality express reservations about comparable worth, saying that it reinforces the sex-stereotyping of work, rather than promoting strict
equality through the breakdown of categories based on gender.
While arguing that women's work should be considered as valuable
as men's, the comparable worth movement does not directly attack
the gender boundary line or the assignment of women to particular
jobs. Nor does it encourage women to change their occupational
preferences and enter male fields. Reskin (1987, 1988), for one,
finds this reinforcement of existing gender typing in comparable
worth very troubling. Her major concern is simply that the maintenance of gender difference, in any form, will always lead to male
domination in some form.

Others argue, from less essentialist positions, that raising wages
for women's work encourages women to remain in traditional fields
(Alstott 1986; Roback 1986). Such an outcome is considered troubling because it leaves open the possibility of future devaluation,
falls far short of integration objectives, and rewards women for rejecting androgynous choices. This position resembles the classic
liberal belief in "free" individuality (Mill and Mill 1970), that is,
that all should be free to compete in the meritocratic labor market
to the fullest exercise of their talents, unhampered by any ascribed
traits. From this perspective, evidence of difference between the
sexes will merely be used, as in the past, to justify the perpetuation
of circumscribed opportunities. Roback (1986, 42, 43), for example, writes: "The true goal of women's liberation today ought to
be to help women obtain the fullest range of options consistent
with their abilities and desires. . . . [Comparable worth] is a policy
that abandons many of the noblest of the early feminist goals."

Such classically liberal views probably represent the far right
wing in feminist discourse today. Nevertheless, affirmative action
in many respects exemplifies this liberal, androgynous vision of
gender transformation. Although some conservative critics dis-
agree (Bell 1976; Glazer 1975), the policy aims primarily to ensure
equality of opportunity in the labor market; it strikes down barriers
assigned according to ascriptive traits and gives preference to mem-

bers of underrepresented groups in order to equalize competition.[13] For feminism, it has represented a job integration strategy, one that has succeeded in demonstrating that women's capacities are indeed the same as men's. And while the accomplishments of affirmative action have been limited (as I discuss in the next chapter), the policy ironically played a crucial, if unintended, role in the development of comparable worth (see Chapters 3 and 4). For although it represents an integrationist vision of gender transformation, affirmative action legitimated gender-based discourse— specifically, the notion that women workers *as women* are entitled to demand special treatment to redress past discrimination.

Although most feminists support both policies in practice, affirmative action stands in sharp analytical contrast to comparable worth. Affirmative action attempts to push women into *male* fields, and in so doing it implicitly accepts the devaluation of women's work and reinforces the greater social esteem accorded male activity. In contrast, comparable worth contests women's devaluation, extending the focus of radical (or cultural) feminism on rescuing female spheres from the denigration of a misogynist culture (Alcoff 1988). This valorization of women's distinct traits, particularly women's relational qualities and familial orientation, has been incorporated into other strands of feminist discourse in the past decade (e.g., Gilligan 1982; Kessler-Harris 1987). While treating gender difference as socially constructed rather than biologically given, such "postmodern" feminism nonetheless emphasizes the value of women's "different voice" and envisions a transformation of the sex/gender system in which both difference *and* equality might be embraced (e.g., Alcoff 1988; Eisenstein 1988). This approach has already begun to influence legal debates (e.g., Lewin 1988) and, to some extent, the popular media. In fact, media accounts suggest that this postmodern version of feminism appeals to women who have not identified with feminism in the past (e.g., Dionne 1989; Rimer 1988). Comparable worth exemplifies this new emphasis on difference and equality; therefore, I suggest, it can play an important part in building a feminist future.

13. According to Daniel Bell (1976, 260–261), for example, affirmative action tries to legislate equality of outcomes, and, in his words, government should not try to "make people equal."

Two

National Gender Politics

Affirmative Action, the Feminist Movement,
and Comparable Worth

In this chapter, which sets the stage for the two case studies that follow, I cover much ground before finally arriving at the emergence of the comparable worth movement. This approach allows me to detail the two most important influences shaping comparable worth: the legacy of affirmative action policies, and the presence of class conflict in the feminist movement. By the time comparable worth became an issue, the rhetoric of affirmative action and the principle that women, as women, were entitled to preferential treatment were firmly established in the national political discourse. Nevertheless, the enforcement of affirmative action was erratic, and the ultimate benefit to working women was far more modest than the expectations raised. The resulting frustration, spelled out now in the context of a new discourse of gender politics, explains the rise of the comparable worth movement. The new vocabulary, however, arose not only from the civil rights movement and federal policies, but also from a feminist movement with a long history of conflict over which women would be best represented.

Affirmative Action:
The Rhetoric and the Results

The Federal Government

Affirmative action refers to the removal of formal barriers to the entrance of women and minorities into fields from which they have been excluded. More important, it includes positive preferences, with goals and timetables for increasing the numbers of the under-represented. The notion that disadvantaged groups must be not only brought up to the starting line in the race for occupational attainments but also given a handicap or head start to ensure a fair contest was central to many of the Great Society social programs and reforms of the 1960s. This sentiment was aptly expressed in a 1965 speech by President Johnson:

> Freedom is not enough. You do not wipe out scars of centuries by saying, "Now you're free to go where you want and do as you desire." You do not take a person who for years has been hobbled by chains and liberate him, bring him up to the starting line of a race, and then say "You're free to compete," and justly believe you have been completely fair. Thus it is not enough to open the gates to opportunity. All of our citizens must have the ability to walk through those gates; and this is the next and most profound stage of the battle for civil rights.

> (Cited in Thornberry 1983, 49)

Affirmative action policies evolved out of the "passive" antidiscrimination edicts first issued during World War II. As much a protection against wartime labor shortages as an endorsement of increased opportunities for minorities (Leonard 1984a, 1), these edicts carried few sanctions. After the war executive orders barring racial discrimination in all areas of employment were issued by Presidents Truman and Eisenhower, but these orders were also passive, establishing neither means nor methods for enforcement. Finally (reflective of both the growing civil rights movement and the need to consolidate black electoral support for the Democratic administrations of Kennedy and Johnson), antidiscrimination efforts moved from passive edicts to positive requirements that employers demonstrate increases in the integration of their work forces (Steinberg 1984b, 9–10).[1]

The significant legal and institutional changes these requirements brought at the federal level included passage of Title VII of the 1964 Civil Rights Act and issuance of Executive Order 11246 in 1966. Title VII prohibited discrimination in all employment practices and established a federal enforcement agency, the Equal Em-

1. Also important were affirmative action requirements in education, barring discrimination and requiring increased representation of women and minorities in educational institutions, enacted in the 1970s.

ployment Opportunity Commission (EEOC), to investigate and conciliate complaints and grant complainants the right to seek remedies in court. Later amendments gave the EEOC the power to bring suits directly against employers and added state and local governments as employers within the EEOC's jurisdiction.

To give more force to civil rights law, Executive Order 11246 required written affirmative action plans from all employers receiving federal contracts of over $50,000 (later amended to $10,000) (Segers 1983, 65). Such plans require documentation of the racial composition of the work force in nine broad occupational categories, a comparison with the local labor market, and goals and timetables for increasing the underrepresented. They do not, however, require quotas; the "goals and timetables" do not specify that particular numbers be hired, or that any *less*-qualified candidates be given preference. Affirmative action plans do require that special efforts be made to recruit *equally* qualified members of underrepresented groups within reasonable time frames (Ferree and Hess 1985, 151).

To provide enforcement of the affirmative action plans of federal contractors, the Office of Federal Contract Compliance (OFCC) was established, with a mandate to conduct contract reviews and, if necessary, hold up funds, cancel contracts, or even bar contractors from receipt of future contracts (Greenberger 1980, 118–122). Because approximately one-half of all private-sector, nonagricultural employment is provided by firms that are federal contractors, the potential of the executive order to integrate the workplace was quite far-reaching (Benokraitis and Feagin 1978, 60–62).

These original equal opportunity reforms were aimed solely at race discrimination. Yet they had obvious appeal for the resurgent feminist movement as well, which lobbied for their extension to sex discrimination. In the end, however, sex was included in Title VII only because of an unlikely alliance between the few women in Congress and conservatives seeking to discredit the Civil Rights Act (Samuels 1975, 102–105; Steinberg-Ratner 1980, 11n7).[2] Furthermore, early EEOC commissioners and staff, feeling that it was not the intent of Congress to enforce such provisions, brought very few sex discrimination suits (Greenberger 1980, 109; Johansen

2. See note 21 below on the inclusion of sex in Title VII. Executive Order 11246 also did not originally include sex discrimination; it was added in amendments several years later owing to feminist pressure (Greenberger 1980, 118).

1984, 34). Nevertheless, the legal and institutional framework was in place for women to utilize equal opportunity policies, once sufficient political pressure developed.

Although such pressure did increase in the 1960s and 1970s, the federal commitment to these policies was erratic. Indeed, many have accused the government of a lack of sincerity verging on duplicity, complaining of huge backlogs of uninvestigated complaints, bureaucratic confusion (with some sixteen different agencies having distinct yet overlapping requirements), vague guidelines, and excessive leniency toward business interests (Benokraitis and Feagin 1978; Foster and Segers 1983; Greenberger 1980). The lack of vigorous enforcement is the most frequently cited reason for the limited impact of affirmative action on women's economic status. But government enforcement has depended on the needs of different administrations to respond to different constituencies, some significantly more powerful than women. Private-sector opposition, for example, may help to explain the lack of enforcement during the Nixon and Ford administrations (1969–1976).

Owing to inadequate budgets and low staffing, the backlog of uninvestigated complaints at the EEOC had reached 100,000 by 1974 (Segers 1983, 93) and, by 1977, 130,000 (Johansen 1984, 18).[3] Moreover, in the first twelve years of the EEOC's existence (1965–1977), the commission had eleven different chairpersons; this lack of continuity was a serious liability, both organizationally and in terms of policy (Johansen 1984, 18). One study of Title VII cases brought against employers between 1965 and 1975 documents the ineffectiveness of legal efforts in this period, finding that the courts allowed for class actions and class relief in only 13 percent of all sex discrimination cases (Greenberger 1980).[4] This low incidence is im-

3. It is interesting to note, however, that fear in the Nixon and Ford administrations of the determination or zeal of those choosing to work for civil rights agencies may have led to even further restrictions on staff size. For example, Greenberger (1980, 122) cites a 1977 report indicating that the Office of Civil Rights, during several previous years, had returned, unspent, millions of dollars to the Treasury. At the same time, more than two hundred *authorized* staff positions had remained unfilled, representing over one-fourth of the agency's entire staff.

4. The rate for race discrimination cases was 24 percent, race being considered a more "odious" form of discrimination by many legal authorities (Greenberger 1980, 111). These figures do not imply, however, that racial discrimination was adequately addressed by federal efforts; 24 percent is likely quite low considering the full extent of racial segregation.

portant because such suits, which are brought on behalf of all those "similarly situated to the plaintiffs in the case," result in more effective and sweeping remedies than individual suits (Greenberger 1980, 110–111). Remedies in class actions are also likely to be far more costly to employers, thus serving as better deterrents to other organizations (Reskin and Hartmann 1986, 86). Overall, reviewing the first decade of national policies, sociologists Benokraitis and Feagin (1978, 116, 169) concluded that affirmative action efforts to regulate industry amounted to more rhetoric than action, and were more symbolic than effective.

Under the Carter administration serious attempts were made to step up Title VII enforcement. The Carter government reorganized and streamlined the federal bureaucracy involved in this area, increased budgets and staffing, and assigned very strong civil rights advocates to key positions. The most significant of these appointees for gender politics was Eleanor Holmes Norton, professor of law and former human rights commissioner in New York, who took over the chair of the EEOC. Under Norton, the EEOC saw more settlements, fewer complaints were dismissed for lack of cause, and the backlog of cases was greatly reduced (Reskin and Hartmann 1986, 86). In the Office of Federal Contract Compliance similar improvements were made. For example, during the four years of the Carter administration, thirteen companies were barred from receiving federal contracts—half of all firms to have ever been barred (Noble 1985). Still, Leonard (1984c) notes that this number is very small considering the tens of thousands of firms covered. In 1980, for instance, less than 0.2 percent of all protected employees at establishments that had undergone contract reviews received back pay awards. As Greenberger (1980) concluded, with discrimination in the workplace seemingly so pervasive, this level of action was shockingly low.[5]

The Carter administration generally had stronger alliances with minority and feminist voters, who provided crucial electoral support. During this time the comparable worth movement also gained important validation from within the federal government (a point I return to at the end of the chapter). Although pay equity was not

5. Leonard (1984c) also found that the first step toward *any* sanction was taken in only 1–4 percent of all contract reviews, with the typical result being merely a finding of "basic paperwork deficiencies."

fully endorsed by either the courts or the executive branch, the actions of the EEOC in this brief period opened up important opportunities for local efforts (the results of which will be noted particularly in the next chapter's discussion of the San Jose case).

Conversely, the Reagan administration, which counted on little or no support from minority and women's groups, moved to dismantle much of the civil rights bureaucracy and appointed outspoken critics of former policies to key positions. Under the first five years of the Reagan government only one firm was barred from receiving federal contracts, and the number of administrative complaints and back pay awards was cut by nearly one-half (Noble 1985). The EEOC under Reagan emphasized individual rather than class action suits, moved to a more restricted interpretation of Title VII (Reskin and Hartmann 1986, 87), and allegedly "warehoused" comparable worth complaints (Grune 1984). Repeated attacks and ridicule of the principle of comparable worth by federal officials became common (Pear 1985a, 1985b; Turner 1984; U.S. Commission on Civil Rights, 1985b). To date, support does not appear to be forthcoming from the Bush administration either, although in campaign rhetoric Bush tried to co-opt the issue by repeatedly citing women's need for economic equality (NCPE 1988b, 4).

Interestingly, the weak enforcement of antidiscrimination policies in the private sector contrasts sharply with much stronger efforts made within the public sector itself. As Segers (1983, 92) observes, one of the victories for affirmative action has been the "partial determination of the Federal Government to put its own house in order." Overall, women's and minorities' share of public-sector employment grew substantially, even during the Nixon-Ford years (Benokraitis and Feagin 1978, chap. 3). Between 1960 and 1970, the primary years of the civil rights movement, the proportion of blacks employed in the public sector increased from 13.3 percent to 21.4 percent (Wilson 1978, chap. 5). Even after the recessionary economy slowed growth in public employment, women's share continued to increase, rising from 43.8 percent to 48.2 percent between 1973 and 1981 (U.S. Department of Labor, Women's Bureau 1983, 71). Also during this period minority women became heavily concentrated in state-sector employment; by 1981 the public sector employed 12.9 percent of white men, 17.5 percent of white women, 18 percent of black men, and fully 26 percent

of black women (Malveaux 1985, 10–11). In addition, 1980 census
data indicate that blacks employed at managerial and professional
levels are found disproportionately in the public sector (U.S. Bureau of the Census 1986, 385). Although much of the increase in
minority and female government employment was in newly created,
low-paying, low-skill positions, significant upward mobility did occur in civil rights–related and social welfare agencies (Benokraitis
and Feagin 1978), the most politically visible sites.[6]

The fact that affirmative action had a stronger impact in public
employment than private indicates both the greater visibility and
higher political stakes associated with action or inaction in the public arena and the greater ease of implementing changes in that sector. Public employment is historically a politically sensitive issue.
Ever since the days of "machine-controlled" politics and patronage
systems the allocation of state-sector jobs has generated skepticism
in the popular mind. Because public employment remains a vulnerable point for any government, it was, as Wilson (1978) suggests, a necessary area for response to the civil rights movement
and later to the women's movement. Providing an increase in jobs
for women and minorities also offered officials a means for con-
structing or strengthening political alliances with the core movement organizations, and this occurred at both the national and the
local level. (These same factors help to explain the location of comparable worth efforts in the state and "quasi-state" sectors).

Organized Labor

The reaction of organized labor to federal affirmative action policies
has been mixed. Although the AFL-CIO played an important role
in the passage of Title VII, these policies have sometimes antagonized labor unions because the "goals and timetables" for increasing the representation of underutilized groups threaten that
cornerstone of workers' rights, seniority. It has been easier for labor to support affirmative action in hiring, during periods of expansion, than in firing when economic slowdowns occur. For example,
when the "last hired—first fired" women at General Motors (GM)

6. One example of a politically visible site was the Office of Civil Rights in the
Department of Health, Education, and Welfare. In the 1970s the office was staffed
largely by black males from the civil rights movement (Gelb and Palley 1987, 109).

complained that seniority rules had a discriminatory impact, the AFL-CIO executive council argued vigorously against any modifications. The council stated that seniority rules would not be relaxed to retain women, that neither job sharing nor shorter workweeks would be imposed on higher-seniority men to prevent layoffs of women, and that the only solution for women and minorities would be full employment (Balser 1987, 179–182; Foner 1980, 526).

Of course, the labor movement is not monolithic. Other voices less conservative than those of the AFL-CIO leadership have supported affirmative action more fully, even calling for "superseniority" to protect women and minorities during periods of layoffs. Such voices argue that straight seniority is discriminatory, for it protects only a small, white, male elite among workers (Quinn 1982; Rice 1983; Wcislo 1983, 1985).[7] The Coalition of Labor Union Women (CLUW), an organization of women active in the AFL-CIO, experienced sharp internal divisions over affirmative action issues, particularly in the case of the women autoworkers. Although the national leadership refused to break with the AFL-CIO leadership, the California branch supported the women suing GM and the UAW over discriminatory layoffs (Foner 1980, 532; Withorn 1976). Despite this conflict, however, the mainstream view within the AFL-CIO contends that the burden of correcting racism and sexism should be entirely on management; it will not acknowledge that seniority can function at the expense of women, minorities, and the unorganized (Balser 1987, 179–183; Buswell-Robinson and Kelly 1982).[8]

Affirmative action policies antagonized organized labor not only by threatening seniority rights, but also by holding unions legally and financially liable for discriminatory contracts, even if they had attempted to bargain or litigate against such practices. Under the Carter administration, this antiunion emphasis was removed, and the law was modified so that if a union can show good-faith efforts to end discrimination, it is relieved of culpability (Portman, Grune, and Johnson 1984, 231). This shift may help account for more re-

7. Some groups outside the labor movement advocating this position included the U.S. Commission on Civil Rights (during the 1970s), the National Lawyers Guild (Women's Labor Project 1980, 70–71, 93), and the National Organization for Women (Foner 1980, 525).

8. For an important discussion of racism and affirmative action in organized labor, see Hill 1987; and *New Politics* 1987.

cent cases in which AFL-CIO leadership has favored voluntary affirmative action plans, as in the famous reverse-discrimination case *Weber v. Kaiser Aluminum and United Steelworkers*. In this case, two black men were admitted to a craft training program over Mr. Weber, a white man with greater seniority. The AFL-CIO, however, defended the plan voluntarily negotiated between the Steelworkers' Union and Kaiser, earning praise from civil rights and women's groups (Foner 1980, 545). Certainly, labor is also less likely to oppose affirmative action in the era of reverse-discrimination cases, in which suits are brought against voluntarily bargained plans already in place and in which unions can therefore be liable, as they were in *Weber*. Moreover, the changed political context created under the Reagan administration, with its twin assaults on organized labor and civil rights gains, made organized labor more supportive of affirmative action policies.

Employer Responses and Employment Patterns

The results of affirmative action have been contradictory. On the one hand, the fundamental idea that sex discrimination, like race discrimination, is inherently unfair has become widely accepted (e.g., NCPE 1985a). The corollary—that women, as women, are therefore entitled to equal treatment and opportunities for advancement—has also been largely accepted and institutionalized. Without these developments, the comparable worth movement would not have been possible.

On the other hand, the concrete effects of affirmative action with regard to occupational segregation and the economic standing of women have been very limited. Perhaps a greater proportion of new jobs in growth industries went to minorities and women than would otherwise have been the case; but the benefits of affirmative action have not reached the majority of employed women, who remain concentrated in low-paying, female-intensive fields. In fact, press coverage of recent improvements in the male-female wage gap has been quite misleading, implying that women made great progress in the 1980s (e.g., Pear 1987). According to the National Committee on Pay Equity (NCPE), women's wages have increased slightly from the famous "59 cents" level, that is, from the much-publicized level at which women earned on average just 59 cents for every dollar earned by men (e.g., Mansbridge 1986, 36–44). However, the gap between women's and men's earnings has hovered around 60 percent since 1955, so the currently touted 70 percent figure remains well within "the range of historical precedent" (NCPE 1989a, 3). Furthermore, the weekly earnings averages cited by the media inflate women's share, owing to the effects of temporary, part-year, and overtime work. The use of annual earnings (the basis for the original "59 cents" figure), in fact lowers women's average income to 65 percent of the male average. Finally, it is important to note that *fully 30 percent* of the so-called improvement in women's wages reflects a *decline in men's earnings* caused largely by the drop in high-wage industrial jobs. If men's wages had *not* declined, women would be earning just 63.4 cents for every dollar earned by men (NCPE 1989a).

Employers have responded with ambivalence to federal affirmative action requirements. One study, conducted under the auspices of the Conference Board, surveyed the top firms listed by *Fortune Magazine* and found that affirmative action was initially resisted as a disruptive government intrusion (Shaeffer 1980, 307).[9] This resistance arose because, like other government interventions, affirmative action limits each firm's managerial prerogative to control its internal labor force (Edwards 1979, esp. 160–162, 207). During the Reagan era, however, many business leaders supported affirmative action against the administration's attack (e.g., *National NOW Times* 1986a).

Business support for affirmative action, such as during the Reagan years, is not wholly irrational; the policies can bring benefits to individual employers, which offset the loss of managerial control. Such bureaucratic interventions, according to Edwards (1979), serve to remove conflict from within individual firms. Because they redirect conflict over the allocation of jobs to the government, regulations like affirmative action protect individual employers. In addition, while initial implementation involves costs and disrup-

9. The Conference Board is a private research firm dedicated to improving the "quality and effectiveness of business leadership" that depends largely on corporate funding (Shaeffer 1980, 309n5). The fact that such a study was conducted indicates the strong reactions of the corporate community to affirmative action, and the subsequent pressures felt to comply with federal policy.

tions, affirmative action policies are rather easily incorporated by
bureaucratized firms, becoming simply additional rules governing
the internal mobility of workers. And once they have become a part
of a firm's personnel management system, such policies cease to be
regarded as onerous intrusions. This is particularly true of large
firms, able to accommodate the broad EEOC occupational categories fairly easily to their own labor force requirements.[10]

Shaeffer (1980, 307) also found persuasive evidence that many
firms, after initial resistance, came to view affirmative action as a
"good management tool." For example, one executive listed the
benefits: "As a corporate program, there has been an overall upgrading of the workforce. Objective criteria for employment decisions have become practice, hence all persons are considered for
positions on the basis of merit. Previously untapped human resources are now available. Healthy competition for advancement
exists" (Shaeffer 1980, 303–305). Other commentators have reached
similar conclusions about the impact of affirmative action. In fact,
the authors of an article entitled "The Female Takeover: Threat or
Opportunity" have observed that "in the end, such a practice is
just good capitalism" (Woodworth and Woodworth 1979, 47). (Of
course, it is possible that pay equity might also become such a
management tool, particularly in large organizations, an issue I return to in Chapter 6).

This acceptance of affirmative action as "good capitalism" does
not mean, however, that businesses would have been likely to
adopt such policies in the absence of external pressure. Because
affirmative action policies were so broad based and part of a much
larger sociopolitical and economic climate, it is difficult to isolate
their precise effects on employers and organizations. Yet most researchers agree that federal policies did have some influence on
employer practices. Again, Shaeffer (1980, 279) found that "many
major corporations now say they equate a preventive managerial
approach to avoiding difficulties under Title VII with the basic affirmative action approach called for under the Executive Order
[11246]." Moreover, after the large back-pay award paid by American Telephone and Telegraph (AT&T) in 1973 to settle sex discrimi-

10. Small business, which relies less on bureaucratic controls and faces a more
strained employment market, has generally opposed affirmative action and called
for the restoration of managerial prerogative (see, e.g., Noble 1985b, 1986b).

nation claims brought by the EEOC, "all major U.S. corporations were forcefully put on notice that . . . they have significant non-discrimination obligations not only to minorities but also to women" (Shaeffer 1980, 278).[11] That employers were aware of this "notice" is confirmed by a 1976 government study that found some type of affirmative action plan in place at the majority of firms subject to federal regulations (Reskin and Hartmann 1986, 88–89).

If the corporate community so widely accepted affirmative action, why were there not larger gains for women, including a larger reduction of the wage gap? In fact, the acceptance may have signaled merely the extent to which the policy was "domesticated," spurring the rationalization of personnel systems more than the integration of the workplace. Although it is difficult to isolate the impact of affirmative action on employer practices, a comparison of the current occupational distribution of women with that before the adoption of national policies (see Appendix A, Table A-2) reveals only modest changes.[12] This is not to say there have been no gains. Some doors have been opened to women, particularly to enter managerial and (male) professional fields formerly closed to them. The increase in women gaining degrees in law and medicine is impressive, as is the increase of women in management (see Appendix A, Tables A-3–A-4).[13] Yet a sizable body of research also shows that, for most women, such open doors remain out of reach (see Blum and Smith 1988).

Several careful studies demonstrate that affirmative action has made measurable, if modest, inroads against the occupational segregation of both minorities and women. Beller examined national

11. The AT&T case has been much studied, as it involved the nation's largest firm, which the EEOC described as "without doubt, the largest oppressor of women workers in the U.S." (cited in Segers 1983, 91). The settlement also included the adoption of a model affirmative action plan, the mixed results of which are included in my discussion in Chapter 5.

12. Making inferences from such aggregate data is problematic, as O'Farrell and Harlan (1984, 267n21, 270) detail: census data are not current enough, occupational codes are too broad, the Labor Department's Establishment Survey does not include breakdowns by sex, data from the private sector consists of that information which firms choose to make public, and none of the national aggregate data sets control specifically for program interventions.

13. The timing of the sudden increase of women completing law and medical school (see Table A-3 in Appendix A) indicates the role played by national affirmative action policies in education, adopted in 1972 (see Epstein 1981).

data on 262 detailed occupations and found that occupational segregation declined during the 1970s at a rate three times greater
than in the previous decade. Beller's index of occupational segregation, for which 100 represents total segregation, fell from 68.32 to
61.67; she attributes much of the decline to federal policy changes
(1984, 11–12). Leonard arrived at a similar conclusion after examining longitudinal data from the Office of Federal Contract Compliance on 68,690 firms with over sixteen million employees. He
found that minority males, and to a lesser extent minority females,
made statistically significant gains between 1974 and 1980; their
earnings and employment shares increased more in firms with federal contracts, subject to OFCC regulations, than in noncontractor
firms (1984a, 5–7, 11–13).

These positive results, however, are hardly grounds for rejoic-
ing. Although Leonard concludes that affirmative action works, the
statistically significant increases he cites are in fact quite small.[14]
Moreover, as he acknowledges (1984a, 15), minorities and women
enjoy the greatest gains in growing firms generally, whether or not
they are federal contractors. Reskin and Hartmann conducted a
comprehensive review of the impact of federal antidiscrimination
efforts for women. They conclude that federal policies have made a
difference but that this impact is primarily attributable to *active*
enforcement efforts such as litigation, repeated contact compliance
reviews, court-monitored consent decrees, or special industry targets (1986, 84, 94–96). Unfortunately, as I have shown, such active
enforcement efforts on the part of the federal government have
been inconsistent.

In addition, Bielby and Baron caution against overinterpreting
even the modest progress that women appear to have made. Despite the decline in occupational segregation found by Beller, the
index tells us that over 60 percent of women would still have to
change occupations to achieve integration. Furthermore, Bielby
and Baron's studies with establishment-level data (for several hundred California firms) suggest that even detailed occupational data

14. Leonard (1984b, 7–8) explains: "Between 1974 and 1980, the ratio of black
male to white male mean employment income for full-time, full-year workers increased by 2.3 percent, from .684 to .700." He estimates that approximately
30 percent of this increase "may be due to occupational advance induced by affirmative action."

conceal nearly complete intraoccupational segregation: men and women are separated by both job title and work setting (1984, 1986). Although Beller, for example, identifies management as one of the largest areas in which progress in integration has been made, Bielby and Baron (1986, 789) suggest that firms may have "a broad view of what constitutes a managerial job when classifying women and minority workers." Such a "broad view," which can be discovered only by examining firm-level data, no doubt helps employers to show compliance with affirmative action goals and timetables. But at the same time, it inflates our sense of women's present status and of the gains that can be credited to federal policies. In fact, such problems lead Bielby and Baron to conclude that the nine wide occupational categories used to monitor affirmative action by the EEOC are of little value.

Research on the distribution of new occupational opportunities among women is less extensive, but most suggests that the primary beneficiaries of affirmative action have been college-educated white women. Again, Beller reports that the occupations that have become less male dominated are in the managerial and professional categories; at the same time, "little or no change occurred among the blue-collar occupations" (1984, 19), which might have provided good opportunities for working-class women. Studies by Shaeffer and Rosenbaum confirm that college recruiting was the preferred strategy for many firms in meeting affirmative action goals (Shaeffer 1980, 308), with those most likely to benefit being recent graduates of high-ranking schools (Rosenbaum 1984, 233).[15]

Minority women in particular appear to have benefited little from federal affirmative action policies. Although women of color have entered fields traditionally occupied by white women, a shift in which affirmative action likely played some part, Malveaux (1985, 1985–1986) discounts the notion that black women's status is converging with that of white women, noting that black women are crowded into the lowest-paying jobs even within the pink-collar ghetto. For example, in 1985 the low-wage, service occupations employed some 17 percent of white women, but fully 31 percent of black women (U.S. Department of Labor, cited in Reskin and

15. Rosenbaum (1984, 1985) examined personnel records for ten to fifteen thousand employees in a large corporation during a period in which affirmative action plans were implemented. He concluded that, overall, effects were limited.

Hartmann 1986, 6). And while the earnings of women of all races fall far behind those of white men, they fall furthest behind for women of color (see Appendix A, tables A-6 and A-8). O'Farrell and Harlan (1984, 270) conclude: "The negative effects of race and sex are compounded for both hiring and promotion of minority women."

In summary, even if we accept the most optimistic interpretation of recent employment trends, such as Beller's, we are left noting the very limited accomplishments of affirmative action. Segers (1983, 90) summed up the situation well when she wrote:

in aggregate terms, the situation of blacks and women in American society has not improved. . . . For blacks as a whole and for women as a whole, then, it may be the case that affirmative action has not made [for] much progress. . . . Of course, we can cite single cases of individual women and blacks who have succeeded in attaining high places. . . . [But] society is not becoming less inegalitarian.

This review indeed has shown that the actual results of affirmative action belie the rhetoric. The claims for intervention to promote the mobility of the "underrepresented" were in fact far greater than were ever fulfilled. Yet the national consensus on the principles underlying affirmative action is apparent in the rhetoric of every presidential administration; even those whose enforcement efforts were the weakest decried all forms of discrimination. For women, the legitimation of a gender-based discourse has become more significant than any change in employment patterns. Such gender-based claims arose, however, not only from federal government action, but from the resurgence of feminism in the 1960s as well.

Class and Gender in the Feminist Movement

Public opinion polls indicate that by the late 1970s—a decade in which resurgent feminism captured national attention—the gender-based discourse legitimated by affirmative action had become widely diffused. Both a high identification with "women" as a category and a widespread perception of the illegitimacy of sex discrimination had developed among women of all classes and races (Ferree and Hess 1985; Katzenstein 1987). Because of this raised consciousness, many social movement scholars judge the American women's movement a success (Fulenwider 1980; Gelb 1987; Klein 1987; Mueller 1987). However, the contemporary feminist movement faces a paradox: one the one hand, widespread adherence to its basic tenets, and on the other, relative political weakness and a narrowly based core constituency (Belkin 1989; Dionne 1989). Black women and working-class women, whose agreement with feminist tenets has been quite high, have generally not identified as part of the movement (Klein 1987). Moreover, in contrast to less popular European movements, American feminism can boast of few concrete accomplishments for low-income women (Katzenstein 1987; also Dionne 1989).

The emergence of the comparable worth issue must be understood within the context of the class and gender politics that have shaped American feminism. The paradox of widespread ideological adherence but a low sense of membership accounts for much of comparable worth's appeal, both to movement insiders hoping to enlarge the movement and to low-paid women who have felt excluded. Comparable worth offers the hope of healing the historical class antagonism that divided American women's activists for decades. At the same time, however, the political significance of class differences among women persists, and may even have been strengthened by the limited success of affirmative action; these differences may ultimately limit the success of comparable worth as well—a point I return to in Chapters 6 and 7.

Prehistory: Women's Rights Issues
Before the 1960s

The history of class antagonism on issues of women's rights dates back at least to the end of the suffrage era and the winning of the vote for women. During the "first wave" feminist struggle for the vote, trade union women (against some pressure from male union leadership) worked with elite suffrage groups like the National Woman's Party and played a major role in the campaign to pass the Nineteenth Amendment (Flexner 1975).[16] After the amendment

16. Unfortunately, this type of cross-class alliance was less successful across race differences. According to Giddings (1984, chap. 7), although black men and women strongly advocated women's suffrage, many white activists were willing to use racist tactics in the South.

was in place, however, these coalitions broke down as unionists and elite groups—with very different women in mind—developed competing approaches to the cause of women's equality (Foner 1980, 56–60). Winning the passage of an Equal Rights Amendment (ERA) proclaiming women's absolute equality before the law became the major objective of the National Woman's Party. Most union women, in contrast, strongly opposed the ERA because it would have invalidated special, protective labor laws for women. Both groups were working for women's rights, but conflicting class interests led to a forty-year fight over this issue (Hole and Levine 1971, 52–107).

Sociologists Rupp and Taylor view the pre-1960s campaign for the Equal Rights Amendment as an "elite-sustained stage" of the women's movement, characterized by a small number of professional women who pursued passage "doggedly and single-mindedly" (V. Taylor 1986, 3). The fight for the ERA was seen as a direct continuation of the earlier struggle for the vote. Allied with the National Woman's Party were groups like the National Federation of Business and Professional Women's Clubs and the associations of women in law and medicine. These small, elite groups emphasized the formal legal and property rights most relevant for women of their standing—white, middle- to upper-class, highly educated, professional women. This emphasis antagonized both black women and union women, who were more interested in gaining such substantive protections as labor regulations and enforcement of voting rights (Rupp and Taylor 1987, 50–51, 200). Mary Anderson, a leader of the Women's Trade Union League (WTUL) and first director of the Women's Bureau of the Department of Labor, went so far as to accuse the National Woman's Party of embracing "a kind of hysterical feminism with a slogan for a program" (cited in Hole and Levine 1971, 79). For their part, women in the WTUL and Women's Bureau came to put greater effort into opposing the ERA than into either of their two original goals: organizing women workers and fighting the exclusionary practices of the American Federation of Labor (Foner 1980, 138–139; Rupp and Taylor 1987, 5–6, 144–153).

Trade union women and their allies opposed the ERA because the amendment would have nullified their own lengthy struggles to gain special protections for women workers, such as restrictions on the hours and conditions of women's employment—laws that did provide at least some actual protection from exploitive, dangerous working conditions.[17] Unfortunately, protective legislation also justified occupational sex segregation and women's lower pay and restricted labor market opportunities for women by invoking traditional notions of women as mothers and "the weaker sex," who required special government attention. As a consequence, protective legislation was vehemently opposed by the pro-ERA feminists, whose concern was with discrimination against women in elite male fields; thus they defined women's rights strictly in terms of equal treatment.

The issue of protective legislation is much debated by feminist and labor historians. Some argue that the National Woman's Party, in promoting strict legal equality, represented the only group with "a truly feminist standpoint" (Lehrer 1987, 239; also Hole and Levine 1971). Others argue, in contrast, that the WTUL members should be considered "industrial feminists," who pursued special legislation because, given the constraints faced, it was the most effective strategy available to better conditions for working-class women (Kirkby 1987; also Feldberg 1980).[18]

Freeman (1987) points out that the class divisions represented in the ERA issue also involved political parties and business interests.

17. Support for protective legislation was not the only basis for the antagonism between union and pro-ERA women, however. Union women in the Women's Bureau and WTUL, as well as black women of the National Association of Colored Women, were also antagonized by the single-minded tactics of the pro-ERA National Woman's Party, which included tokenism, the financing of front groups, red baiting, and a cavalier attitude toward coalition building. Rupp and Taylor (1987, 135–165) conclude that the Woman's Party tried to create an impression of black and labor support for the amendment, yet never made sincere efforts to address these groups.

18. Admittedly, as Lehrer (1987) argues, the class and gender lines were not as simple as my brief discussion might suggest. Some groups of women workers opposed protective laws, particularly women displaced as a result of night-work restrictions. Also, some WTUL members and officials of the Women's Bureau were middle-class reformers who identified as allies of labor. Nonetheless, the largest groups opposed to the legislation were employers and elite women using laissez-faire, antilabor arguments. And the largest groups working for the protections were the trade unions led by the WTUL and the Women's Bureau, who maintained that the number of women displaced was very small compared to the many thousands in the "women-employing" industries to be protected (Foner 1980, 148–150; Kirkby 1987). Both Rupp and Taylor (1987) and Harrison (1988), focusing on the post–World War II period, agree that the conflict over the ERA was primarily one of class.

Although the issue was not high on the agenda of either party, in this period Republicans, conservatives, and major business interests tended to favor the ERA, which was seen as compatible with a laissez-faire, antiregulation stance. In fact, many Woman's Party members shared a conservative view of the labor market, in which legal intervention for women workers was undesirable, serving only to handicap them and make them less competitive. Those opposed to the amendment, in contrast, tended to be Democrats, but they were scarcely a majority of their party (Freeman 1987, 217). For many years, then, the efforts of the two small groups of women's rights advocates mainly canceled each other out. It was not until 1970, within the context of "second wave" feminism and a new generation of activists, that a broader feminist consensus in favor of the Equal Rights Amendment was reached.

Class divisions among women's rights advocates also colored efforts for the Equal Pay Act. First introduced in Congress in 1945, the act failed to gain passage, as it did in every subsequent session until 1963. Unlike the ERA, "equal pay for equal work" had long been a labor movement issue, promoted both by women's advocates and by union men concerned that men's wage levels not be undercut (Steinberg-Ratner 1980, 29–30, 46). During World War II, for example, the War Labor Board required that women receive equal pay when taking over men's jobs for the duration. This policy had been extended to include a comparable worth standard of "equal pay for jobs of equivalent value" by the war's end, but this extension was never enforced (Milkman 1987a). After the war, union women in the Women's Bureau made a federal equal pay law, initially intended to include a comparable worth standard, their primary goal. This equal pay measure was seen as anti-ERA. For one thing, it took attention from the amendment as *the* women's rights issue; moreover, it left protective legislation intact, and it was to have been enforced by the Women's Bureau, the long-standing antagonist of the pro-ERA feminists (Freeman 1987, 219; Mansbridge 1986, 9–10; Rupp and Taylor 1987, 175).

For its part, the pro-ERA National Woman's Party remained publicly neutral regarding equal pay measures, unwilling to give the impression of being against working women. However, the elite group worked against the Equal Pay Act behind the scenes, arguing, as they had against protective labor legislation, that interventions only hurt women's ability to compete in the labor market. More specifically, they said that pushing up women's wages would only restrict job opportunities by lowering employers' incentives to utilize female labor (Freeman 1987, 219). Sadly, unionists in the Women's Bureau later claimed that they continued to fight the Equal Rights Amendment in the 1960s primarily because the Woman's Party had fought them on the Equal Pay Act (Rupp and Taylor 1987, 176).[19]

The repeated failure of the Equal Pay Act was indicative of the lack of any coherent or organized working-class women's constituency behind the Women's Bureau's efforts (Johansen 1984, 31–33). But despite this weakness, the Women's Bureau gained greater access to the federal government during the Kennedy administration,[20] becoming institutionally expanded through the establishment of national and state branches of the President's Commission on the Status of Women (which functioned as research and advisory bodies). With the decision to drop the comparable worth standard in favor of the narrow equal work criterion, the Equal Pay Act was finally passed in 1963 (Johansen 1984, 33). Its passage is considered part of the prehistory of the contemporary women's movement, though it was in fact a major victory for women. But the context of class divisiveness from which the Equal Pay Act emerged left a legacy that proved difficult for the new generation of women activists to escape (Rupp and Taylor 1987, 192).

19. The duration of this conflict indicates the extent to which the class-based antagonism between these two groups took on a life of its own, transcending any specific policy questions. Rupp and Taylor (1987, 559–564) also comment, in a similar vein, that the antagonism between elite and union women persisted long after the original legal basis to the ERA-protective legislation conflict had eroded. In the earlier part of the century, most labor legislation affording protections to *all* workers was rejected by the courts (as "unreasonably" restricting the "free" labor contract), and only by arguing on the basis of women's special needs was it possible to have legislation upheld. Seen in this light, the ERA posed a significant legal threat. After the New Deal, however, labor regulations applying to both men and women were deemed valid and "reasonable." Yet the antagonism between elite feminists and union women remained well entrenched for another thirty years (also see Lehrer 1987).

20. Steinberg (1984b, 9) attributes this improved access to the critical electoral support of the labor and civil rights movements in the Democratic victory of 1960, as well as to the first stirrings of resurgent feminism.

The "Second Wave": Gender and Class in
Contemporary Feminism

The "second wave" resurgence of feminism during the 1960s is typically seen as arising from a convergence of forces, including relative increases in the educational levels and labor force participation rates of women, as well as civil rights and New Left politics (Carden 1974, 1978; Evans 1979; Ferree and Hess 1985; Freeman 1975; Fulenwider 1980). The new generation of women created a new organizational context for feminism, which drew on the legacy of both the elite Woman's Party and the unionist Women's Bureau. At least through the first decade, however, resurgent feminism, with its emphasis on the ERA and equal treatment strategies, tended to replicate the earlier class bias of the "elite-sustained" stage. Only with the failure of the ERA and the rise of the antifeminist backlash has contemporary feminism attempted to become a more inclusive movement, embracing strategies like comparable worth that are directed at working-class women.

As is obvious from the previous discussion of affirmative action, the feminist movement owes a substantial debt to black activists. It has built on many of the organizational, ideological, and legal contributions of civil rights struggles, and the analogy constructed between sex and race underlies many of the gains made by women (Ferree 1987, 176–177). In fact, the race analogy directly provoked the foundation of the National Organization for Women (NOW) in 1966, considered the birth of the "second wave." As we have seen, Title VII of the Civil Rights Act of 1964 was finally passed with the added prohibition of sex discrimination, enforcement of which the majority of EEOC commissioners and staff opposed. They considered the provision to have been adopted without serious intent, to discredit the principle of equal opportunity rather than promote sex equality.[21] Two "pro-woman" commissioners suggested pri-

---

21. This peculiar incident also occurred because of the alliance between pro-ERA elite women and conservatives. Because Woman's Party members saw Title VII as a possible "foot in the door" for the ERA, they played a key role in getting sex added. The conservatives who voted for the addition of sex very likely wanted to discredit the entire act, but they also may have reasoned that if such discrediting failed, at least white women should get the same legal benefit as black women. Therefore, as Rupp and Taylor (1987, 176–178) points out, Title VII was not an

vately that to have sex discrimination treated seriously external pressure groups like the civil rights organizations were needed (Freeman 1975, 54; Rupp and Taylor 1987, 178–180).[22] Then at the third national convention of the Commissions on the Status of Women, a resolution urging the EEOC to treat sex-based cases as seriously as those that were race-based was vetoed even before it reached the floor. A small group of angry delegates immediately concluded that the "pro-woman" EEOC members were right: an independent, nonpartisan organization was needed, to function like an NAACP (National Association for the Advancement of Colored People) for women (Ferree 1987, 176; Freeman 1975, 54–55; Fulenwider 1980, 11–12). NOW became that organization.

Once formed, NOW expanded quickly, becoming the largest and most broad-based feminist organization. Yet even though it incorporates both union and professional women, echoes of previous class antagonisms remain. Core membership, for example, has consisted largely of well-educated white women, as in the earlier "elite-sustained" stage (Carden 1978; Eisenstein 1981; Freeman 1975; Fulenwider 1980; Klein 1987). Although such issues as reproductive rights have been important, the organization's central aim, particularly in the first decade, reflected the integrationist goals of the civil rights movement: "to bring women into full participation in the mainstream of American society" (statement of the original charter, cited in Carden 1974, 104). Winning passage of the Equal Rights Amendment, symbol of this equal citizenship, therefore became NOW's top priority, much as it had been for the National Woman's Party.

Although NOW and other second-wave organizations were never as elitist as the Woman's Party, the stress on equal treatment un-

---

unexpected gift to the women's movement; the Woman's Party had been trying to ride the coattails of the civil rights movement since the mid-1950s, if in an opportunistic fashion.

22. In addition, the EEOC was reluctant to enforce the sex discrimination provision because it wanted to avoid the controversy over protective legislation, that is, whether Title VII would invalidate special protections by requiring equal treatment in all employment practices. Although the National Woman's Party hoped this would be the case, paving the way for passage of the ERA, the EEOC left the issue for the courts to resolve and did not issue guidelines until 1969 (Steinberg-Ratner 1980, 50n32; Hole and Levine 1971, 34–35; Rupp and Taylor 1987, 178).

intentionally extended the earlier class bias. Equal treatment policies, as Wilson (1978) has pointed out, tend to benefit those who
already have greater resources. Much as occurred in the black community, those women with more education and greater family resources were best situated to take advantage of the newly opened
opportunities (particularly as the opportunities tended to be concentrated in high-visibility, professional areas). In both cases—civil
rights and feminism—largely middle-class movements followed
strategies that unwittingly best reflected their own narrow interests. Women of color objected to NOW's single-issue focus on the
ERA because of this narrow class-biased agenda (Giddings 1984,
340–348). In general, as Ferree (1987) points out, American feminism's reliance on the race-sex analogy and policies requiring equal
treatment has had a two-sided result: American working women face
far fewer overt barriers than European women but, at the same
time, receive far fewer substantive benefits. Obviously, it is those
with fewer resources who dearly need such substantive benefits.

Nevertheless, and again like the civil rights movement in the
black community, contemporary feminism in the United States has
been concerned with representing women of all classes, and may
be moving in a more class-inclusive direction. The contemporary
campaign for the ERA, in contrast to the earlier "elite-sustained"
effort, was marked by a high level of consensus among women's
right activists. There were several reasons for this, which I briefly
digress to explain.

As late as 1967, most unions still supported retaining protective
legislation and therefore opposed the ERA (Johansen 1984, 40).
But just as with the Equal Pay Act, measures "protecting" women
were favored primarily because they reinforced sex segregation
and protected *men* from job competition with women. In the 1960s,
changes in the occupational structure and an increase in women's
labor force participation made such discriminatory effects more apparent (Hole and Levine 1971, 30–39). At the same time, a small
but active number of union women, frustrated by their lack of influence within organized labor, began to view their interests differently. Working against protective measures, they began to construct ties to the feminist movement and to organize for more of a
voice within the labor movement (Johansen 1984, 40). This effort

culminated in the 1970 endorsement by the Women's Bureau of the Equal Rights Amendment (Rupp and Taylor 1987, 183).[23]

Independent of this shift, by the late 1960s Title VII cases were coming before the courts and protective legislation began to be struck down. The requirement of equal treatment in employment practices was invalidating protective laws on a case-by-case basis, despite the fact that the ERA had not passed (and the EEOC had failed to issue guidelines on sex discrimination). The original legal need for the special treatment argument had long since eroded; labor regulations protecting *all* workers had been accepted by the courts since the New Deal (see note 19). Thus, the traditional basis of labor's opposition was finally neutralized.

By the early 1970s, with the changed legal context and the changed stance of women unionists, a nonpartisan consensus developed in favor of the amendment (Freeman 1987, 220–221). There was little opposition, in fact, when it passed the Congress in 1972. However, while the ERA had been seen as an antilabor, "free market" issue easily supported by conservatives, with the new labor-feminist alliance it became part of a liberal, interventionist agenda. The traditional class and gender positions became very nearly reversed as internal changes in the Republican party also edged out moderate women and brought the New Right antifeminists to power. Opposition hardened, ratification by the states stalled, and ultimately the campaign for the ERA failed (Mansbridge 1986).

It is most important here to note that the failure of the ERA led to questioning of the feminist agenda and to an awareness of the political weakness and narrow base of the movement. NOW leaders had originally thought that implementation of the ERA would provoke a broad range of changes, including improved economic status for women through stepped up enforcement of federal policies. When efforts at ratification stalled, the amendment was pro-

23. This changed stance also led to the formation of the Coalition of Labor Union Women in 1974. CLUW has always been a small group—it numbered about six thousand in 1979 and was up to eighteen thousand by 1986 (Balser 1987, 199). It has been fairly successful in promoting women "insiders" to leadership positions in the AFL-CIO and serving as a top-down check on national union policies. It has been far less successful in promoting grass-roots organizing, though it has given greater voice to working-class women's concerns within NOW (Balser 1987; Johansen 1984, 41–42; Milkman 1985; Sexton 1978).

moted explicitly on economic grounds, with the slogan "59 cents" widely used. Although the economic consequences of the ERA would likely have been minimal (Mansbridge 1986, 36–44),[24] the slogan also signaled the changing feminist agenda and a willingness to address economic issues more directly (Johansen 1984, 2, 67).

NOW also made other attempts to address working-class women. At the organization's tenth annual convention in 1976, for example, issues originating from a labor task force were featured, including an endorsement of union organizing (Johansen 1984, 41–42). And in 1978 comparable worth received official support (Johansen 1984, 139). In addition, when feminists gained a foothold in the federal government during the Carter administration, their demands moved beyond an elitist gender politics to the needs of low-income welfare and wage-earning women (Eisenstein 1981, 232, 244–248; Ferree and Hess 1984, 125).

Figures on the size of the movement illustrate its relative political weakness. Generally it is estimated that, in the late 1970s and 1980s, major movement organizations had 200,000 to 300,000 members (Carden 1978; Mueller 1987). The membership of NOW may have peaked at some 220,000 in 1982 with the last-ditch efforts to get the ERA ratified (Ferree 1987, 173); by mid-decade that figure was reportedly about 150,000 (Brozan 1986). Still, the constituency is somewhat larger than paid memberships in movement organizations would suggest. The circulation of *Ms.* magazine, a good rough indicator, has consistently been around 500,000 (Katzenstein 1987, 4).[25] Gelb (1987, 283) estimates that in 1981 only 4 percent of all American women gave money to a women's rights organization, and that only one out of three hundred was involved in some feminist activity.

In addition to the failed ERA campaign, awareness of the changing family economy also led to some shift in emphasis by the feminist mainstream. The stagflation economy, the decline in industrial

24. In strictly legal terms, Title VII already made employment law gender-blind, undermining much of the argument for the ERA. However, it is probably true that the ERA would have sent a strong message of public commitment to the courts, encouraging broader interpretations of Title VII. In fact, as Mansbridge (1986, 42–43) notes, this might have led the courts to endorse a comparable worth standard for bringing sex-based wage discrimination suits.

25. It is also significant that, as Fulenwider (1980, 65) found, approximately 90 percent of *Ms.* magazine's readers are white and college-educated.

employment, and the sharp rise in female-headed households throughout the 1970s made all types of families more dependent on women's earnings. Currie, Dunn, and Fogarty argue that during the 1970s women's earnings became critical for working-class, married-couple families to protect against an eroding standard of living, as "a kind of social speed-up" required putting more family members to work (1980, 13).[26] In addition, households with a married couple dropped from 78 percent to 61 percent of the total (Bianchi and Spain 1983, 9); and while the number of female heads-of-household in the labor force doubled (Cain 1984, 142), unless a single mother had a managerial or professional job she was virtually condemned to poverty or near-poverty. In 1977, for example, 42 percent of single mothers had incomes below the poverty line, a rate six and one-half times higher than for married-couple families (Currie, Dunn, and Fogarty 1980, 12). Sociologist Diana Pearce (1978) first described this phenomenon as "the feminization of poverty" (also Pearce and McAdoo 1981). In fact, between 1966 and 1985 the percentage of families in poverty headed by women increased from 30 percent to 48 percent (Chavez 1987). But the term also captured the more general sense that many women, rather than benefiting from increased opportunities, actually faced worsened or more precarious conditions. *Ms.* magazine highlighted the feminization of poverty in its tenth-anniversary issue, commenting that what had been a "decade of liberation" for some had been grim for many others (Ehrenreich and Stallard 1982).

Yet despite this attention to women's poverty, the very terms of the "feminization of poverty" discussion exposed some lingering class and race bias within mainstream feminism. Advocates for black and poor women were antagonized by an analysis that stressed only gender as a cause of poverty and by a movement that voiced concern only when large numbers of white, formerly middle-class women began to fall into poverty (particularly when poverty rates for black women remain three times as high; Burnham 1985). For example, Sparr (1984, 9) wrote: "Proponents of that argument may leave a mistaken impression that sexism is the fundamental prob-

26. By 1983, 21 percent of employed women had husbands earning less than $15,000 per year. Another 26 percent had never married, and 19 percent were divorced, widowed, or separated (U.S. Bureau of the Census, cited in Diamond 1984).

lem. They fail to examine thoroughly the nature of the capitalist economy, which requires and maintains an impoverished class." And Malveaux (1985, 10), citing Sparr, added: "To the extent that this impoverished class is black . . . a set of policy initiatives that solely addresses the 'feminization of poverty' may have limited interest for black women" (also see Burnham 1985).

In sum, while contemporary feminism may be moving to a more class-inclusive agenda, American gender politics and the construction of women's rights issues have traditionally involved considerable class antagonism. The extension of formal rights of equal opportunity in the workplace and equality before the law symbolized by the Equal Rights Amendment speaks more to the interests of middle- and upper-class women and has a history of antagonizing labor-identified women's advocates. Even after the demise of protective legislation and the resulting consensus behind the ERA, the resurgent feminist movement has continued to represent a narrow constituency. Although many of its tenets have become quite broadly diffused, actual membership is small, and the sense of identification among working-class and minority women is low (Klein 1987). Nonetheless, in response to both the limitations of earlier strategies and a more hostile political and economic climate, the movement has become more sensitive to women it previously marginalized. Its embrace of the comparable worth issue can be understood as a part of this response. Issues like comparable worth, which might heal the class schism that has so impeded progress in the past, have the potential to greatly increase the effectiveness of the feminist movement. Although comparable worth emerged locally, primarily in distinct grass-roots efforts, by the mid-1980s it was being claimed as one of the few successes for the national women's movement (Chavez 1987; Lawrence 1985; Lawson 1985a).

The Comparable Worth Movement
State and Local Emergence

The comparable worth issue began to emerge in different parts of the country during the 1970s, primarily within public-sector employment at state and local levels, but also to some extent in the private sector over settlement of wage discrimination issues originally raised during World War II.[27] Generally, comparable worth efforts, in both sectors, involved women who had not benefited from previous equal employment policies but who had, nonetheless, gained a sense of entitlement as women. Frustration with the limits of federal policies led women remaining in female-dominated jobs to voice new demands. Yet these demands attracted little national attention until Eleanor Holmes Norton took over the EEOC under the Carter administration and made comparable worth a priority issue (Steinberg 1984, 13).

Activities in Washington State were among the earliest in the country, although implementation occurred only much later. As early as 1973, employees represented by the American Federation of State, County, and Municipal Employees, along with the state branch of the Commission on the Status of Women, requested a job evaluation study to compare wages of equivalent male- and female-dominated jobs. Such studies rank jobs on the basis of factor points assigned for skill, effort, responsibility, and working conditions. The measurement techniques used actually developed over the past century as a corollary of scientific management, and were originally used to increase managerial control over wage setting, to rationalize the wage structures within large organizations, and to defuse employee reaction. Now pay equity proponents look to job evaluation because it offers a means of "objective" measurement and is often already in use, in some form, in many large organizations (Treiman 1979). Washington State officials could not easily reject the employee request, since a study of the top managerial and official positions had just been completed, and salaries increased, on the basis of similar methodology (Remick 1984, 101–102). The employee study, however, completed the following year, is considered the first use of job evaluation techniques to examine sex-based wage inequities specifically.

27. Specifically, the International Union of Electrical Workers (IUE) continued its efforts to gain equal pay for women in the electrical industry by setting up a Title VII compliance program. When patterns of job segregation and lower pay grades for women persisted, the IUE targeted one firm, Westinghouse, to take to court. While the case was ultimately successful, it was decided on the basis of *intentional* discrimination on the part of the employer, and not on a comparable worth criterion, that is, on the basis solely of the lower wages for women's work (Bureau of National Affairs 1981, 7; Steinberg 1984b, 13).

The results of the Washington study were unexpected by many; women's jobs were found to pay only 75–80 percent as much as the equivalent men's jobs, with virtually no overlap in male and female salaries in any given factor-point range (Remick 1984, 102–103). Widespread attacks on the validity of the study results and resistance to proposed remedies led to a decade of frustrated efforts by comparable worth advocates, and finally to a major lawsuit. In 1983 the district court found the state guilty of violating Title VII and awarded employees nearly $1 billion in back pay and benefits, in addition to future comparable worth adjustments (Johansen 1984, 55).[28] Although this controversial decision endorsing pay equity was reversed on appeal two years later, the political momentum was sufficient to implement comparable worth without a court mandate. Over $46 million was spent on adjustments in 1986, with an additional agreement for $10 million each year until 1992 (NCPE 1986; Turner 1986).

Concurrent with its efforts in Washington State, AFSCME began to promote comparable worth strategies on the national level. AFSCME represents over a million public-sector employees, of whom nearly half are in female-dominated clerical and semiprofessional jobs (AFSCME 1983). By the late 1970s many AFSCME locals around the country had taken up the issue in some form, as had other unions representing public-sector workers. Another early AFSCME effort developed in Connecticut—although, as in Washington, it did not lead to early implementation. As described by Johansen (1984, 60–64), complaints from state clerical workers led the Commission on the Status of Women, in conjunction with the union, to draft an "Upward Mobility Program." Two years later, when this program had accomplished little, members of clerical and health-care employee unions, the commission, and feminist state senators joined together to lobby for a job evaluation study following the Washington example.

Local-level activity had also emerged by the late 1970s from within the women's professions. In 1977, for example, librarians in

28. Interestingly, Phyllis Schlafly (1984, 251–255) made much of the fact that the federal district court judge who presided over the Washington case endorsing comparable worth was a Carter appointee. This indicates another area where the increased access to the federal government of feminists and civil rights advocates, while not extensive, had positive consequences.

San Diego, California, brought a sex-based wage discrimination lawsuit against the city. Their own study indicated that, although grouped with other professionals for purposes of affirmative action reporting, 80 percent of librarians were in the lowest one-third of the salary scale for city-employed professionals. When this case became known nationally among library workers, their professional association, the American Library Association, also began to advocate comparable worth (Grune 1980, 167–168; Selden et al. 1982, 5).

Similar developments occurred in the nursing profession. In 1975, to cite one instance, nurses in Denver, Colorado, sued the city, claiming they were paid less than male employees with whom they should have been considered (at least) equivalent, including tree trimmers and sign painters. The presiding judge ruled against the nurses because there was no intentional discrimination (as there would have been, for example, if they had been barred from becoming tree trimmers) (Bureau of National Affairs 1981, 7, 111; Cady 1980, 165–166). The judge in this case also was responsible for the infamous remark, "This case is pregnant with the possibility of disrupting the entire economic system of the United States of America!" (Bureau of National Affairs 1981, 111).

The comparable worth movement gained an important voice at the national level, outside the federal government, with the formation of the National Committee on Pay Equity. In 1979 state and local activists met with sympathetic experts in a conference sponsored by AFSCME and the Women's Bureau, where it was agreed that a national umbrella organization to coordinate activity and lobbying efforts was needed. The result was the NCPE, which brings together feminist, civil rights, and labor groups. NCPE's first actions included the publication of a guidebook on pay equity that urged women to work at the local level, and the creation of "an integrated diffusion network" for what had previously been a movement of scattered grass-roots efforts (Johansen 1984, 43–44).

Actions of the EEOC

After Eleanor Holmes Norton became chair of the EEOC in 1977, she moved judiciously toward setting national policy on comparable worth. This was accomplished by means of careful review and implementation of available legal strategies and academic research findings. Two major resources for local activists resulted from these efforts: a partial legal breakthrough in the Supreme Court decision in *County of Washington v. Gunther*, and a landmark report on comparable worth by the National Academy of Sciences (NAS).

Before the *Gunther* decision, comparable worth was unsuccessful in the courts. For example, the nurses' case mentioned above, *Lemons v. City of Denver*, failed both when originally heard in 1977 and again in 1980 on appeal (Bureau of National Affairs 1981, 111). In fact, litigation under Title VII was becoming a dangerous tactic for comparable worth advocates. Not only were the proceedings lengthy and expensive, but the decisions were setting and reaffirming damaging precedents as the courts continued to view sex-based wage discrimination by the narrow standard of *equal* work established by the Equal Pay Act (Johansen 1984, 44).[29] Under Norton the EEOC followed a more careful strategy in litigation, proceeding with cases that could, by narrow arguments, move the courts incrementally toward validating comparable worth (Bureau of National Affairs 1981, 51).

The 1981 Supreme Court decision in the *Gunther* case explicitly refrained from endorsing comparable worth. However, it opened the door for further litigation by allowing the wage discrimination charge without meeting the equal work standard (Roberts 1982; Sorenson 1982). The case involved female jail matrons, underpaid relative to male jail guards according to the county's own job evaluation system; the female jobs had been evaluted as worth 95 percent of the male jobs but paid only 70 percent, while the men were paid the full amount of their evaluated rate. The important point for the court, and in the EEOC's shaping of the case, was that the evaluations themselves were *not* being contested. Therefore, the case could be decided without addressing comparable worth, strictly on the basis of *intentional* discrimination in failing to pay women at their evaluated rate (Bureau of National Affairs 1981, 5–6; Treiman and Hartmann 1981, 3–6).

Following Reagan's electoral victory in 1980, Norton's incremental legal strategy was cut short after *Gunther*. Even so, the decision

29. This standard was incorporated as a part of Title VII in the Bennett Amendment, which provides that an employer may differentiate by sex in determining compensation as long as the equal work standard set by the Equal Pay Act is not violated (Bureau of National Affairs 1981, 5–7).

did open the door to many local efforts during the 1980s, including the Washington State case, and the threat of litigation has provided important leverage in collective bargaining and legislative efforts for comparable worth (Johansen 1984, 20–21). For example, lawsuits were successfully used to press for implementation of comparable worth in Hawaii and Wisconsin, and in such cities as Los Angeles, Chicago, and Philadelphia (AFSCME 1983; Cook 1985, 1986; NCPE 1989d).

Recent dismissals in suits against California and Michigan, however, may signal the end of this tactic's effectiveness. Proponents had hoped to set a precedent by arguing that the maintenance of a sex-segregated work force, with a substantial wage gap between male and female jobs, constitutes intentional discrimination because explicitly discriminatory wage scales adopted more than fifty years ago have never been corrected (NCPE 1989c, 5). But in both cases the judges ruled that women's wages reflect the marketplace, not deliberate discrimination. Despite this setback for the comparable worth movement (one activist described it to me as a "sock in the stomach"), the *New York Times* report concluded that litigation in the 1980s had been an important "conduit of change"; and, more important, comparable worth is "flourishing at the bargaining table" (Lewin 1989b).

For those at the bargaining table, the EEOC under Norton provided another crucial resource in a report published by National Academy of Sciences on comparable worth, commissioned in 1980. This report, *Women, Work, and Wages: Equal Pay for Jobs of Equal Value* (Treiman and Hartmann 1981), presented a scholarly appraisal of the wage gap that validated the notion of comparable worth as well as the use of job evaluation techniques for its implementation. For example, the authors concluded: "Jobs held mainly by women and minorities pay less at least in part *because* they are held mainly by women and minorities. . . . The consistency of the results . . . and the lack of evidence for alternative explanations strongly suggest that wage discrimination is widespread" (p. 93; original emphasis). Although the NAS committee members noted the "underdeveloped nature of [job evaluation] technology" (p. 96) and the many areas pervaded by subjective rather than scientific criteria, they nevertheless recommended that this technology be used in establishing comparable worth policies (pp. 72–73, 96).

The NAS report primarily reviewed literature well known to academics, and it was overly cautious in its conclusions,[30] but it expressed a clear, expert consensus in favor of comparable worth that is often seen as definitive. The report, therefore, provides local activists and nonexperts with the legitimation or authority they may need to bring pay equity into the political arena.

In short, in the brief opening provided by the Carter administration, the EEOC was able to introduce comparable worth as a valid issue for policy consideration, to disseminate scholarly opinion in support of the principle, and to create at least the temporary threat of success through the courts. A measure of these accomplishments is found in critics' protests that Norton grossly exceeded her jurisdiction as head of the EEOC. For example, in an address to the American Bar Association, one prominent attorney accused Norton of "a carefully orchestrated campaign to nullify the will of Congress, . . . overturn the decisions of the courts, and otherwise trample over the sanctity of the law" (Spelfogel 1981, 31, 39; also see Bureau of National Affairs 1981, 18). Since then, such attacks on comparable worth advocates have only increased—although, of course, opponents are now the "insiders" in the federal bureaucracy.

In the Reagan years in particular, the federal government made a concerted effort to discredit comparable worth. The chair of the Civil Rights Commission derisively called it "the looniest idea since Looney Tunes" (*New York Times* 1984b), and the commission urged rejection of the concept (U.S. Commission on Civil Rights 1985a, 1985b; Pear 1985a). The EEOC followed such "advice," ruling soon thereafter that federal law does not require equal pay for different jobs (Pear 1985b). But despite this counterattack, the comparable worth movement has continued to grow on both the state and the local level (*National NOW Times*, 1986c; Stein 1988), and the accumulation of actions around the country has greatly reinforced the validity of comparable worth demands (Lewin 1989b).

According to the latest count by the National Committee on Pay Equity (1989d), action on comparable worth has been taken in all

30. For example, it skirted many political issues or issues of conflicting interests, treating these primarily as questions of subjective values and calling for either further research or a consensus (from an unspecified process) between employers and employees (Blum 1983).

but five states. Six are in the process of full-blown implementation, twenty have seen some wage adjustments made, in twenty-three job evaluation studies have been conducted, and in forty-three preliminary research has been completed. As for localities—cities, counties, school districts, and so forth—1,739 are taking action, although the great bulk of these, 1,392, are in Minnesota, the first state to require implementation at the local level; the remainder are in twenty-eight states and the District of Columbia.

Finally, comparable worth has proved to be a highly successful organizing issue at several prestigious private universities. These cases, particularly the strike of clerical workers at Yale University, attracted national attention out of all proportion to the small numbers affected. Such cases demonstrate the capacity of pay equity to mobilize vigorous grass-roots action among previously unorganized women workers (Cerullo and Feldberg 1984; Frank 1986; Serrin 1984a, 1984b). This radical potential of comparable worth and its broader implications were not lost on journalists covering the events. One writer noted that the success of women at such a prominent, and antiunion, university as Yale "shows office workers can be attracted to unions" (Serrin 1984a). He concluded with obvious admiration: "The workers, mostly women, showed immense solidarity, the kind often found today only in labor-history books" (Serrin 1985).

It is apparent that the national context out of which local comparable worth efforts emerged was filled with inconsistencies—between the rhetoric of affirmative action and its concrete effects; between the traditional class bias of the feminist movement and its need for a broader, more inclusive base of support; and between the growing success of comparable worth and the resulting resistance of the federal government. These inconsistencies created both opportunities and constraints for local activists. The following chapters explore how these challenges were addressed in two specific cases. In the first, female city employees in San Jose, California, explicitly feminist-identified, raised comparable worth as an affirmative action issue until frustration led to a union approach. But in Contra Costa County, my second case, women were initially labor-identified and felt little tie to the feminist movement until becoming involved in comparable worth efforts.

Three

"Tough Politics"

The Comparable Worth Movement in San Jose

The city of San Jose and the county of Contra Costa, although both in the greater San Francisco Bay region, are quite different in character. San Jose, located approximately fifty miles south of San Francisco, is the center of an affluent metropolitan area, with a strong ethnic and racial mix and a liberal political milieu. Thirty years ago San Jose was an important agricultural center, but it is now the capital of the high-tech industries of the Silicon Valley. Contra Costa County, in contrast, sprawls over a large area from the northeastern edge of San Francisco Bay out to the eastern valleys; there, large stretches of undeveloped hillsides remain alongside shining new housing, shopping and office developments in the central county, the poor black ghetto of the west county, and the oil refineries in the north.

I chose these cases because the differences in local character shape distinct class and gender relations. Nevertheless, both localities were the site of strong affirmative action efforts in the early 1970s and intense comparable worth campaigns a decade later. I will show in the next two chapters the distinct paths to mobilization followed by low-paid women in each locality as they moved from the limits of affirmative action to the more radical comparable worth demand. Although a similar convergence of class and gender identification resulted in the two cases, in San Jose activists began from a stronger gender-based vocabulary, and in Contra Costa a class-based discourse defined the opening moves.

In 1981 the San Jose case became one of the first major victories for the comparable worth movement. The city had undertaken a job evaluation study and verified the same sizable wage disparities indicated in the earlier Washington State study, and in July of that year the San Jose activists in AFSCME Local 101 became the first to call a strike over pay equity. Because this brief strike was a success, winning substantial wage adjustments for low-paid women and attracting extensive national attention, the San Jose case is often treated as exemplary. In this chapter I examine the origins and conduct of the San Jose effort by means of in-depth interviews with participants, documentary evidence, and secondary sources; in Chapter 4, then, I turn to the Contra Costa case. (See Appendix B for details of the research methodology and specific case references.)

From Affirmative Action to
Comparable Worth

Although San Jose was the fourth largest city in the state and seventeenth largest in the country in the 1980s, it employed only some nine hundred women and three thousand men. The women worked primarily in the female-dominated occupations: over half (54 percent) worked in clerical jobs, and semiprofessionals (library and recreation workers) made up just under 20 percent of female employees.[1] The larger number of men employed is due to the fact that San Jose, like most cities, provides police and fire services, which are predominantly male jobs.

The city of San Jose first began writing and implementing formal affirmative action plans in 1973, largely in response to the demands of the local Hispanic community. Since then a degree of racial and ethnic integration has been achieved,[2] although only at the lowest levels (see, e.g., Acuna 1978; *San Jose Mercury News* 12/22/76, 1/21/74).

1. This figure for semiprofessionals is my estimate, as extrapolated from affirmative action reports and comparable worth memos, since EEO categories are too broad to give a precise figure for this occupational grouping. Despite the lack of exact figures, clearly a large majority of female city employees work in female-dominated jobs.

2. For example, full-time minority employment increased from approximately 10 percent of the work force in 1973 (*San Jose Mercury News* 2/13/76) to 30 percent in 1984 (City of San Jose 1984, 44).

The appearance of a strong feminist voice in local government was prompted by the growth of feminist activity in the community (Flammang 1985, 1986, 1987). In 1974, for example, a banner year for local feminists, the San Jose chapter of NOW hosted the organization's statewide convention (*San Jose Mercury News* 10/27/74) and filed a sex discrimination suit against Philco-Ford, a large aerospace firm (*San Jose Mercury News* 9/26/74).

One of the top priorities for feminists in San Jose was the election of women to local public office. Local chapters of the National Women's Political Caucus and the League of Women Voters worked hard toward this goal, and were quite successful—more so than groups in many other localities around the country. In 1974, in addition to a woman being elected to represent San Jose in the state assembly, former councilmember Janet Gray Hayes was voted in as mayor—the first woman in the nation to head a city of that size. Hayes and other women leaders thus proclaimed San Jose "the feminist capital of the nation" (Flammang 1985). By the time of the comparable worth strike in 1981, women held a majority of seats on the city council, Mayor Hayes had been reelected, the deputy city manager was a woman, and the city's slogan had been inflated from "the feminist capital of the nation" to "the feminist capital of the world."

The city's internal employment policies were clearly responsive to these changes. Community women's groups worked hard for affirmative action in city employment, as I learned in an interview with a former president of the local NOW chapter, who also served as the women's representative to the City's Affirmative Action Advisory Committee during this period.[3] The city's response to these concerns was apparent in the creation of a full-time women's coordinator position. While the city affirmative action officer was responsible for implementation in general, the women's coordinator worked on affirmative action issues for the city's female employees specifically.[4]

3. At the time of our interview, this woman was employed as a top city personnel relations official.

4. In fact, the city's commitment to affirmative action for women may have sparked some resentment in the minority community. In 1976 the *San Jose Mercury News* (2/13/76) reported that one Hispanic leader spoke out because he felt the city was favoring white women to the exclusion of minorities in meeting its affirmative action goals and timetables. By the time of my research in 1984, however, the position of women's coordinator had been eliminated.

The city's commitment to affirmative action is further evident in the changing distribution of women in the city work force. Women began for the first time to enter management positions, as well as some traditionally male blue-collar and technical bastions such as public works and the police department—if to a very modest degree. This gradual integration has continued, despite little overall growth in the size of city employment (Pifarre 1985).[5] However, as in other organizations, the gradual move toward less strict occupational segregation by sex—a significant accomplishment in itself— materially benefited only a small number of women. At the same time, though, it sent a strong symbolic message to all female employees, enhancing women's aspirations for upward mobility. In fact, one city official concluded: "While becoming the high-tech capital of the world, San Jose was also gaining its reputation as a feminist power center. . . . Women's strong advocacy of affirmative action programs in the early 70's had led to significant employment gains. . . . But as workplace parity was gradually realized in many areas, other issues began to arise" (Farnquist, Armstrong, and Strausbaugh 1983, 359).

Clerical Women

By the mid-1970s many women were becoming frustrated with the city's affirmative action policies as, acting on newly raised expectations, they sought individual promotions. This was especially true for clerical workers, who generally lacked the college credits required for upward movement out of secretarial work. In fact, frustration with this educational requirement led to the formation of a clericals' group called the City Women for Advancement. One of my respondents recounted the group's history, explaining that city management never made exceptions, even for women with many years of experience but lacking college courses: "It was very obvious to some of us, the clerical people who were working next to

5. Some figures can give an idea of this gradual movement. By 1978 women held 12.4 percent of technical jobs (Acuna 1978), and by 1984, this had increased to slightly over 20 percent (Pifarre 1984). Furthermore, by 1980 twenty-four women had become police officers, (5.6 percent of the total police force) and by 1984, thirty-nine (6.8 percent). Also, by 1981 there were thirty-two women in management positions (13.2 percent of total managers), and in 1985, sixty-seven (15.7 percent) (Pifarre 1985).

professional people, that there was no reason we couldn't handle those jobs just as well." When a new entry-level professional position, administrative aide, was created in 1973, the experienced clerical women, thwarted in their attempts at upward mobility, felt provoked to take action: "We applied for the jobs, about twenty, maybe thirty clericals, we all applied for the job. . . . We actually had several informal meetings and we decided to apply for the job. And we were all turned down! They disqualified us from taking the exam!"

Together, the women appealed this decision to the Civil Service Commission, turning for support to feminist organizations: "I drafted a letter to various women's groups in the area, NOW, and the Santa Clara County Commission on the Status of Women, and some others . . . and asked that they send letters of support. We outlined that [together] we had over three hundred years of clerical experience, and that we felt this was sufficient qualifications for the position—and that we should at least be allowed to test!" It was in these letters that they first called the group City Women for Advancement. "And so several groups did respond. And the Civil Service Commission ultimately did decide that in certain clerical classifications experience could be equated for the education. *Mine* was *not* one of them, however!" The irony of this outcome was not lost on the women employees: "There were about ten or twelve that were able to take the test. And the overall pass rate on that test was about 30 percent but 80 percent of clericals passed—even if only one gained the promotion."

Several important lessons came from this experience. First, the women, each interested in an individual promotion, found that they confronted a common problem of blocked mobility. Second, the women's use of a gender-based frame for their complaint was affirmed as a positive approach, both by the support gained from community feminist groups and by the partial capitulation of the Civil Service Board. But importantly, despite a fairly effective protest, the gain was so limited that women felt a need to press for further changes.

The City Women began holding lunchtime meetings about once a month, and eventually made several presentations to the city council that linked their complaints to the city's affirmative action program. The desired reforms seemed to fall well within the scope of existing policies, as actions that ought to follow from promises of "aggressive efforts" to assist women's advancement in the city system.[6] The biggest issues continued to be the substitution of experience for educational requirements, the creation of bridge classifications linking clerical to professional career tracks, and the creation of expanded job ladders within the clerical field itself. These demands represented elaborations or extensions of the affirmative action model, since advancement was defined as the movement of women into different jobs, at higher levels within the organization (even if this required expanding the job hierarchy). And many of these women hoped to move up and ultimately *out* of clerical work into male jobs.

My respondents estimated that twenty to twenty-five women at a time had attended the City Women's lunchtime meetings. One woman I spoke with considered such gatherings to have been primarily social, a "consciousness-raising type of activity." However, another pointed out that they attracted women office workers from many different departments, allowing them to get to know one another; and as she said, "They did a really good job. They got the women together, and they got the facts down, and [later] they presented them . . . [to the union and to the City Council]."

Throughout this period, the City Women for Advancement also edged toward the idea of comparable worth as they grappled for more effective strategies to assist clerical women. They became increasingly aware that only a few women were moving into better-paying jobs. Although they continued to press for such opportunities, they felt provoked to draw comparisons between the jobs they seemed stuck in and the higher-paid, male-dominated jobs. At first, as several women explained, these comparisons were drawn only very informally.

One longtime office worker described the evolution of her thinking. According to civil service requirements, a clerical, no matter how long she had been with the city, had to have a written test, a skills test, and an oral interview each time she applied to move up the job ladder. My respondent resented this as "constantly having to prove yourself"; because she had progressed up the clerical

6. Official affirmative action rhetoric includes such statements as the following: ". . . positive and innovative action to assure that all possible barriers to employment of members of minority groups and women . . . are eliminated. . . . This includes initiation and continuance of *aggressive efforts* to attract and assist members of these groups to qualify for employment and advancement within the City system" (City of San Jose 1984, 6; emphasis added).

track from entry-level typist to executive secretary, she felt she had proved herself many times over. She complained to other women office workers that the men in city jobs were not constantly being tested: for many of their jobs, she knew, only an interview was required. Over time she became progressively more angry. Finally, in one of the secretarial exams a question asked: "Would you run errands for the boss's wife?" This so enraged the women test takers that they stormed up to the personnel office to protest. My respondent clearly developed a sense of the inequities clerical women face, and she understood them within a gender-based frame. This orientation contributed to her later support for comparable worth. When we spoke in 1985, she told me that five years earlier she had known all the male-female comparisons for clericals (from the comparable worth study); she said she'd had them all "down cold."

Another longtime secretary for the city explained how she began to compare the men and women, framing her complaints in gender terms. Each time salary raises came up, she saw that the men were receiving larger increases than the women: "There was a group of women who *for years* talked about how unequal we felt the pay raises were in the city between the primarily male and primarily female jobs."

Since educational requirements had been the initial point of contention with the city and the most overt cause of the clericals' blocked mobility, several women began drawing informal comparisons with the educational requirements of male-dominated jobs. When they found that many men in categories requiring only an eighth-grade education were better paid than they were, the women became resentful. One respondent explained how angry they were when they realized they made less than men who washed cars for the city! The City Women for Advancement began to document these education-salary comparisons more formally. My second respondent quoted above described this effort in some detail:

We did a study, years and years ago [approximaely 1975 or 1976], and at that point it wasn't called comparable worth. It was just kind of a study to see how different the salaries were for female-dominated and male-dominated classes—which evolved [several years later] into the comparable worth thing. . . . We didn't go to the outside or look at what other cities did. We just looked at classifications versus education versus salary, just to see where all the classes fell.

At that time, it wasn't related to the union [AFSCME Local 101] at all.

But afterwards, after we'd made the charts, we started talking to people in the union about it, asking if it could be used as a basis for salary negotiations. But we didn't really delve into it in any great depth—we didn't really push for it. We always had kind of talked about the inequities that existed, whenever a group of women would get together. But we didn't really begin to push for any changes to be made until we started talking about the Hay [job evaluation] study.

An important step toward comparable worth was taken in 1977, when the City Women for Advancement presented their report, "Affirmative Action and City Women," to the city council. The report made some twenty recommendations for increasing the mobility of clerical women. In addition to the need for bridge classifications and credit for work experience, recommendations included increasing recruiting and training for nontraditional jobs and instituting job sharing and flexible hours. Such recommendations (with the possible exceptions of job sharing and flextime) again reflect the affirmative action model of mobility, with its advocacy of increased opportunities for job movement. Furthermore, as one woman explained, the recommendations were not actual *demands* for which the women were prepared to fight; they were merely requests for the council and city management's consideration and eventual managerial implementation. Female employees, however, had great immediate interest in the proposals, and over two hundred women packed the council chambers for the presentation (Gruber 1977).

Although the report of the City Women emphasized enhanced opportunities for job mobility, it also proposed one very new idea: that women's jobs no longer be paid according to "their normal value in the marketplace" (Farnquist, Armstrong, and Strausbaugh 1983, 359). In salary negotiations that year, clerical women requested a *27.5 percent* increase, based on their study comparing male and female job requirements and their new idea that the market value for clerical work was unfair, or simply wrong. At that time, however, the wage request was primarily a symbolic gesture from which little actual gain was expected. The women were not prepared, so early on, to press for nonmarket, comparison-based wages, in part because of the novelty of the idea, but also because of the nature of the "top-down" affirmative action framework and their own lack of labor identification. As several writers have observed, however, increasing people's awareness of gender-based pay inequities can be like opening the proverbial Pandora's box (e.g., Farnquist, Armstrong, and Strausbaugh 1983; *Oakland Tribune* 7/7/81).

Two women's comments illustrate the excitement generated by the comparable worth issue in contrast to affirmative action. The first woman explained why she thought many women would eventually share this excitement: "People will begin to see over time, okay, here is a way to get me, and me, and me, and *all* of us typists or whatever [female job holders] *more money*—instead of just *one* of us getting promoted." The other woman, who had benefited personally from affirmative action, explained: "Eventually I believe women will choose other [nontraditional] fields. But women who are working *now* should not have to pay for that *eventual* adjustment. I know that many clericals are *very* capable—more than professionals." Many other women echoed these comments—for example:

The pay inequity between male and female jobs . . . it's something that went back to when girls grew up, they got married, they stayed home. The husband went out, he worked, and he supported the family. That's *not* a reality anymore! People started realizing, "Hey, that's fine. But that's a fairy tale in this day and age." And . . . because society had said this is how it's operated for hundreds of years *doesn't make it right!* It *has* to be changed. It has to start somewhere!

Ironically, the city's appointment of a full-time women's coordinator contributed to the clericals' growing politicization. I had the opportunity to interview the woman who held this position in the late 1970s. She had a strong background in civil rights, having worked on equal opportunity issues in the Vista Program and then as equal opportunity specialist for another California community. As part of her job in San Jose, she became involved with the City Women for Advancement and assisted in the writing of "Affirmative Action and City Women." Her presence in an official capacity lent added legitimacy to the group's actions, even as they increasingly came to oppose city management.

In addition to working with department heads to increase the representation of women in male-dominated jobs, the women's coordinator supported comparable worth, explaining she felt it was a just claim for women workers. The best approach for achieving comparable worth in her view, however, was the "top down" model of affirmative action; for employees, it was appropriate only to present recommendations to the city administration and the council, and to leave actual policy making to them. She did not support comparable worth as a union strategy and, in fact, held rather anti-union views. She vehemently opposed the 1981 strike: "In the past, I felt I was in conflict with the union. We did work together, but there was not a good mutual feeling. I had a problem with the whole strike issue. Certainly things couldn't have been accomplished as quickly [without a strike]. And comparable worth was a timely thing with the media and the mayor being a woman. But strikes are a *dirty* thing."

Despite such antilabor sentiments, the women's coordinator did cooperate, within the City Women for Advancement, with AFSCME Local 101 business agent Maxine Jenkins.[7] Jenkins, credited with introducing the formal notion of comparable worth to the clericals, had arrived in San Jose with a background in both feminist and union activity and a commitment to integrating the two (see Balser 1987, 129–130; Foner 1980, 503–504). With the participation of both a city official and a union official, the City Women became an important channel between nonunion and union women. Although not a labor-affiliated group, some of the City Women members had been union members, though inactive ones; the presence of Jenkins, along with joint support for the comparable worth issue, led to increases in union membership and activity. Two women, for example, told me that it was while active in City Women that they first realized the need for unions, as they saw the need for real power in bargaining. Thus, the City Women for Advancement not only built support for comparable worth, but also legitimated a union presence, illustrating that a labor strategy could be used to address gender issues.[8]

7. Jenkins, AFSCME Local 101 business agent in the late 1970s, left in 1980, before the job evaluation study was finished and before the comparable worth strike. I was unfortunately unable to contact her for this study, and later in this chapter when I refer to my interview with the union business agent I refer to her successor, Bill Callahan.

8. Analysts concerned with the "organizability" of clerical workers reach similar conclusions on the importance of some prior form of association both to expose women to a union approach and to illustrate that unions can be appropriate for women. One activist, for example, writes that prior forms of organization can represent "the phase of building a sense of collective identity and the will to organize which must precede the traditional union organizing methods" (Cameron 1986, 109). Strom, in her historical studies of women's organizing, also notes the necessity to convey the message that unions are appropriate for women (1983, 381).

Librarians

During the same period, San Jose's predominantly female librarians were also struggling to extend the goals of affirmative action
and moving toward an embrace of comparable worth. Approximately seventy-five library professionals were employed by the
city, of whom 80–85 percent were female (Pifarre 1984, 1985). In
the mid-1970s this group had formed its own organization, the
Concerned Library Active Workers (CLAW). CLAW, like the group
for clericals, City Women, was formed to deal with the specific advancement issues facing library employees, who confronted a different situation from office workers. These women professionals
also desired greater socioeconomic attainment, but the idea of
moving into male jobs, as affirmative action would require, had
little appeal. Many of these women had invested a great deal in
their education (or in gaining the equivalent on-the-job experience), as library jobs require bachelor's or even master's degrees in
library science (or the equivalent experience). This investment
would be forfeited if they changed fields. As in most traditional
women's professions, however, librarians face an essentially flat
lifetime career trajectory and earnings curve.

Aside from requiring the loss of investment in their careers,
many librarians felt that the affirmative action model of mobility
was insulting, for it implies that women who have chosen traditionally feminine fields are to blame for their low earnings (Remick
and Steinberg 1984, 294–295). In interviews, several women commented that city officials stated that if they wanted the higher rewards, they should go into male jobs. Librarians in San Jose, in the
atmosphere created by affirmative action efforts, came deeply to
resent this implication, and felt strongly that no woman should be
forced to change jobs merely to receive fair pay. For library employees, the struggle that developed in the mid-1970s represented
an attempt to achieve upward mobility *within* the library field,
whereas clericals focused on the requirements and practices involved in moving up and *out* of clerical work. Both groups, however, pushed the limits of what affirmative action policies can offer.

One librarian explained the bureaucratic mechanisms involved
in their early efforts to gain special salary increases. Employees in
any job class could appeal a pay raise by showing *external* labor

market comparisons to justify special adjustments (over and above the general increase). Librarians, of course, could not easily draw external comparisons demonstrating underpayment, as nearly all library work is performed by women. Another avenue, then, was to contest the job specification—to argue that it did not include the full range of actual responsibilities and that therefore a salary adjustment was warranted. But with either approach, the appeal process was lengthy and frustrating. Another librarian involved with CLAW during this period recalled:

I started in the library ten years ago [1974]. . . . When we'd say we wanted to raise our salaries in the library and they'd say [and here she imitated their feigned innocence]: "Okay, sure, fine. What are librarians in the next jurisdiction getting?" [She laughed softly.] Well, of course, we were all getting coolie wages because there was no sense comparing me to another coolie in another jurisdiction!

I then asked if they had ever gotten any special increases. She replied: "We did get some *small* increases, but it took *years* to lay your case for it." Later this woman commented with great vehemence on the pejorative aspect of affirmative action: "I *don't* want to leave librarianship to make an adequate salary in some field that pays more money but is . . . is . . . . *Why* is that [field] more financially rewarding and less emotionally satisfying, less intellectually satisfying? The only explanation I could come up with finally was because it's [library work is] run by *women*, and that's why it's not valued."

Another librarian and CLAW activist also explained what was wrong with an affirmative action approach:

The city has said: "We *really* think what we really need to do in the long run is to get the women into these male occupations." Well, then *who the heck* is gonna do the other jobs that are important?! . . . What they're saying is that those jobs [our jobs] are not important . . . whereas we say they are important jobs. And some people have an interest in doing surveying, and some people have an interest in working in libraries, and some people have an interest in working with computers—and we're *not* all the same. But that doesn't mean that one job is less important, or less valuable, or should have less status or less money than the others!

In such comments one can see how affirmative action provoked the changing consciousness of these "semiprofessional" women.

They had perceived the offers of enhanced advancement opportunities, yet when they reached for tangible returns they were slapped back down. The pejorative implications became clear, and women reacted angrily to any suggestion that their choice of occupation was to blame for their low earnings. Librarians were provoked to reframe their complaints in gender terms as well, for the crux of the problem seemed to be that their work, a traditionally female profession, was considered of low value compared with male fields. In fact, one of the few male librarians, Mike Ferrero, told me that when he first heard of the comparable worth notion, "it was just like a light going off [sic] in my head," because it so precisely illuminated the library workers' experience.

The emergence of comparable worth among librarians echoes earlier strains or sentiments common to the female semiprofessions as a whole. As occupational sociologists have defined them, the semiprofessions lack the full authority and autonomy within their employing organizations of the classic professions. Therefore, the ongoing dilemma for such fields is how to establish professional status and gain more autonomy within organizational settings. Because they cannot claim a monopoly over any systematic body of knowledge and theoretical training, it is difficult for groups such as teachers, nurses, social workers, or librarians to claim the status of such occupations as medicine, law, or the traditional academic fields (Etzioni 1969; Ritzer 1972). For women in these fields in the mid-1970s, the promises held out by affirmative action, as well as the contributions of feminist discourse in general, only reinforced the "role strain" already present. Certainly, in San Jose this occupational role strain became reframed as a gender issue and recast as part of the larger problem of female subordination. Without the larger social context, or the immediate local environment in which affirmative action for women was high on the public agenda, such occupational issues would not have taken on the same "gendered" formulation.[9]

Semiprofessionals have also typically had difficulty embracing

9. Recent attempts in the teaching field to impose greater "professional" standards represent a response to semiprofessional role strain that does *not* use a gendered formulation. By imposing such things as proficiency exams and more complex certification procedures for primary and secondary instruction (predominantly female fields), some hope to justify much higher salaries (Spencer 1988, 182).

An interesting, but nonfeminist, framing of semiprofessional role strain as a

union strategies, because the labor union stance and blue-collar image detract from the fully professional status they emulate (Etzioni
1969; Ritzer 1972). Librarians, for example, experience this ambivalence; as one CLAW leader commented: "I don't think librarians
are used to unions, and many librarians have shied away from
unions as being unprofessional" (Fischer 1981, 2084). Yet she also
explained that in San Jose the librarians came to feel that collective
bargaining was their only viable strategy for achieving comparable
worth. Therefore, in 1978 library employees from CLAW became
active in the Municipal Employees Federation (MEF, the sub-
group of AFSCME Local 101 of Santa Clara County representing
City employees), becoming officers in order to push for comparable
worth.

The courts are not going to help us very much, and legislation takes a
while and may or may not be implemented. The courts are not particularly favorable to pay equity. . . . The San Diego case hasn't been settled
yet. It's been in the courts six years or so, and litigation is very expensive. . . . The only way I see of achieving pay equity is through unions.
. . . No one is going to give you money, and it's a lot of money . . . so
it's well worth fighting for. . . . That's why you need a strong union.

(Fischer 1981, 2084)[10]

Recreation Professionals

A third group that entered union activity at the point of the comparable worth effort was recreation workers, some fifty to fifty-five
employees of the Parks and Recreation Department who work in
neighborhood recreation centers throughout the city. This field
was mixed with just under half of the job occupants male (Pifarre
1984, 1985), but it was viewed overwhelmingly as female sex-typed
work because it involves working with children as a direct extension of the public schools. One woman's story is instructive in re-
counting the changing awareness through this period.

---

gender issue occurred in social work during the 1950s. To counter the negative
"feminine" image of the field, efforts were made to recruit men, as well as to make
social work more "masculine" by making it more scientific and rational (Collins
1988, 190).

10. Librarians in San Jose were very aware of the suit brought by women librarians against the city of San Diego, California, where the affirmative action officer had failed to act on their report of salary inequities among professional employees (Galloway and Archuleta 1980, 168–169).

This respondent had been a recreation professional with the city since the late 1960s, although she had initially planned to become a high school teacher. In college she had begun working part-time in an after-school playground program; she "developed a real love for the recreation field," changed her major area of study, and took a full-time job when one became available. By the mid-1970s, however, with the effects of affirmative action beginning to be felt, she became increasingly distressed that her chosen field was a "dead-end street" as far as any further advancement was concerned. It bothered her that recreation work was not taken seriously, and she began to realize that this was because it was women's work. She then began to notice what the librarians, her fellow female professionals, were doing: "Actually, library professionals face the same sorts of barriers in employment that recreation professionals do. People have to fight real hard to be looked at as professionals."

Consequently, this respondent decided to become more active in MEF, as the librarians had, and got elected to the negotiating team to "make more noise" for the recreation employees. Like the librarians, however, she found that her motives, which initially were narrowly construed for the benefit of her own profession, quickly became enlarged and extended to women workers in general. She had already had the sense that her work was denigrated because it was women's work, and therefore she quickly became "embroiled in the comparable worth issue" once on the negotiating team. Describing her attitude at that point, she told me: "We were fighting like anything for the women's jobs."

For this woman, as for many librarians, concern with her own advancement, fueled by the notion of entitlement that affirmative action gave women, led to a broader politicization. She came both to reframe her concerns as gender issues and to enthusiastically endorse union activity to pursue her new sense of interests as a woman worker. In fact, she later left city employment to become a full-time union employee, organizing other women and working for comparable worth in other localities.

The Union: Women Professional and Clerical Workers

The realization that they could not attain their goals through traditional "top-down" approaches led many San Jose women workers to become interested in union activity. Interestingly, the tendency of affirmative action to produce this unintended consequence was noted in an earlier analysis. An organizing manual written specifically for public-sector women noted that one result of affirmative action implementation generally is women's development of higher aspirations; but because these expectations are not met, the author notes, "employers are actually driving women and minorities into the arms of unions" (Samuels 1975, 240). Put differently, what is first framed as a gender issue, as *women's* blocked mobility or the denigration of *women's* work, converges with a class perspective as women discover the usefulness of unions to promote their interests as devalued *workers*.

In San Jose the union, MEF of AFSCME Local 101, had been primarily concerned with the male occupations, since male workers—engineering technicians, surveyors, construction inspectors, and most city maintenance workers—were most active prior to 1977–1978 (the police and fire departments have separate employee organizations). The women, although represented by MEF, did not participate actively until the emergence of the comparable worth issue in 1977.[11] As one long-time city clerical told me, "I was a member of the union for less than a year. I joined when I first came to the city [appoximately 1975]. But I quit because the technicians got such a big raise that year, more of a raise than us, so I wanted to keep the dues money for myself."

As women began to agitate for their own demands, and as these began to center on wages for women's work rather than opportunities to change jobs, the usefulness of the union as a collective bargaining authority became clear. Women from both City Women for Advancement and CLAW became active union members in the late 1970s. In 1978, in fact, librarians took over most of the official positions in MEF. As one librarian commented in a published interview, "Within CLAW, several articulate people surfaced around the issue of pay equity, and we decided that the union was the best vehicle for pursuing pay equity. . . . I don't want to say that we took over the union, but the real activists in the union, which is a broad-based union, were library employees" (Fischer 1981, 2080).

The new interest of women employees in union activity was en-

11. MEF represents some two thousand city employees (*Labor Notes* 1981b), but several respondents estimated that only half that number were dues-paying members.

hanced by the fact that the local's business agent was a woman. By all accounts Maxine Jenkins was a central figure in building support both for affirmative action reforms for women and for comparable worth. Through her involvement with City Women for Advancement she was able to create a more positive image of union activity among women who were described to me as "just never having been exposed to a union mentality before."

For librarians, comparable worth was the catalyst that prompted both involvement in the union and a sense of identification with women workers outside their narrow occupational group. Comparable worth was "the light going off" that connected their perceived interests as "professionals" struggling for greater recognition with the interests and struggles of other women workers. Although tensions remained between the groups, this connection was crucial politically and moved the group closer to framing their concerns in class terms.

After the women had taken over their union in 1978, they made comparable worth the top bargaining priority, and quickly circulated a position paper to this effect (Beyette 1981). Yet because there were few examples of successful comparable worth efforts on which to model their tactics, activists were not sure how to proceed. Maxine Jenkins had come to San Jose specifically hoping to use comparable worth to organize clerical workers, and the national AFSCME leadership had begun to promote the comparable worth strategy (see, e.g., Grune 1980, 131, 152–153). Yet San Jose women were also aware of the stalled Washington State efforts, which involved "sister" AFSCME locals (as well as the stalled case of the San Diego librarians mentioned above). Washington efforts had been initiated in 1974, with the authorization of the first job evaluation to compare male- and female-dominated jobs. While this study had found large discrepancies between male and female salaries for equivalently ranked jobs, the legislature had declined to appropriate any funds to remedy the inequity. An update of the study corroborated the earlier results, but by 1978 Washington employees had still seen no action (Johansen 1984, 19–20; Remick 1984, 102–104).

Nevertheless, it seemed to San Jose activists that a formal study was a necessary first step toward equitable wages. But the city immediately rejected a proposal to that effect, in large part because of the passage of state Proposition 13, which drastically cut property taxes (Farnquist, Armstrong, and Strausbaugh 1983, 359).[12] Ironically, later that year the city contracted with Hay Associates, a national management consulting firm, to conduct a similar salary and classification study of all *management* positions. According to one union source, this action was a response to "grumbling" by women managers, who may have picked up the idea from their women workers (McGuire 1982, 12). The city manager, however, maintained that the managerial study was being conducted to establish internal and external equity in order to retain management employees in the booming Silicon Valley market, not to compare male and female salaries (Flammang 1986, 816, 833). Still, AFSCME members saw their opportunity and jumped, demanding that if management were to have such an equity study, nonmanagement employees should also. When the city "reaffirmed that it was not interested in studying the relationships between male and female salaries" (Farnquist, Armstrong, and Strausbaugh 1983, 360), AFSCME members began several months of agitation aimed specifically at gaining a formal study.[13]

Because women's blocked mobility had already been a point of contention for several years, the issue of the job evaluation became politically volatile by 1979, especially given the announcement of the management study. Agitation included intensive lobbying of the mayor and councilmembers, who were concerned with their public appearance and "feminist" credentials (Mueller 1985, 14). In addition, AFSCME organized a one day sick-out of clericals, in which 80 to 125 women participated.[14] As one respondent com-

12. The state also instituted a wage freeze as a condition for receiving bailout funds from its large surplus. The following year, however, the state Supreme Court ruled the freeze an unlawful restriction on the provision of the funds (Farnquist, Armstrong, and Strausbaugh 1983, 359). In addition, as Flammang (1986) documents, the healthy local economy helped San Jose to recover quickly from the aftershocks of Proposition 13.

13. The cost of the study may have played some part in the city's rejection. Hay Associates was to charge the city $96,000 for the study of nonmanagement positions (Fischer 1981, 2085), and the total estimated cost to the city including staff and employee time off-the-job was $500,000 (Keppel 1981; *Labor Notes* 1981b). Yet with a total city budget in 1980 of $400 million and personnel costs of approximately $95 million (Flammang 1986), the cost of the study was certainly not the major reason for the city's opposition.

14. The low estimate originates from the city administration (see Farnquist,

mented, "A hundred twenty-five clericals from City Hall went out in that sick-out. And a week after that, the study was agreed to by the city."

Although the city did then agree to the study, it would make no promises on implementation; it merely agreed to review the results. Thus for almost all of 1980 the study itself, while just the first step from the union's point of view, became the focus of activity and attention. The union maintained all along that the study would reveal serious underpayment of women, yet, as several respondents explained, the city manager had selected Hay Associates because he was confident their methods would find no inequities. Concurrent Hay studies of Wisconsin and Minnesota state employment in fact did reinforce the status quo; Hay consultants justified what disparities were found according to market factors. However, there was no union involvement in those studies (Grune 1980, 131, 153), and as my respondents pointed out, San Jose's city manager had not expected the union to stay involved in the evaluation process. In fact, AFSCME had already won a major concession: Maxine Jenkins had persuaded the council (against the city manager's advice) to instruct Hay to deemphasize market factors for a fair result (Flammang 1986, 831).

Politics and Science: The Job Evaluation Study

The entire job evaluation episode in San Jose exemplifies the tension between science and politics in the control of state policy making, a tension that several social theorists have identified as peculiarly characteristic of contemporary society. Following Max Weber's analysis of politics in modern bureaucracies, Habermas (1971, 1975) posits that science, considered the realm of value-free inquiry, becomes a legitimating ideology for governmental action. This process obscures both the class and power relations served by and represented within such action. Moreover, the ideology itself has a tendency to reframe moral and political questions as merely technical issues; that is, questions of what our rights to specific en-

Armstrong, and Strausbaugh 1983, 360), while the upper estimate originates from a union activist among my respondents. My respondent also stressed that this number was significant, being out of 515 clericals in the city; the sick-out did not include female professionals.

titlements should be are reduced to questions of the efficiency or appropriateness of techniques, and questions of what ought to be are reduced to discussions of what is empirically verifiable. Because of this "scientization of politics," according to Habermas, politics in turn becomes "depoliticized." In other words, control by bureaucratic managers and technical experts increases, while broad-based participation in public debate over policy goals is precluded.[15]

In San Jose, these tendencies can be seen in the struggle over the job evaluation study at its various stages. On the one hand, city officials attempted to keep control of the evaluation process, mystifying the methodology used in order to foreclose debate. For example, the city had originally planned to include only one employee representative on the ten-member evaluation committee, and had not intended even to provide the union with a copy of the completed report (Fischer 1983, 2081). Hay Associates also contributed to this mystification, as they certainly had an interest in protecting their copyrighted techniques; by 1981 Hay had conducted more job evaluation studies nationwide than any other firm (Van Beers 1981, 42). On the other hand, the union activists, who were aware of their threatened loss of control, had to balance the need for validated empirical proof of their claims against the need to question and contest the methodology—that is, to question its purposes and the interests it was designed to serve. In fact, as was mentioned in Chapter 2, job evaluation techniques are hardly neutral. Originally designed to promote managerial control over wage setting, they primarily rationalize existing job hierarchies, and are thus problematic for establishing pay equity policies (Sorenson 1982, Treiman 1979).

The president of AFSCME Local 101, librarian Mike Ferrero, explained why activists pushed for the Hay study despite the potential for "scientization" of the process:

I saw the study mainly as an avenue to use . . . a *tough politics* we could develop to raise salaries for my members, a good many of whom were women and had been underpaid for a long time. . . . You know, when you

---

15. Other examples of this scientization of politics are numerous. One can point to debates surrounding the issues of poverty and of arms control as two examples. So often these debates have become mired in technical questions, such as how best to measure poverty (Plotnick and Skidmore 1977; Zeitlin 1977), or how much a particular weapons system will cost. And a consideration of the ends at stake or the interests represented is lost.

go into negotiations one of the things you always need no matter what is
data. . . . So what this was, when we decided to do the study . . . was a
gamble that out of that study would come a lot of data that would be a
valuable tool for us. . . . We assumed going in that if we didn't lose some
kind of contact with the study, some kind of *control,* the study would
show fairly substantial inequity between men and women's jobs.

I think that at that point the *entire* strategy was, what did we need
to do to keep the study on track? So if the politicians got cold feet they
couldn't dump it; so they couldn't in some way sabotage it; so they couldn't
get the results of it skewed in some way that either the results did not
come out the way they should have, or that someone could yell "foul
play," or that in some way the credibility of the study was questioned. . . .
I felt if we could have a *lot* to do kind of with the internal dynamics of the
study and doing the evaluations, that the results would be pretty positive—even if there were some problems. By and large, the results would
be something we could use, they'd be tangible.

I asked at that point what he and other union activists had known of
the Hay system, and he responded quickly:

[If we were] getting into squabbles with the city at that point over whether
to use Hay or use some other system to do the study, then they could just
reject the Hay. And I was afraid then we'd just be "out to sea without a
paddle." So it was pretty pragmatic in deciding to just go with Hay.

In looking at it, the Hay methodology—at least as far as I could analyze
it, I didn't see any clear way we could get hurt by it. . . . The city was also
trying to be very careful not to let a lot of information about the methodology out so you could grab ahold of it. But we managed from different
sources to get some substantial information on their methodology. We got
some help from our national union, who was *not* a real big fan of Hay Associates. But by that time, that was *the* game in town. So I wasn't about to
say we weren't going to play.[16]

Another library activist explained that while the city was very
secretive with information on the Hay techniques, library workers
did extensive searches in business and management publications
for references to the methods. Eventually they found articles reviewing the Hay system, including copyrighted charts and techniques. It is ironic that the occupational or professional skills of this
group, so underrated, served them so well politically.

16. Very likely the national union's animosity toward Hay Associates was due
to the experiences in Minnesota and Wisconsin discussed above. Both these cases
also were instigated by AFSCME locals (Grune 1980, 131, 152).

The union stayed involved in the study process, combating the potential "scientization" of comparable worth, primarily in two ways: by contributing to the job description process, and by participating on the evaluation committee. Once it was decided to use Hay Associates, Hay's procedures did determine the parameters of the debate. The activists succeeded in influencing the results only by intervening at these key preliminary stages. As Ferrero, the union president, had said, to get the study and keep it on track *was* the entire strategy at that point. But the need for legitimated measurement of wage discrepancies, crucial for future bargaining, overrode concerns with the shortcomings of the methodology.

Job Descriptions

The first step of the Hay method involves writing job descriptions. Employees begin by filling out questionnaires regarding the tasks and responsibilities of their jobs. These questionnaires are then collected and analyzed, and job specifications written by personnel analysts are sent back to employees for their approval. Because of the direct involvement of employees, job description was an obvious area in which San Jose comparable worth activists saw an opportunity to exert influence. Union clerical and library activists organized lunch-hour workshops on the questionnaires. They emphasized that women should train other women in this task, and that every subtle possibility for enhancement of one's job description should be used, as the specifications would later become the basis for the assignment of factor points.[17]

One clerical activist described her involvement in some of this training. She explained that clericals had a fairly negative attitude at first because from their perspective, earlier classification studies, conducted by and for the city administration, had never accomplished anything. She felt she was able, however, to convince the women that this study would be different, and that their participation could make a difference. Her major goal, she explained, was to keep women from writing "the run of the mill kind of thing," to keep them from writing, "'Oh well, my job isn't very important;

17. In the Hay system (and other factor point job evaluation systems), jobs are assigned points according to a set of weighted compensable factors. Total factor point scores are then the basis for the ranking of jobs into salary grades. (See next section on the evaluation committee for more details.)

I just do this, and this and this,' but to [get them to] look at it on a
more positive level and say: 'I make these decisions. I have these
responsibilities.'"

From all reports the library workers particularly excelled in this
aspect of the job evaluation process. Patt Curia, a library activist,
when interviewed on comparable worth for the *Library Journal*,
said: "The librarians knew that this step was really important because the job description was the basis for evaluating the worth of
each job. We protested some descriptions three or four times because we wanted all of the important things we do included. . . .
The library job descriptions were probably the most thorough [in
the city]" (Fischer 1981, 2080). Two librarians I interviewed corroborated Patt Curia's point. One, for example, commented: "I
worked with a lot of individuals on what terms to use, how to best
portray their jobs." And the other added: "Library people went
over them and over them, and said, 'No, this isn't right. No, this
has got to be changed.' We had the perception that this would be
the basis for the assignment of points."

When I asked what they had emphasized in the descriptions,
they responded that they knew what kinds of things the Hay methodology emphasized. In addition to supervisory responsibilities,
they knew it was important to stress the amount of money or proportion of the budget one was responsible for. One gave as an example of what a librarian might write, "I'm a supervisor. I'm also
responsible for this building because the public is in the building.
I'm responsible for whether we're buying the right books with the
$30,000 a year of taxes in book money." The other librarian agreed,
adding that instead of just writing, "Well, I help people get books,"
the librarians would put down: "I'm responsible for a $1.5 million
book collection."

In fact, the librarians were so successful in this aspect of the
study that other groups were resentful. One engineering technician, a woman who had switched to this male-dominated job category, told me that she felt personnel ought to have looked at "what
people *really* do, and not at how they describe what they do. Because some people are just better at describing. . . . Librarians are
in the word business anyway." She also commented that the technicians had just taken the whole study "very casually," while the
librarians obviously had not.

In addition to affecting the job evaluation outcome itself (that is, influencing the job specifications to gain more points in the scoring), this training process served an educational purpose. Focusing attention on the questionnaires and on how best to describe one's job helped promote the idea that women's work is underpaid, helped women find new esteem in their jobs, and generally helped build interest in the study and a sense of anticipation for the results. As one activist put it: "We went through a tremendous information-education campaign to teach people about comparable worth when we taught people how to fill out the questionnaires. It was about a year and a half of constant articles in the newsletter, special meetings, lunchtime workshops, and special leaflets. . . . And if we hadn't of done that I don't think we'd have gotten the support that we did by 1981." And one of the librarians quoted at length above commented:

At the beginning some of the outstanding [i.e., politically active] clerical women had to practically beat it into the heads of the other women that your job *is* more responsible, more involved, a higher level than that guy out there who is cutting the grass. And they had to just drum it, and drum it, and drum it, and drum it—because people are affected by the way their job is seen by other people.

One of these "outstanding clericals," when asked whether she felt the training had been effective, attested to its educational value: "I felt it was very effective because it accomplished a couple of things. It made some people who were in lower-level [job] classes . . . feel better about what they're doing. . . . I also felt that it made a great many more aware of what was going on, and a lot of them got excited about the possibility that they could be in on a history-making event."

The Evaluation Committee

The makeup of the ten-member evaluation committee, whose task it would be to review the job specifications and assign points to approximately one hundred benchmark jobs,[18] became the next point

18. Benchmark jobs, selected for their representativeness, were chosen by a labor-management steering committee, although where they felt it necessary the evaluation committee later added several benchmarks. The points on the benchmarks are used to assign points to all other jobs, after which the male and female jobs can be compared.

of contention between the union and city management. The city manager had intended to have only one union representative present; the rest would be management employees. But the union protested this immediately, personnel relented, and the committee ultimately consisted of nine nonmanagement employees, with two nonvoting representatives, one from city management and one from Hay Associates. The voting members were to be selected from different departments and job categories, from among the "best" employees, that is, long-term employees with good knowledge of their job class and the other jobs in their department. Although candidates had to be formally approved by personnel, Ferrero, AFSCME Local 101 president, said this was only a minor problem—the "best" employees were often those most involved in the union and comparable worth efforts. Furthermore, personnel's involvement only gave the evaluations more credibility. Ferrero remarked that it would have been less effective had the job evaluations been seen as "just a union study." Again, the union's desire for legitimacy had to be balanced against the need for control of the procedure.

The final committee included Patt Curia, the senior librarian quoted above; the woman recreation professional also quoted above; a legal secretary; a gardener; one employee each from the general services and planning departments; a representative of the trades; and a police records clerk. Several respondents pointed specifically to the makeup of the evaluation committee, in addition to the fact that comparison was being made of male and female jobs, as making San Jose's a precedent-setting study. The clerical activist mentioned above commented further that in the job description workshops the knowledge that the specifications would be evaluated by one's peers contributed to the excitement felt about the study itself.

Evaluation committee decisions were made by consensus; members would discuss each job until a unanimous agreement on its score could be reached. (The evaluation committee met two days a week for some four months to score the benchmark positions.) However, the compensable factors, their components, and the assigned factor weightings were predetermined according to the "Hay Guide Chart-Profile Method," the copyrighted techniques of Hay Associates (Hay Group 1982).

One question I asked all my respondents was whether they felt the Hay measurement techniques were in any way biased in how points were assigned to jobs.[19] Many did not know exactly how the points were assigned; they just hoped that having every aspect of one's job included in the job description, described in the best possible language, would lead to the highest possible score. Beyond that, they felt that having their representatives on the evaluation committee would prevent any unfair scoring. For example, one union activist not on the evaluation committee commented that the process "was removed and complex enough that on the outside, we don't know—we don't see what kind of weights were given by the Hay system." Most respondents did not explicitly consider the possibility, which several feminist social scientists have raised, that the construction of the compensable factor components and weightings can itself contain a deeply embedded bias against women's work.[20]

I interviewed two women who were on the evaluation committee. The recreation professional told me how uncomfortable she had felt with the Hay methodology:

We had a sheet with little boxes and you wrote numbers in. . . . And I just didn't see how . . . looking over all these little areas and deciding what levels all these things were at and then writing down numbers was really going to come up with an accurate evaluation of the job. . . . We'd talk about the job for forty-five minutes, and then we'd start assigning points to it. We'd each go and write our points up on the overhead projector. . . . At first . . . staring at this sheet with numbers, and picking one from column A and two from column B, and writing a number down at the bottom—it was a little scary.

She explained the attitude of the women on the committee, remarking that, despite the Hay charts' limitations, "we fought; I mean all the women were saying: 'We're going to make sure that

19. Most job evaluation procedures, including that of Hay, assign points on the basis of four criteria generally accepted to be "universal": (1) skill and knowledge, (2) mental demands or level of problem solving involved, (3) accountability, and (4) working conditions. Each factor is broken down into components, and varying weights are assigned. The sum of the various weighted factor points gives each job a total score (Farnquist, Armstrong, and Strausbaugh 1983, 361; Hay 1982; Treiman 1979).

20. Sorenson (1982), for example, has pointed out that the skill and knowledge factor in the Hay system is operationalized such that skills characteristic of women's work receive less weight. Van Beers (1981) has made a similar point regarding the working conditions factor. Moreover, Remick (1978) has suggested that many significant aspects of women's work go unmeasured entirely, because most factor

the women's jobs get more points than any others.' Even though a lot of people will tell you: 'Oh no, we were really unbiased.' But we weren't. We were fighting like anything for the women's jobs. . . . We fought and fought and fought."

Both women I spoke with discussed the one conflict with the Hay system that had arisen in the evaluation committee, over the notion of "job stress." Library workers wanted job stress included as a compensable factor, and the other union members backed the suggestion. The Hay consultant argued, however, that job stress was not a factor to use in a proper evaluation, explaining: "What is stress to one person is excitement and glory to another." According to my respondents, the fight became so intense it nearly stopped the entire evaluation process.

Although "stress" is a topic of serious academic research (e.g., Kahn 1981), as well as a virtual "buzzword" in media and pop psychology (e.g., Bolch 1980), it is often only vaguely defined. One researcher identifies the "common element" in stress as "emotional arousal to threatening and unpleasant aspects of life situations" (Kahn 1981, 28). But a survey reported in *Science News* (1981) called stress "a sign of the times" produced by "our society in transition," particularly by "the new social roles of the sexes." When I asked respondents what *they* meant by the term, they gave imprecise answers. The woman recreation professional gave a long reply, beginning with many troubling aspects of her own job:

Well, outside of cramped working conditions, personal security was a real problem. . . . I worked in an inner-city park that was real isolated—and sometimes I was there by myself until ten o'clock at night. [Then she listed:] The ability to meet deadlines and put on programs with shrinking budgets. The constant need for interaction with the community, which was real diverse. Working with community groups from "low rider" clubs to some of the gangs that had developed, to neighborhood associations and merchants' associations. . . . And being the only one responsible for it.

She then spoke of the woman police clerk on the committee: "She made a really good argument for stress. . . . She was booking

---

point systems such as Hay's have been modeled on male jobs. (Summarized in Blum 1983; more recently see Acker 1987, 1989; Remick 1984; Steinberg and Haignere 1987; Treiman 1984).

suspects . . . *and* having to deal with cops and that whole cop mentality."

It seemed to me that the main point in this definition was to underscore how hard the women's jobs were, or what was "effort-full" about them. In a sense, this reproduces the notion of comparable worth itself. To these women, saying "My job is extremely stressful" was as if to say, "My job is damned hard work, work as hard as what men do." The women were aware, of course, that the belief that women's work is somehow "natural" and thereby less taxing, less like "work" than men's jobs, is widespread in our society. In fact, one of my interviews with a male technical worker bore this out: it was his opinion that recreation and library employees did not deserve higher pay because they have "cushy jobs," jobs that are "all fun and games."[21]

In this dispute, then, the issue of stress took on what amounted to symbolic importance. It signified the women's resistance to the evaluation of their jobs being defined and controlled by technical experts, as well as their skepticism toward the Hay procedures. It expressed their suspicion that the process was not wholly scientific or interest-free, that the Hay factors might be biased against considering the full value of women's work, and their frustration at not being able to control the evaluation process. In the end, however, because they did not have the power to redefine the parameters of the study, they decided to "play the game." As the recreation professional explained, "we finally had to make a decision about the value of stopping. . . . And we decided that it just wasn't worth it. We decided to give it a shot, since we knew it was the only shot we were going to have [at comparable worth]."[22]

The Trend Line

One technical element of the job evaluation procedure on which comparable worth activists had little influence was the determina-

21. Women have internalized such stereotypes as well. One woman commented to me when discussing this conflict, "You know, I could *not* understand it when librarians and library workers talked about stress. Because they are all in nice buildings, they help people find books. I did *not* see how that was stressful."

22. For a somewhat similar incident, with conflict expressed around the notion of stress, see Acker 1989.

tion of the "trend line," the regression line of average salaries for the various factor point levels.[23] The technical nature of the trend line, on which the eventual wage settlement was based, obscures the underlying political dimension. Yet the line itself, the central gauge for determining the wage disparities and adjustments, represents a political compromise as much as an objective measure of the wage inequities. Activists well understood that the averages on which the trend line was based had been biased downward by including the lower wages of the female-dominated jobs. That is, if a trend line had been calculated from the male jobs alone, average wages for each level would have been much higher, resulting in even greater disparities with women's jobs.

Even so, the final Hay report documented sizable wage inequities; thus the comparable worth activists can be considered successful in their efforts to politicize other aspects of the procedure. The Hay report indicated that, on average, male jobs were 8 to 15 percent *above* the trend line, while female jobs were 2 to 10 percent *below*, with many jobs falling even lower (Van Beers 1981, 11–12). On the whole, then, the study found that female-dominated jobs paid 15–25 percent less than the comparable male-dominated jobs, amounting to an average of $3,000 less per year (Beyette 1981; Johnston 1981, 164). The extent of such wage disparities verified by the study made a strong impression on employees (leading ultimately to the strike), as well as on the community. Some of the more glaring inequities were widely reported in the media. For example, the *Los Angeles Times* (Beyette 1981) highlighted five dramatic comparisons:

the mayor's secretary earned 47 percent less than a senior air conditioning mechanic;

a nurse earned $9,120 a year less than a fire truck mechanic;

a senior librarian made $5,304 a year less than a senior chemist;

---

23. The salary trend line represents the regression line expressing the relation between job evaluation points and median salary for each of the fifteen salary grades. These salary grades were determined by rank ordering all jobs according to their factor point scores and grouping them. A distribution was then plotted that determined where each job stood in relation to the trend line (Farnquist, Armstrong, and Strausbaugh 1983, 362; Fischer 1981, 2085; Hay 1982).

a legal secretary made $7,288 less a year than an equipment mechanic;

a neighborhood recreation supervisor earned $710 biweekly, whereas a gardening coordinator earned $831.

Such results, when added to the weight of the earlier Washington State findings, were compelling evidence for the justice of comparable worth.

Although the union in San Jose was willing as a practical concession to accept the Hay calculation of the trend line as they had accepted other elements of the Hay methodology,[24] activists did not see this acceptance as final. Nor did they see the trend line as an interest-free statement of the facts. Rather, activists sensed the limits of their power to contest further the quasi-scientific techniques. In interviews they made it clear that they intended to fight "beyond the trend" in the future—especially when management salaries had been promptly raised to 10 percent *above* trend after their Hay study. I heard several such comments; for example: "I'm working for beyond the trend. . . . We don't want to be equal to a depressed salary. We want to be equal to a reasonable salary, which we figure is an average of *men's* salaries. Because you pay men what you are supposed to pay for a certain level of work and for their family support." And this:

You're not going to hear about it [changing the trend line] from managers, but I think they realize it [can be changed]. When they adjusted *their* salaries it went above . . . no problem with that concept. Suddenly when you're talking about our salaries you're talking about a mythical trend line. And then, when they talk to us, they're very careful not to even talk trend line. "Within a 10 percent margin of error that Hay recommends" [said sarcastically]. They mix their figures a lot. It's a problem, because if you average an adequate salary with a depressed salary, you get a depressed salary level. And then you expect me to be pleased that you've raised my salary to that level. . . . Well, I am pleased, but I am *not* satisfied!

---

24. What San Jose activists could not have foreseen was the negative precedent this pragmatic decision would set for later cases, particularly for the Minnesota counties required by state law to implement pay equity. According to Evans and Nelson (1989, 151–160), many counties followed the San Jose example of using the lower "all-jobs" trend line as a cost-containment measure.

The Strike

When the study was completed, anticipation ran high among employees. Although all employees were told of their new salary grades, the full extent of the wage disparities was not initially made public. In fact, the city did not originally intend to give the union a copy of the completed report. (In negotiations prior to the study's completion, union representatives had walked away from the bargaining table for two weeks until the city agreed to give the union a copy of the report and to reopen salary negotiations; Fischer 1981, 2081). Even so, despite the city's attempts to keep study results confidential, copies of the salary trend line were widely circulated.

That people were well informed of the study's results was clear in my interviews. One woman, a legal secretary, not only could tell me that her job was 18 percent below the trend line, but she also wrote out a list from memory of the dozen male jobs with which her job had been rated equivalent; these included electrician, air conditioning mechanic, senior carpenter, and electrical inspector, to name a few. And a recreation professional (not the woman on the evaluation committee) reported that her job was found to be 27 percent below the average for its point level.

Negotiations for comparable worth wage adjustments began during Christmas week 1980, but they stalled after the city refused to offer what the union considered either adequate general increases or comparable worth adjustments. In fact, the city's offer took funds for comparable worth out of funds allocated for general increases (Johnston 1981). By the spring, employees' frustration was great. A very successful one-day sick-out was held, called "Hay Fever Day," to insist the city act on the study results. The city's resistance caused additional anger because the newly completed management study had been immediately implemented with, according to one respondent, "no quibbling." Some managers' pay was increased as much as 30 percent, and the city manager received a $13,000 a year raise (Fischer 1981, 2081). One angry woman told me, "They assumed the points were valid for them, and they were paid by the points—so we should be too!"[25]

25. Similarly, in Washington State an impetus for demanding the comparable worth study came from observing a management study and its implementation. There, management salaries also had been raised, but when female employees

Negotiations dragged on for several more months, but in July, when the contract expired and the city's position had changed very little, a strike was called. Ferrero, president of AFSCME Local 101, recounted the events leading up to the strike:

When the study results did come out there was a great deal of real excitement. By and large, the study had come through with the kind of results we had all dreamed it would. . . . There was a lot of anger created out of management getting those increases, and then our bargaining being held up over that same issue. There was a lot of deep-seated anger in the women, even in places where we weren't terribly well organized. . . . A lot of them [women clericals] thought: "It's wonderful that the union is forcing this study, and making sure that the study is going to be done. But once the study's done, then that's when the city will move in, recognize the problem and deal with it"—and treat them fairly and justly. And when that didn't happen—now, to you and I that may be real naive, but to a lot of them that was a real awakening. And that's where the anger came from.

As he explained, many employees had expected the Hay study to effect change without any further employee pressure, although most activists had realized that "the facts" were not going to speak for themselves. Awakening to the reality that "tough politics" rather than scientific techniques would be necessary generated the momentum for the strike.

The strike lasted only nine days. A state mediator was called in, but formal bargaining did not begin until the sixth day, following informal discussions. In the meantime, the city manager sent letters to all employees threatening those staying out with termination; strikers responded by gathering at a noon rally to burn their letters in front of City Hall (Fischer 1981, 2083). In bargaining, union and city negotiators initially thought they had reached agreement, but the city council rejected the proposed settlement in a closed-door session (reportedly because of unwillingness to commit to a four-year plan). Union members were outraged. Several stormed the council chambers, and some fifty activists picketed the mayor's house.[26] Finally, on Tuesday, July 14, the city council ap-

argued that their salaries ought to be raised according to the same methodology, that methodology was suddenly called into question (Remick 1980, 407–408).

26. Seven and a half years later I recontacted one union leader by phone; she still got very agitated recalling this turn of events.

proved a two-year offer and settlement was reached (Fischer 1981; McGuire 1982).

The two-year contract included $1.45 million for comparable worth adjustments to some 750 workers in sixty-two female-dominated classifications. This was not much more than the city had originally proposed, but the union also won a general cost-of-living increase of 15.5 percent. Initially, city management had offered only minimal cost-of-living raises, intending to fund comparable worth out of money for the general increase. Some respondents saw this as an attempt to pit men and women against each other and divide the union, but AFSCME members would not settle until both adequate equity adjustments *and* cost-of-living increases were agreed on.

The new contract was considered a victory for the union, but it did not bring full wage parity, which all parties agreed would have to be phased in over a longer period. The contract did bring the average level of the female-dominated jobs up to the 10 percent margin, or "cone," of error often cited by Hay consultants. The average adjustment was 9.6 percent, with the adjustments based primarily on how far one's salary level fell below the trend (thus, the largest adjustments went to those jobs farthest from the regression line) (*Comparable Worth Project Newsletter* 1981, 2; Farnquist, Armstrong, and Strausbaugh 1983; Flammang 1986, 826; *Labor Notes* 1981a; McGuire 1982). Ferrero of AFSCME Local 101 summed up the victory that this contract represented by saying: "They [the city] basically accepted the first two years of our four-year plan" (McGuire 1982, 14).

Ultimately, the dramatic image of the strike that was conveyed beyond the community may have been more significant than the actual contract. This image was created in large part by media attention, which in turn was gained by capitalizing on external events.

Comparable worth activists had received an enormous boost to their cause when, one month before the San Jose contract expired the U.S. Supreme Court announced its decision in the *Gunther* case, affirming sex-based wage discrimination in a situation of sex-segregated jobs (see Chapter 2). This announcement focused national attention on comparable worth, as well as on the situation brewing in San Jose (e.g., *Newsweek* 1981). To use the Supreme Court action to full advantage, AFSCME Local 101 immediately

filed an EEOC complaint against the city for failing to implement
the Hay study results.[27] Although this may actually have hardened
the city's opposition (Beyette 1981; Keppel 1981), it certainly attracted even more attention, providing impetus for the union to
make the dramatic move of a strike.

An entirely unrelated incident that coincidentally occurred at
this same time drew national media attention to San Jose as well. In
the summer of 1981, California was in the midst of the Medfly crisis (an invasion of the Mediterranean fruitfly), and Governor Jerry
Brown had taken a controversial stand against aerial spraying of the
insecticide malathion, a program slated to be based at San Jose airport, a city-run facility. During the comparable worth strike the
union took advantage of this debate by picketing the airport heavily, particularly on the day Brown was scheduled to speak and the
media were out in force.

These efforts were very successful. The San Jose strike made
page one of the *New York Times* (7/6/81) and was covered in the
Washington Post, the *Wall Street Journal*, the *Los Angeles Times*,
and the major newsweeklies (*Time* and *Newsweek*), as well as on
television news.[28] One librarian commented that this "media blitz"
put a lot of pressure on the city to work for a settlement (Fischer
1981, 2082–2083). But Bill Callahan, the AFSCME business agent
who succeeded Maxine Jenkins, explained that he considered much
of the strike effort to have been "media hype":

Out of the two thousand we represented, we said three-quarters were on
strike. And there were probably only five hundred out at the height of the
strike. But we created the image that a lot was happening. We said that
sixteen out of seventeen libraries were closed down, and that was not
true. We said the city was considering closing down the airport, and that
was not true. We really could only last a few days. But we wanted to em-
barrass the mayor, who was more interested in her future political career. . . . And people did not really check the numbers out. But the im-

27. This was precisely the issue of liability in the Washington State case, which
was also filed soon after the *Gunther* decision (Remick 1980).
28. In fact, Mayor Janet Gray Hayes and AFSCME business agent Bill Callahan
were flown to New York during the strike to appear on "Good Morning America,"
the national morning news program of the ABC network. Ironically, the segment
was never seen on the West Coast owing to the announcement that President
Reagan had nominated a woman to the Supreme Court; apparently one feminist
news item was considered sufficient (see Achenbach 1981).

age became true, because other women saw the image of San Jose and were impressed by it.[29]

As Callahan maintained, capturing national attention for the demand that women's work be reevaluated was probably more significant than closing down city services. After all, unlike the private sector, the public sector has no profits to cut into with production stoppages or slowdowns; and public-sector budgets are politically negotiated more directly than profit rates can be. Regardless of the numbers on strike, after the nine days of media "blitzing" or "hyping" the settlement was reached that activists in San Jose and nationwide considered the first major victory for comparable worth.

Although the San Jose strike was relatively brief, like any strike situation it had an intense impact on those centrally involved. As business agent Callahan told me, "The strike was very dramatic. . . . It changed the lives of everyone involved. It was like being in gridlock for nine days on the L.A. freeway." Many of the strongest feelings of activists had to do with who went out on strike and who did not, as illustrated in these comments:

I went out on the sick-out and the strike. . . . Nine out of eleven in my section of Accounts Payable went on strike, and they all knew where *I* stood!

Every legal secretary went out on strike [fifteen or sixteen total]. We all belonged to the union. . . . I was proud because our jobs were at risk, but we went out anyway.

The five women I supervised pushed me to join the union originally. But then I went out and they didn't! . . . I've been on strike twice in my working life, and I hope never again. It's so hard to strike, too hard; it's hard to see so many union members *not* go out.

My biggest disappointment was that the clericals from the council offices did not join up and did not go out with us.

As these comments suggest, comparable worth was only partly successful in San Jose as a tool for organizing women and building

29. Some did check, but this never seemed to hurt the union's credibility. For example, the *Los Angeles Times* reported that "the strikers have not brought the city to a standstill. While the union contends that 50–60% of its workers are out, the City placed the number at closer to 20%" (Beyette 1981). For a good example of the prounion image, see Goligoski 1981.

participation in the union. Some women workers did not join the union, and some union members did not participate in the strike. While exact numbers are hard to come by, AFSCME Local 101 president Ferrero has stated that five hundred new members joined the union during the three major years of the comparable worth effort, 1979–1981 (Flammang 1986, 829); I suspect, though, that this claim was exaggerated. Ferrero told me, "Comparable worth *was* an attempt to organize the clerical workforce. And we met with some success. But it was always kind of astounding to me why we didn't have *more* success with that." Business agent Bill Callahan commented similarly: "Clericals are the most difficult to organize. Everyone was real disappointed that there wasn't any large rush in membership, especially after the strike was settled."

However, a woman activist pointed out that no concerted effort was made after the strike: "We didn't go into an organizing drive after that [the strike]. Nobody knew how to organize. On one day I did go around City Hall and I actually signed up twenty people, which was unheard of. But everyone was too tired out after the strike. We expected people to love us after we won the strike. But we really fell down as a union." And, reflecting on the whole experience, two activist librarians defended inactive women: "What you see as inactivity is really just a lack of urgency. Things are rolling along now"; and "They are low-paid people who don't have a lot of time between their jobs and their families to get involved. They don't have the money to go out to eat instead of fixing supper for their families. And they perceive that the leadership has them in mind."

After the strike period, with its excitement and intensity, the campaign for comparable worth slowed considerably in San Jose. Of course, this relaxing of effort was to an extent understandable. A great deal had been accomplished: significant wage adjustments were won, comparable worth was included in contract language, and the union became better incorporated into local politics. By the time of my interviews in 1984 and 1985 many activists described themselves as "burnt out," but smaller adjustments continued to be gained in successive contracts. In addition to the 1981 and 1982 adjustments won in the strike, $116,000 was spent on comparable worth in 1983, another $171,000 in 1984, and $341,000 in 1985 (Flammang 1986, 819–822). As one secretary told me: "As long as we have the precedent set for comparable worth, we'll keep asking for equity adjustments."[30]

Women workers generally expressed agreement with business agent Callahan's conclusion, that is, that their primary accomplishment was the image of militance conveyed to so many women around the country. People commented that "they paved the way," or that "they were the first." Although a few resented this image,[31] most I spoke with seemed very proud of their role. One secretary, a mother of six and a grandmother, was particularly inspirational:

I felt I'd done something really important. It was rather incongruous, myself and another woman, both of us grandmothers, going in front of the city council, and picketing! We'd say: "What are *we* doing here?" But my children were really proud of me. And I knew it was at least as important as the Geraldine Ferraro nomination. Maybe it was more important, because we were just the average people, everyday average people.[32]

In terms of theory, the San Jose movement is significant in two respects. First, it illustrates the role a limited governmental reform may play in galvanizing political action for more far-reaching demands. Specifically, affirmative action reforms legitimated women's desires for mobility but provided actual benefit to very few, thus they both raised and frustrated women's aspirations. Struggling within the context of affirmative action, women also developed a collective sense of gender interests, which was reinforced by the strong feminist presence in the city. But as comparable worth emerged from these efforts, women's collective gender interests were reframed in terms of both gender and class, and many realized the only effective way to gain comparable worth was through union action.

Second, the San Jose movement illustrates the effectiveness

30. Continued attention to the issue is necessary because, despite successive adjustments, full parity has not been reached. Moreover, as one clerical activist pointed out, as long as cost-of-living increases are proportional and the wage gap remains, male-dominated fields continue to gain disproportionately.

31. One employee was quoted in the *Los Angeles Times* as commenting, "We're sort of the sacrificial lambs to the labor issue of the 80's" (Beyette 1981).

32. It may already be difficult to recall the excitement with which women greeted the Democratic nomination of Representative Ferraro for vice president in 1984, the first appearance of a woman on the presidential ticket of a major party in American history.

of the "tough politics" approach employed by the union, which wrested at least partial control of the technically mystified job evaluation process from management "experts." Although such use of technocratic ideology generally characterizes contemporary bureaucratic institutions, the San Jose case exemplifies a largely successful attempt to counter the "depoliticization" of wage setting. Importantly, this was done without sacrificing the needed verification of wage disparities. On the national level, the union's "tough politics" contributed to the accumulation of evidence for comparable worth, while also conveying the image of an aggressive labor *and* feminist campaign. In the next chapter I will illustrate how the San Jose movement for comparable worth inspired female employees in Contra Costa County to press for higher wages both as women, and as women in particular class locations.

Four

"No Fingerprints"

The Comparable Worth Movement in
Contra Costa County

Female employees of Contra Costa County, California, have been actively working to better their employment conditions for over two decades. Their most recent efforts involve a movement for comparable worth begun on the heels of the San Jose strike victory. While the comparable worth effort in the county has been impressive in the extent of its grass-roots support and the tenacity of its core activists, the incremental gains have come more slowly and have been far less dramatic than was the case with the San Jose strike victory. Moreover, what has been touted by some as the Contra Costa "solution" to comparable worth, proponents have described as being "nickel-and-dimed to death."

Contra Costa's comparable worth movement emerged from a different social and political background from that in San Jose. The clerical women in particular have long been a more labor-identified group, framing their interests in stronger class terms than their counterparts in San Jose: while using an affirmative action strategy to get clerks into better-paying jobs, they also worked to strengthen their all-clericals union. Among female professionals, the emergence of the comparable worth issue in Contra Costa followed a pattern similar to that in San Jose. Affirmative action rhetoric added to the professionals' frustration with their depressed wages and at the same time provided a gender-based frame in which to understand the problem. This combination led to eventual support for comparable worth and an alliance with the clerical workers.

The issue of technocratic politics differs for the two cases as well. As in San Jose, in Contra Costa County labor activists had to manage the tension between science and politics that arises from the need to measure wage inequities. But stiff resistance from a wary county administration made their efforts largely unsuccessful. In addition to the county's efforts to avoid (in one activist's words) getting "its fingerprints on the issue" and therefore being legally liable, activists also had to combat serious budget constraints, the fear of a negative impact on local business development, and the recalcitrance of the largest male-dominated union in the county. (See Appendix C for details of the research methodology and specific case references.)

The Origin of Comparable Worth in the County

Contra Costa County has undergone significant changes in the past twenty years. Although the county was once a distinct working-class region of manufacturing and shipping industries, it is now increasingly characterized by a middle-class suburban population and growing service sector. This development took off after the Bay Area Rapid Transit rail system began operations in 1972, linking the county to the urban centers of Oakland and San Francisco. In addition to real estate development (which has increased "at a frantic growth rate"), the central county has become home to the back-office operations of many Northern California firms attracted by lower real estate costs and favorable taxation and zoning policies, as well as an available female labor force (Malaspina 1984; Newbergh 1984a, 1985a; Security Pacific National Bank 1983).

The county employs a work force of approximately six thousand, of whom nearly 60 percent are female. Although this proportion is much greater than in San Jose (where only 23 percent of city workers are women), the concentration of women in traditionally female jobs is similar, with approximately 40 percent working as clericals and one-third or more in the low-paid professions, primarily social work and nursing (Finney 1983). The larger percentage of men working for the city of San Jose is due primarily to cities' jurisdictional responsibility for male-dominated police and fire services, while county-level responsibilities include the administration of female-dominated social and health services.

The county saw a push for affirmative action in the 1970s; a sex and race class action lawsuit, *Croskey, Burt, et al. v. County of Contra Costa,* was settled by the signing of a consent decree in 1975. As in San Jose, the initial impetus for affirmative action policies arose from the minority community rather than from any feminist or women's organizations (*Martinez Morning News-Gazette* 8/10/72). In Contra Costa, however, the minority community is a smaller, less powerful constituency than in San Jose, and politically the county is much less cosmopolitan in outlook.

In contrast to the "feminist capital" of San Jose, which might be thought of as a "best case" scenario of affirmative action, Contra Costa County has been antagonistic to affirmative action and other progressive reforms. Several of my respondents commented that the top county administrators have very traditional views of appropriate sex roles and resisted hiring women for nontraditional jobs. One college-educated woman, hired in 1975 as an entry-level personnel professional, was one of only two women among twenty-five employees at that level. She commented:

The rest [working as personnel professionals] were white males, former military men. . . . They had to hire women [because of the consent decree], but their hearts weren't in it. . . . The head of personnel is a known chauvinist. He hires only young, attractive women. There was not a sincerity in their efforts [at affirmative action]. They want women in very traditional roles . . . and these [men] are still the ones making major policy decisions.

Despite this inhospitable atmosphere, women (as well as minorities) made gradual gains as a result of the county's affirmative action policies.[1] By 1984, 26.8 percent of officials and administrators were women, although they very likely were concentrated in "female" fields such as social and health services.[2] Yet even in the male bastion of the sworn ranks of the sheriff's department, 11 percent were female by 1984, and special efforts were being implemented to re-

1. For blacks employment has risen from 7.5 percent of the total work force in 1975 to 10.7 percent in 1983; for Hispanics the figures are 3.9 percent and 6.2 percent (Contra Costa County 1984). The county's population, according to the 1980 census, is 77 percent white, 23 percent nonwhite (Security Pacific National Bank 1983).

2. Accurate disaggregated figures cannot be ascertained from the county reports.

cruit female applicants (Contra Costa County 1984). In general, however—and perhaps even more than in San Jose—women employed by the county had not materially benefited from affirmative action (Rego 1981).

The community has seen a moderate level of feminist activity. But this activity developed later than in San Jose, perhaps as a corollary of the area's "suburbanization," which brought in the large middle-class population. By the mid–1980s (when this research was conducted), the local branches of both the National Women's Political Caucus and the State Commission on the Status of Women were quite active. The latter, for example, held widely publicized hearings on the feminization of poverty; and the former, founded in 1976, had succeeded in getting two women elected to the five-member county Board of Supervisors, the top decision-making body in local government.

Early Clerical Activism

The female clericals in Contra Costa County differed from those in San Jose primarily in that they had organized an autonomous union in 1969–1970 to contest their low wages, several years before the emergence of affirmative action or other feminist reforms. Their activism was thus of a different character than clerical activism in San Jose. The United Clerical Employees worked hard both to improve mobility opportunities and to increase wages and benefits for those remaining in the clerical ranks. This group is quite impressive in its strong grass-roots basis and in its members' sincerity, energy, and knowledge of the county system. Yet the group's accomplishments over the years have been limited.

Following the San Jose strike, comparable worth quickly became a priority issue for the United Clericals. They turned to comparable worth not only to make greater wage gains, but also because it expressed a construction of class and gender interests they had been acting on, with little external validation, since their original organizing activities. Their early activism anticipated many of the moral claims underlying comparable worth, particularly that women have a right to a decent, family wage regardless of the marketplace. This concern was expressed most notably in their 1972 strike, the first strike by clerical workers in the state's history.

The facts of the 1972 strike can be stated very briefly. Approximately six to seven hundred clerks (out of a thousand) struck over wage and benefit issues. Several male-dominated unions joined the strike in support of the women, but also with their own issues. Other unions refused to cross the picket lines, and county services were severely disrupted (Hollis 1972 f; *Martinez Morning News-Gazette* 7/1/72, 7/6/72). Women also received strong backing from the county's Central Labor Council; this support strengthened their identification with the larger labor movement and led eventually to their affiliation with AFSCME as Local 2700. After three and a half weeks, the clericals settled with the county. They agreed to half the wage increase originally demanded, but gained a key "gender" demand: increased sick leave to stay home with sick children (*Martinez Morning News-Gazette* 7/22/72).

Although their activities anticipated comparable worth, the Contra Costa clericals were much less gender-identified, and more class-identified, than clericals in San Jose. An original organizer of the clerical union and its first president recalled a story that demonstrates this fact; it involved a meeting held twenty years ago, in which the director of personnel was to answer questions regarding the clerks' low wages. This meeting was one of a series that precipitated the organizing of the United Clericals.

He had Bay Area–wide diagrams [of clerical wages]. . . . They always threw [wage] comparisons at us. Those comparisons were always making us look bad. . . . But there weren't any clericals organized in the whole state—so what did it prove if we all had the same wages!

Women interrupted him and made him take questions about raises. His response was that clericals have sugar daddies and live at home with their men!

So he left, and we voted to organize that night . . . to be independent and keep it strictly clericals.

This story reveals both the parallels and differences between the Contra Costa and the San Jose women. Like San Jose officials, the director of personnel responded to the clericals' questions about their low pay with external labor market comparisons (that is, comparisons to clerical wages in other public agencies). In San Jose in 1978, when women met this type of response they reasoned: "Of course we all have the same low wages—you are comparing us to other *women*." But in Contra Costa County, eight years earlier, the women responded: "Of course we have the same low wages—you are comparing us to other *nonunionized workers.*" It is interesting that the director of personnel responded by framing the situation in gender terms, expressing the county's view that, as female workers, the clerks did not require more than "pin money." Again, however, the women's response was different from that in San Jose: they decided to organize and agitate on a class basis, as a labor union, rather than as women claiming sex discrimination.

These county employees were fully aware of the "gendered" aspect of their situation—that is, that their group was all-female and that their work was "women's work." But they saw themselves, first and foremost, as women in a particular class location. Their former AFSCME bargaining agent, Diana Doughtie, explained the strength of their working-class identification: "Before becoming a bedroom community, Contra Costa County had a very big union base. All the industries, steel and the oil refineries, all were unionized. The county had a very high proportion of union membership. Many clerical women were [or had been] married to those men."

The strong identification as working-class women is clear in these comments made by long-time members of the United Clericals as well:

I joined the union as soon as I took a county job. . . . We went from several hundred originally to now thirteen hundred members, and there used to be *no* men. . . . We would do anything to further the women's status, the pay, and the way we were looked upon.

Originally the union came about because we clerks were not receiving the increases we should have. . . . The county wasn't recognizing that the majority of us were single mothers who needed better pay and benefits.

When I started at the county, I was divorced and had two kids, and I made as much take-home pay as I had gotten on welfare. . . . And I was *always* labor-oriented. My father had always been in the plumber's union.

When I first went back to work, I was packing plastic gloves. And I was in the union, the steelworkers. I was an officer. When I came to work for the county, there was no union. So I was one of the founders of the United Clericals.

These clerical women, who identified strongly as women *workers,* did not, however, align their interests with those of *all women,* or with a larger feminist movement. This is hardly surprising given the middle-to-upper-class orientation of the mainstream feminist movement at that point. These clericals were not the middle-class,

college-educated women who were busy making San Jose the "feminist capital of the nation." Rather, they were an autonomous working-class group of "middle-aged, polyester pants–suited women,"
as one observer later described them. The remark of one clerical
activitist helps to explain the lack of connection to a larger women's
movement in those early struggles: "I never considered myself a
feminist, until I discovered [years later] that I actually was."

The press also made no connection between the clericals' struggle
and the broader feminist movement. The larger urban newspapers
did not mention the gender dimension to the conflict, apparently
seeing no relation between the battle for state ratification of the
Equal Rights Amendment—which often put feminist issues on the
front page that year—and the struggle of a group of backwater
clerks for better pay (*Los Angeles Times* 6/28/72, 7/23/72, 7/24/72;
San Francisco Chronicle 6/28/72, 7/19/72, 7/22/72; *San Francisco Examiner* 6/29/72). Coverage in the local papers presented
the gender issue (that is, that the strike involved an all-female
group) but did not connect this to the larger women's movement.
The one brief mention of such a connection ironically implied
antagonism. The caption under a photo labeled "One Cheerful
Striker" reported, "A group of Women's Liberationists handed pam-
phlets to some of the strikers while another group [of striking
clerks] called out: 'this is better than Women's Liberation!'" (*Martinez Morning News-Gazette* 7/7/72). Unfortunately, the motives
of the liberationist pamphleteers cannot be discerned.

The 1972 clericals' strike demonstrated that these women had a
strong sense of what a decade later would become identified as the
feminization of poverty (Ehrenreich and Stallard 1982; Pearce and
McAdoo 1981). County clerks were acutely aware of the precarious
economic situation they faced, despite their membership in the
full-time, paid labor force. They continually referred to themselves
as the "working poor" (*Martinez Morning News-Gazette* 7/6/72;
Vogt 1972a). For many, the precariousness was due directly to the
loss of the male breadwinner in the family. According to the first
president of the United Clericals, fully half of the members in the
early years were "the sole support of one or more children." Even
when a male breadwinner was present, the clerical paycheck was
very likely becoming indispensable as the stagflation economy of
the 1970s decreased the value of working-class men's paychecks.

Statements made by the clericals during their strike exemplify the class and gender consciousness of these women, (as well as their anticipation of comparable worth claims). For example:

Our members have reached the point of desperation where management's counter-proposal is tantamount to no offer at all. What difference can an additional 6 or 7 dollars take-home a month mean to a *breadwinning mother* who can't afford to put meat on the table for her kids to eat?

Ours is a truly *oppressed class*, penalized for being *women* and paid generally as if we were a bunch of kids fresh out of high school and still living at home with Daddy. Our ranks include highly skilled technicians who earn a top salary that is hundreds of dollars *less than most unskilled labor earns*. We approached management with a modest proposal this year and got kicked in the teeth for our efforts. Our intention now is to kick back.

(*Martinez Morning News-Gazette*
6/20/72; emphasis added)

The clericals' awareness of their economic marginality was also premised on their day-to-day experience in the workplace. A large number worked in the Social Services Department and were in daily contact with welfare recipients, many of whom were single mothers receiving Aid to Families with Dependent Children (AFDC); as clerical women gained familiarity with their situations, they could see that their lives were at least potentially similar. At one point, as a negotiating tactic, a group of clericals filled out welfare applications and brought them into a bargaining session. The United Clericals' first president recalled: "There wasn't one of us who wouldn't have been better off on welfare. We took those applications in to negotiations that year—and management's response was to say we'd probably filled the forms out wrong! But then we said: 'The same clerks did these as do welfare applications every day at work!'" And during the strike one local paper reported: "As a whole the clerical workers are [the] lowest paid group of county employees and contend their wage rates are below subsistence level and should be implemented by resortment [sic] to welfare aid" (*Martinez Morning News-Gazette* 6/21/72).[3]

3. In fact, while the office workers' strike was vehemently opposed by the local taxpayers' association, women received the support of the local Welfare Rights Organization (*Contra Costa Times* 7/11/72).

In addition to the early awareness of the feminization of poverty, Contra Costa clerical women also anticipated comparable worth's emphasis on raising the social esteem for women's work. For example, during the 1972 strike one press story began, "Clerical Women Want More Respect," and continued:

pickets explained that the strike is a fight to force Contra Costa County administration into realizing that clerks are more than drones operating an 8 a.m. to 5 p.m. shift among the typewriters and file cabinets.

"Management thinks we're semi-literate or less intelligent. They have no idea what a clerk does. I have doubts whether management could walk in and do what a clerk does," declared [one woman on the picket line].

(Vogt 1972b)

Later Clerical Activism

After the county signed the affirmative action consent decree in 1975, the United Clerical Employees—by then organized as AFSCME Local 2700—focused some of its energy on moving women up and into men's higher-paying jobs. The creation of career ladders, bridge classifications, and enhanced promotional opportunities became part of the AFSCME Local 2700 agenda. According to my informants, however, such affirmative action reforms were seen from the start as limited, and the need for continued union strength was recognized. In contrast, women in San Jose, lacking a strong union identification, had believed more deeply in the individual mobility that affirmative action invoked. Yet even in Contra Costa, the idea that women's path to success lay in breaking down the barriers to men's jobs was very much "in the air" during the 1970s. The *Contra Costa Times*, for example, a local newspaper, ran many such success stories (Feder 1979; Ghent 1978; Grossman 1978; Vogt 1978; Witt 1978), and the local League of Women Voters provided assistance to women desiring entry into male jobs (Sestanovich 1979).

One of the AFSCME Local 2700's achievements along such lines was the development of a bridge classification, accounting technician, to make possible movement from the (female) account clerk series into the professional-level accountant series, the entry point for many college-educated (white) males. This "bridging" of clerical and professional job ladders also allowed account clerks to sub-

stitute experience for some college credits, an important concession to the clericals, as it was in San Jose. Yet, as one longtime
clerical activist explained, this achievement, the union's biggest
success in enhancing upward mobility, has meant a promotion of
only about eight women into the bridge position, and two into the
professional accountant level.

One woman account clerk's experience of blocked mobility
might be considered illustrative. She explained that the first person to win a promotion into the new bridge class was, ironically, a
man who had never even belonged to the clerical union.[4] The reason management gave for promoting him over any female candi-
date was that he had a family to support—to which this woman angrily retorted: "As if half the women here aren't single with kids to
support!" Management's sexist attitudes had changed little since
then: "They still believe the old idea that the man's the breadwinner and the women don't really need the money." In addition, she
pointed out, although a few women have moved up, the total number of openings is very small. She, for one, had acquired more than
enough experience and night-course units for the accountant series, but had yet to make it even into the bridge class. It is not surprising that in the meantime she has become a union activist and
strong proponent of comparable worth.

In the Social Services Department, after a long and tough fight,
the clerical union had recently won a bridge class to allow clerks to
move up into professional social work.[5] For movement into this
predominantly female occupation, the county agreed to the partial
substitution of experience for education. The AFSCME Local 2700
president commented that they hoped to develop up to twenty-five
positions in the bridge class, but she acknowledged the limitations
of such career ladder strategies: "If we saw *two* people eventually
move beyond the bridge we'd feel we'd been successful."

Another woman, more cynically, said that such career ladders
are "fake"—"you just move to the first step and get stuck there."
She was concerned that these "reforms" would only undermine
efforts to get comparable worth adjustments for women who were

4. At the time of my interviews the clerical union did have a small number of
male members, perhaps six, according to the current president.
5. See note 10 below for an explanation of the two categories of jobs in this
field: eligibility work and social work.

stuck in the "bridges," since management could argue that minimum qualifications had been eroded—a particular problem in social work, already an undervalued, female-typed field.

A clerical woman who had been with the county ten years may
be more typical in her balanced appraisal of affirmative action strategies and their limits. She commented: "I feel the affirmative action
officer [a black woman] is conscientious. She makes every effort, an
honest effort, like to get women into the firefighters. And they're
getting women into management. I've seen more women filling
management positions in the last ten years. . . . I have no criticisms of the policy. It is working, but it's *slow*." In summing up her
own career mobility, however, this woman noted, with irony, that
despite returning to night school and earning a college degree, "I
started as a clerk and *ended* as a clerk." Not coincidentally, she too
has become active in the clericals' union.

The president of AFSCME Local 2700 was more negative in her
appraisal of affirmative action: "My impression of affirmative action
in the county is that it's done more for racial minorities than women.
I don't think the bulk of women feel affirmative action would assist
in fighting sex discrimination. It has just not accomplished that
much." When I asked whether the clericals' union had pushed for
women moving into other nontraditional jobs, she replied:

We did encourage them to, let's say . . . seven, eight years ago. We still
provide notice of the exams, and information and materials on how to prepare for the exams. But it's my philosophy that women should not have to
go into a trade or craft position. And that's why I'm aligned so strongly
with the comparable worth concept.

So we didn't discourage people [from changing to male jobs]. We still
are very happy for people in our ranks who become sheriff's dispatchers,
which have usually been traditional men's jobs, or firefighters, or whatever. But we make it very clear to the rest of our people that we don't feel
they should have to go those routes to get comparable pay.[6]

As I have discussed, affirmative action can be difficult to address
within a union context; it is often too divisive and individualizing to
be used in conjunction with union tactics requiring group solidarity, particularly as it threatens to override seniority rights. This
conflict was felt by clerical activists in Contra Costa County, even

6. Interestingly, the job of sheriff dispatcher may be changing in both sex typing and composition as a result of affirmative action pressures. See Chapter 5.

as they utilized the equal opportunity model legitimated by affirmative action to push reforms.[7] Diana Doughtie, AFSCME Local 2700 business agent between 1978 and 1984, explored this conflict in our interview: "I feel affirmative action is important, but it's *not* my goal in life. . . . Also, affirmative action irritates me lately because it is used to take away from comparable worth. They [management] use affirmative action to say they're doing enough. . . . Probably those same people fought against it for years who are now using it as an excuse to not pay comparable worth." She explained why, despite her support for job integration, she often found herself opposing the attorney monitoring affirmative action in the county:

I believe in recruiting from the inside, not from outside. I was always saying: "Look at your own work force." [For example,] one time a new position opened up for a medical records technician. Affirmative action [officials] wanted to recruit from outside to increase minorities. So I did my own survey of clerks who worked with medical records and had the necessary experience. I found thirty-six people qualified, of which nineteen were black.[8]

Although affirmative action was not her "goal in life," for Doughtie comparable worth did become a major objective. As a woman unionist, she played an important role in the Contra Costa effort, much as Maxine Jenkins had in San Jose.[9] An articulate and committed organizer, Doughtie explained that she had not always been labor-identified: "Several years ago I would have described myself as a liberal democrat and liberal feminist. But I had *no* worker's

7. Some union activists in San Jose expressed the conflict between affirmative action and a union's collective approach as well. President Mike Ferrero of AFSCME 101 explained that because such issues could cause serious internal conflict the union had to stay clear, despite its formal support of affirmative action; straight seniority is necessary, he said, to hold the group together.

8. Rosenbaum, in his study of affirmative action and organizational mobility (1985), found that affirmative action does tend to benefit women with less firm tenure.

9. As noted in the last chapter, those concerned with building a women's labor movement say that unions need to demonstrate that they are receptive to women and gender issues (e.g., Strom 1983, 380–381). And the presence of women activists, particularly committed feminists like Doughtie and Jenkins, is perhaps the best illustration of such receptivity (e.g., Needleman 1988). AFSCME nationwide has been moving in this direction, as two of its organizers report: "AFSCME, perhaps more than any other union, was willing to reach beyond its ranks when necessary to find staff who could relate to a clerical constituency" (Lynch and Bayer 1986, 98).

consciousness." After several years in low-paying work, however, she became a strong labor activist, and the clericals I interviewed all spoke of her with much admiration. For example, this clerk from the sheriff's office explained: "Six years or so ago I joined the union. My father was a labor-oriented person, a house painter. So it seemed right to me to join. But I never was active . . . not until I got to know Diana Doughtie. . . . Now I'm on the executive board, I write and edit the union newsletter, and I'm a member of the Council 57 Board with the other AFSCME locals."

Even though the comparable worth effort in Contra Costa did not take off until women saw the success of the San Jose strike, Doughtie had been laying the groundwork. In fact she, like Jenkins, first introduced the notion to her community. "I could see this was *the* issue for clericals—I felt it was *very big*," she told me. Her continuing efforts for comparable worth were crucial, as the clerk from the sheriff's office commented: "She was really the driving force—for six years educating people. She was always bringing comparable worth up. Everyone now knows what it is. If they don't know, they must've had a paper bag over their heads!"

Women Professionals

The same forces and circumstances that made the librarians and recreation professionals in San Jose into vigorous advocates of comparable worth also led the nurses and social workers in Contra Costa County to embrace the issue. Yet unlike the professionals in San Jose, who were represented in the same union local as clerical workers, the Contra Costa nurses and social workers had their own bargaining organizations. The county affiliate of the California Nurses Association (CNA), with some 220 members, represented the registered nurses, nurse practitioners, and supervising nurses, while Local 535 of Service Employees International Union (SEIU) represented the approximately 500 social workers and eligibility workers (Cisterman 1983; Finney 1983).[10]

10. Eligibility work is the deskilled, routinized part of what was formerly a social worker's job. The field was divided ten to fifteen years ago. Currently only the actual handling of problem families requiring state intervention (child abuse, juvenile delinquency, etc.) is delegated to social workers, who are required to have master's degrees (or equivalent experience) and are classified as professional em-

Prior to the emergence of the comparable worth issue, nurses and social workers in Contra Costa County, like most members of the women's professions, were generally caught up in separate struggles for greater professional recognition and rewards.[11] With the heightened gender consciousness of the 1970s and affirmative action policies legitimating women's aspirations for mobility, both social workers and nurses in the county began to frame their occupational role strain as a gender issue. As in San Jose, however, they felt that the underlying assumptions of affirmative action denigrated their female-typed occupations. This combination of factors ultimately resulted in their support for comparable worth.

For registered nurses, issues of professionalization have been acutely felt in the past decade, with the increasing division of labor and the creation of new technical and paratechnical fields in health care threatening to erode their status. Within the American Nursing Association (ANA) and its state-level organizations—which are not affiliated with the AFL-CIO and are ambivalent as to whether to model themselves after labor unions or after professional organizations like the American Medical Association—the push has been largely for higher educational requirements to strengthen the position of registered nurses. In the past many registered nurses completed only two-year certification programs and passed a licensing exam, but the trend is now toward requiring the four-year program and the bachelor of science degree in nursing. CNA favors requiring the four-year degree, with those with less training relegated to what one respondent called "technical nursing."[12]

---

ployees. Eligibility workers, in contrast, handle all welfare clients receiving any type of income maintenance or general assistance. Such jobs require only a B.A. degree and are considered technical rather than professional jobs, as the work consists primarily of applying a set of rules to specific instances. One eligibility worker told me that the job classification exists in a kind of limbo, sometimes pulled down to clerical work, other times elevated to social work. However, because they are in the same union with social workers, are college educated, and earn considerably more than clerical workers, I consider them here with the other female-dominated professions.

11. As I discussed in the last chapter, this struggle is typical of the "semi-professions," which occupational sociologists see as lacking the authority, autonomy, and status of the full professions (Etzioni 1969; Ritzer 1972).

12. CNA has not, however, recognized educational differences in contract agreements; salary differentials have been determined strictly according to job descriptions.

Two of my respondents exemplify the dilemma faced by nurses. Both had been in nursing for some time (seven and nine years, respectively), and while deeply committed to the field, they were frustrated by its low status and rewards. With only the two-year training, both had recently made plans to return to school because, as one explained, "I'm too good to be a technical nurse."

Neither woman saw much benefit in affirmative action. They doubted generally whether it would lead to much job integration in the long run. One commented that management would do only the bare minimum required by law, and stated: "There are so many women available to be clerks and for other shit jobs. We should try to get them into other careers—plumbers and whatever. But they're [the male crafts] like closed guilds, like in medieval times." The other commented with similar skepticism: "I don't feel in the long run jobs will be more integrated. . . . When women push, men close it off more."

Further, because neither woman was interested in changing fields, affirmative action strategies offered them little. All four county nurses with whom I spoke explained that upward mobility in their field currently translates only into administrative work; if they enjoy the actual nursing work, the face-to-face contact and care of patients, movement up means a less desirable desk job. Finally, even a top nursing administrator, a black woman who had benefited from affirmative action policies, viewed most such efforts as little more than "manipulation and tokenism." As to her own position, she remarked cynically that with her, the county got "two for one."

It is not surprising that these nurses, aware of affirmative action's limitations, would become activists for comparable worth. As one explained: "I see broad support for comparable worth [among nurses]. Every [nursing] magazine has two to three articles on the topic. It's the major way I learned about it, through CNA or ANA magazines."

Like low-paid women in San Jose, these women also drew comparisons by looking at co-workers in male fields. For example, one woman began to wonder about the rewards she could expect from further education in nursing:

Why should pharmacists be paid twice as much as me? . . . Pharmacists tend to be viewed as professionals, with prestige. Nurses have no prestige, and are viewed as handmaidens. If we had ten times more education, still we would be paid less. . . . I'm guilty of it myself [i.e., viewing the professions this way]. I forget I have had so much schooling. You have this feeling of being "less than" while you're growing up. I think it's the experience of most women to feel "less than."

Another nurse described how she came to support comparable worth:

[After high school] I got a secretarial job. But then I spent my whole paycheck on clothes! I went to college for a while, but dropped out. . . . [Eventually] I decided to go back to school and do something practical— to make more money and do less shitwork [than in the previous clerical job.] [But because of still fairly low pay] now there's an exodus of women out of nursing. Tollbooth collectors make the same amount as we do! I always felt the idea [of comparable worth] was good. I called it equal rights. It's not fair to keep women at such low pay because the man's the breadwinner when it's *not true* anymore.

Another woman, a nurse practitioner (who, with her master's degree, represents the top of the nursing profession), had similar feelings. Before becoming a county employee she had worked at a large hospital, where she learned that predominantly male physicians' assistants made more than female nurse practitioners.[13] Upon coming to the county she became involved with CNA, learned about comparable worth, and began to think about that contrast. Then, she explained, she became furious. Like the other nurses I spoke with, she felt strongly that the male breadwinner stereotype must change: "We must break down the ideas of what a woman needs to earn versus what a man needs to earn. . . . I think the marketplace argument is bullshit!"

Nurses extended this gender consciousness to sympathize with clerical workers. One commented: "I never knew what they [clerks] made until I worked on the Comparable Worth Coalition. When I found out, my mouth dropped open. And then I said: 'There ought to be a law against it!'" Day-to-day reliance on clerical women made the nurse practitioner even more critical of affirmative action strategies that restrict mobility to movement out of women's work:

The receptionists at the clinics make appointments, juggle thirty-five or forty health care providers, make sure patients have insurance, make sure you get your messages. . . . They work as support for me. They handle

13. Nurse practitioners fulfill many of the same functions in large health care organizations as physicians' assistants, a new paraprofessional field. Both occupations take over many of the more routine aspects of primary medical care from

my pay, and find me replacements [when care providers are out]. One
woman does the payroll for two hundred fifty nurses! These people should
get just compensation for their responsibilities. . . . I don't want those
people *to leave to be promoted!*

The occupational concerns and objectives of social workers have
been similar to those of other female professionals. For years they
have suffered from the status anxiety common to the "semiprofessional" fields; moreover, cuts in social service spending in the 1980s
hurt their occupational prospects. In the 1970s, with the advent of
the national feminist movement and local affirmative action policies, the social workers and eligibility workers (about 85 percent of
whom were female) reframed many of their grievances from a gender-based perspective. In fact, in 1976 they attempted to bring an
equal pay suit against the county, even though the case involved a
comparison of men and women in *different* jobs. One leading social
work activist, Lee Finney, explained in our lengthy interview what
had occurred:

There was a lawsuit brought in 1976 by my union [SEIU Local 535] . . . as
an equal pay case on behalf of social workers versus [predominantly male]
probation officers, saying that protective services social workers should be
paid the same as probation officers because they are essentially the same
work. And that was thrown out by the federal district court in San Francisco on the basis of, basically, that probation officers are peace officers,
and we are not. Because they're peace officers, they can carry guns and
they make arrests—so they deserve to be paid more.

In fact, I've been a probation officer in two different places. I've never
made an arrest in my life. I have never carried a gun. And the work is the
same. I know because I've done both jobs, in three different jurisdictions,
in two different states.

Beyond this unsuccessful attempt to use the Equal Pay Act, social workers were also familiar with affirmative action, the other legally mandated route to mobility. Like other members of the wom-
ens' professions, social workers responded to the pejorative aspect
of the job-change model of advancement. Even one of the few
males in social work was bothered by this aspect: "I believe in affir-

physicians; but nurse practitioners are trained in nursing schools, while the physicians' assistant training programs are distinct.

mative action . . . but they say women should move into male jobs if they want more pay. . . . [But] I like being a social worker. Men make good social workers too. I just don't want to be a truck driver!"

Like many of the professionals discussed in the last chapter, these two social workers initially came to union activism only when they felt their individual professional autonomy thwarted. Without such incidents, unions are not so readily embraced, as Lee Finney explained: "I think, like a lot of professionals in professional associations, there's an illusion that you don't need a union. I mean, after all, you're a professional; they're not going to mess with you. But I find that not to be true." In addition, as Finney mentioned in our discussion of the equal pay suit, the social workers' union did not initially know of comparable worth—but when introduced to it by AFSCME's Diana Doughtie, they quickly seized the issue as extending their earlier effort. "It certainly made a whole lot of sense to us," she commented. And Finney spoke of her own "conversion" to the comparable worthy cause; as she puts it, she is now quite "passionate" on the issue. The male social worker also spoke to me about his "conversion" to the comparable worth cause: "At first the female-dominated argument didn't seem that compelling—until you see the [job evaluation] studies and the gaps are actually *huge!*" [14]

The Comparable Worth Coalition: Using Affirmative Action

Following the San Jose strike clerical and semiprofessional employees in Contra Costa County joined together formally in a multiunion coalition to work for comparable worth. County women followed the events to the south closely. The clericals in AFSCME Local 2700 were particularly excited, since they considered the San Jose employees, an AFSCME affiliate, as "their sister union." In fact, some drove down to assist with the strike in San Jose. As one woman said: "I had been fairly naive regarding male/female differentials. . . . [The] comparable worth issue came up when San Jose went on strike. We worked with them on the strike. . . . I be-

14. He was referring to the job evaluation studies of San Jose and the state of Washington, which were quite influential in Contra Costa County, as will be illustrated in the next section of this chapter.

came a lot more enlightened and pretty outraged." Another clerk
concurred:

In the early years of the United Clericals we did make some comparisons
of job skills, test requirements, and so forth, for clerks with janitors, laborers, and so on. Some laborers made three or four times as much—and
their only test was to fill out an application. Window washers just had to
have the "demonstrated ability to wash a window." Comparable worth is
just really a continuation of all our efforts. But nobody had a real good
handle on it until the studies being done in San Jose.

Another impetus to action on comparable worth came from a
more elite level. Sunne McPeak, a county supervisor (first elected
in 1976), avidly watched events in San Jose as well. As a self-identi-
fied feminist politician, McPeak began to carve out comparable
worth as "her" issue.[15] She called a series of meetings with leaders
of the female-dominated unions to discuss the idea, thus stimulat-
ing their formation of the Comparable Worth Coalition in 1982.

That same year McPeak also prompted the first formal move on
the part of county government by persuading the Board of Supervisors to insert a comparable worth resolution into the county's affirmative action goals (*Contra Costa Times* 9/1/82; NCPE 1984,
41–42). Given the past resistance to women's concerns, it seems
surprising that the resolution passed, unanimously in fact, at a time
when local efforts for pay equity were barely under way. One explanation is that the supervisors may not have understood just what
they were voting for. Despite the recent strike in San Jose, several
respondents suggested that comparable worth was often confused
with the established "equal pay for equal work" principle. (Local
press coverage also made this mistake; see *Contra Costa Times*
8/20/81, 9/1/82; Hartson 1981).

A precedent also existed in Contra Costa County for including
wage equity issues under the rubric of affirmative action. For several years the grand jury monitoring compliance had included such
issues in its reports. In fact, as early as 1978 the grand jury had
concluded that the county was violating the "spirit of the law" by
concentrating women in low-paying work (Rego 1979).[16] The fol-

15. The resentment of labor women at elite women's "sense of ownership" of
the comparable worth issue will be taken up in Chapter 6.
16. The review found that 82.9 percent of the lowest-paying jobs, those paying
less than $5,999 a year, were held by women (Rego 1979).

lowing year's review revealed that, on average, female employees earned $6,000 less a year than male employees (*Contra Costa Times* 9/6/80); and the 1980 review recommended that the county begin studying comparable worth (*Contra Costa Times* 11/18/81). The supervisors were thus already under some pressure to address pay equity. The newly formed Comparable Worth Coalition, along with the San Jose example, only increased this pressure.

Although the supervisors made this positive gesture regarding pay equity, top county administrators vigorously opposed even the recommendation to study the issue. They argued that comparable worth was *not* the same as affirmative action, which requires merely that an organization's labor force reflect the local labor pool. As the county had already met "statistical parity" (by employing women in equal or greater proportion to their percentage in the local labor market, absent any consideration of which jobs they were in), management implied that sufficient action had been taken (*Contra Costa Times* 9/1/82).

In rejecting these arguments, the supervisors very likely believed that a resolution agreeing in principle with comparable worth would placate the unions and the grand jury at little or no cost. The labor activists, however, felt, according to one respondent, that they had "pulled one over" on the supervisors. Although the unions made no concerted effort to clarify the difference among comparable worth, equal pay, and job integration policies so long as the confusion worked to their advantage, they clearly understood the difference. One respondent explained it this way:

We were able to persuade the board [of supervisors] to have comparable worth explicitly part of the affirmative action plan. They didn't realize *it would cost them!* But they're *not* similar. Affirmative action has to do with people moving up. It's like the Republican party! It says women should move into male jobs if they want more pay. Comparable worth says, "Hey, there's no such thing as male jobs, just jobs." You don't have to turn everyone into white males!

Science and Politics: The Struggle for Implementation

After the comparable worth resolution was passed in 1982, the tension between science and politics became a central dynamic in the efforts for implementation, much as it had been in San Jose. However, management of the technical issues in gauging wage inequities proved to be more difficult for Contra Costa activists. Familiarity with the San Jose case, as well as with the Washington State case, changed the context in two decisive ways, both involving employer resistance to job evaluation.

First, after San Jose, employers had reason to fear the response of organized employees to job evaluation. Up until the Washington and San Jose cases, management viewed job evaluation as a useful tool to diffuse employee demands and rationalize wage-setting processes; wage setting itself, though, remained firmly in managerial hands (Treiman 1979). However, the results of the studies in Washington and San Jose instigated by comparable worth proponents demonstrated that the methodology is not impenetrable by political pressure by subordinate employees. Moreover, these studies, while still imperfect from the point of view of proponents, provided convincing and accumulating evidence for comparable worth, thereby galvanizing the support of unions, low-paid women, and often the local community.

Second, employers feared the legal liability implied by simply conducting job evaluation studies. This was particularly true during much of the Contra Costa effort, for at the beginning the Washington lawsuit was pending, and then was decided against the state (in December 1983) on precisely this issue. One respondent explained the attitude of county management: "Because of the Washington State case, they're all now terrified of litigation. And they won't put their fingerprints on *anything*, for fear we will sue them when they do." Fears lessened when this decision was overturned on appeal two years later (in September 1985). But the expensive settlement that low-paid women finally won kept alive the greater threat of litigation: the high cost of wage parity (Turner 1986).

Of course, the fear of liability, even at its height (1983–1985), was not always sufficient to prevent comparable worth proponents from gaining job evaluation studies. Many notable cases proceeded with studies at this time, including the states of California and New York and Los Angeles County. In such cases, however, pressure for implementation may have been stronger and political support on the side of proponents greater than in Contra Costa. As the mayor of Colorado Springs, Colorado, an official experienced in pay equity implementation, commented: "Once you do a study, you better be willing to implement it. If you don't, all you do is create evidence so someone can bring a lawsuit against you" (Lawson 1985b; also see Cox 1985; *New York Times* 1984a).

This change in context—with comparable worth activists becoming increasingly knowledgeable about job evaluation and employers increasingly fearing the consequences—combined with the more conservative milieu in Contra Costa (that is, in terms of gender politics) to make implementation lengthier and more arduous than in San Jose.

Implementation efforts in Contra Costa were further complicated by the fact that two very different approaches to job evaluation were considered at various times, with different groups arguing for and against each: (1) a formal job evaluation, like the Hay study in San Jose, conducted by outside experts, using their techniques; and (2) a so-called piggyback study, conducted in-house, in which county job classes would be compared using the results of other formal studies, primarily those of San Jose and Washington, borrowing the factor point scores from similar benchmark jobs. The distinctions between these two types of studies were often obscured, either inadvertently or deliberately, in the political conflict that ensued.

Unlike the San Jose union, the union coalition in Contra Costa opposed having an outside firm conduct a formal study. (In fact, in Contra Costa support for an outside study became a surreptitious form of opposition to comparable worth; see below.) In each case activists saw the need for a study to legitimate and specify wage discrepancies. But in Contra Costa, the labor coalition did not want already scarce funds to go to an outside consulting firm.[17] Knowing the county was dead set against a formal study anyway, the coalition tried to argue for an in-house piggyback study. One labor leader explained:

We also felt like we didn't really need to do a full-blown study—we did not need to spend several hundred thousand dollars paying a consultant to do it. There are enough studies already done. You could do a piggyback that is just as satisfactory. And we have the expertise to do this our-

17. Recall that Hay charged San Jose nearly $100,000 (Flammang 1986, 818), and this was to study a much smaller organization than the county.

selves. . . . I don't want to pay an outsider and take my chances! I mean, in a perfect world what I would do would be to take two years and do an in-house study with labor and management on the committee; with 5 percent adjustments each year as good faith [down payments]; and the remainder of the adjustments phased in after the study. [Commenting wryly:] So, I don't understand why they don't want to do it. I think it's perfect.

Local newspaper coverage indicates that these positions on job evaluation were often misunderstood or misrepresented. One editorial, for example, states that officials should be "unapologetic" for their opposition to job evaluation: not only have the supervisors, who have been "subjected to considerable abuse," shown good "common sense," since such studies are "inherently flawed," but a job evaluation study would subject the county to possible lawsuits and prove financially devastating (*Contra Costa Times* 11/21/85). This statement, however, fails to credit the position of the labor coalition, which repeatedly stated that if the county would agree to a piggyback study, they would be unlikely to pursue litigation, and they would be firmly committed to phased-in implementation according to the county's ability to pay. (Employees certainly had no desire to provoke layoffs or subcontracting.) The coalition also repeatedly pointed out that they would be using only techniques already accepted by many organizations—and saving the county the cost of a consulting firm by using its own members' expertise. In this case, obscuring the technical debate over particular job evaluation methods served to make the coalition's demands appear highly unreasonable.

The Contra Costa struggle for implementation can best be understood by considering the first two consecutive rounds of contract bargaining over pay equity in some detail. The first round began with the passage of the comparable worth resolution in 1982 and ended in the 1984 contract settlement; the second began in 1984 and ended with the next contract settlement, early in 1986. In each round, the county and the labor coalition jockeyed over technical issues, but the coalition failed to gain a job evaluation study.

Round One: Getting a Down Payment

During the first round of negotiations, the Comparable Worth Coalition went through nearly eighteen months of "prolonged, arduous collective bargaining," according to the National Committee on Pay Equity (1984, 40). In this period the strength of the coalition of clericals, nurses, and social workers, which was put to the test several times, was impressive (NCPE 1984, 45). Yet the results of this round—a 3 percent equity adjustment as a "down payment" and an ambiguous agreement to form a labor-management task force— were much less impressive.

The county made the first move in round one. Following the passage of McPeak's resolution making comparable worth an affirmative action goal, the director of personnel, Harry Cisterman, was instructed to review the existing salary structure and "compile information relevant to comparable worth" (Cisterman 1983). But labor and management interpreted this vague instruction from the supervisors in rather different ways. The local press, for example, which saw the action "as a victory" for the female-dominated unions, reported that Cisterman was to use existing studies, coupled with local data, *to start implementing* "the comparable worth concept" (Rego 1983). Yet when Cisterman's report was issued it was nothing like this description; instead it was a thinly veiled attack against comparable worth.

Coalition leader Lee Finney described labor's angry response to this report:

We expected that this report was going to be like a piggyback type of job evaluation study. It was not anything close! They quote some statistics showing an aggregate wage gap of 37 percent, but they had a lot of market data. . . . And they also had a little blurb about studies that have been done in other places: Connecticut, Washington, San Jose. . . . But in even referring to the other studies, it was like less than a page! It talked about basically why they were *not* useful, and cited the National Academy of Science's study [Treiman and Hartmann 1981] that said there really is no "cookbook" way to do it. And that's been the position of the personnel director with regard to job evaluation—that since there is no good "can opener," we can't do it.[18]

When I interviewed Cisterman, he defended the negative approach to job evaluation included in the report: "Washington and

18. Although the National Academy report, commissioned by the EEOC under Eleanor Holmes Norton, did make such statements as the one Finney cited about "cookbook" approaches, it also argued strongly for the further development and use of such techniques, and for the validity of comparable worth claims (see Chapter 2 above).

San Jose's studies were *not scientific!* . . . I believe comparable worth raises a valid issue of wage discrimination. *But* to approach what it is—we don't have the *technology* to assess the difference across jobs." Along with this "technological" argument, Cisterman repeated the earlier argument of county management for the proper, narrow definition of affirmative action: "Our goal really is to integrate the work force. Then comparable worth will not be a problem."

Cisterman's report so irritated the labor group leaders that they named it "the Pink Paper" in a sarcastic reference to its pink cover sheet. In addition, they reexamined the county salary data and, without technical assistance, issued their own counterreport. In Finney's words:

I wanted to look at the material, and I wanted to dramatize it in a way the Pink Paper had not. And the more I looked at the data, the more agitated I got! It was like: "Oh my God!" . . . And I'm not a statistician. But I did what made sense to me. . . . It's not a job evaluation study, and we didn't do class by class comparisons. . . . [But] it shows that women start lower [in terms of twelve salary levels in the county]; the majority are bunched at lower levels, and they end lower. And this is true for the whole county. This is true any way you describe it. And then I did the five largest departments, two of which are female-dominated [health and social services], two of which are male-dominated [sheriffs and public works], and one of which is mixed [probation]. And in all five of them, whether they're male-dominated or female-dominated, the pattern is the same.

Although the coalition's report (Finney 1983) contained few data not presented in Cisterman's "Pink Paper" (Cisterman 1983), it did present this information more dramatically, in the context of an argument for comparable worth, and without the distraction of pages of market wage comparisons. The Finney report stressed both the need for comparable worth and its reasonableness as a wage-setting policy. For example, the report begins by conceding that "job integration may be a desirable long-term social objective"; "in the immediate and forseeable future," however, comparable worth is needed for those in "women's work" (Finney 1983, 1). Also, in response to the argument that the technology does not exist for such a policy, the report states reasonably: "Although no universally accepted job evaluation system, no 'cookbook' presently exists, . . . many public sector employers have and are attempting to initiate bias-free job evaluation systems. . . . The number of studies available to be 'piggybacked' . . . continues to increase" (Finney 1983, 4, 5).

Although Finney told me the labor report was "primitive" and "done by hand," she also felt it was "a real successful tool." Not only was it used to educate the unions' membership, but "we circulated it with women's groups. And we got letters of support from the National Women's Political Caucus and NOW. . . . [We] used it as a position paper. We sent it to every member of the Board of Supervisors. We even shared it with some of the county's representatives at the bargaining table." It was on the strength of this report, moreover, that the labor coalition proposed the 3 percent "down payment" and the joint task force that they eventually did win (also see NCPE 1984, 45).

Despite the strong impression the labor report made, the union coalition faced the greatest obstacle to pay equity in the county's constrained budget. The county fiscal situation had gone from bad to worse in the early 1980s. In addition to the general economic recession, a reduction in federal grants due to Reaganomics, and a decline in revenues due to California's property tax–cutting Proposition 13,[19] the county suddenly discovered a $17 million bookkeeping error (out of a total budget of $315.6 million) (Contra Costa County 1981–1982, 1982–1983; NCPE 1984, 40–43). Not only was comparable worth removed from the bargaining table, but the county asked all employees to take a 5 percent pay cut. Coalition members, however, stood firm in their demands, opposing any wage cuts and insisting on their equity down payment. They also argued for alternative methods to resolve the fiscal crisis and took an active role in ensuring that an alternative would be adopted.

19. Although San Jose certainly faced similar fiscal constraints, the booming high-tech industries in Silicon Valley created a cushioning effect, at least to the "aftershocks of Prop. 13," and city revenues actually increased each budget year after its passage (Flammang 1986, 820). Because county governments provide expensive health and social services that are not a part of city jurisdictions, Contra Costa, though also a growing region, was harder hit by Reagan budget cuts than San Jose. Evidence indicates that, in fact, revenues from state and federal agencies, providing *over* half of total budget revenues, declined each year from 1980 to 1984 (Contra Costa County 1981–1982, 1982–1983, 1983–1984). In contrast, in San Jose the vast majority of funds come from local taxes, which, after a flat year in 1979, increased steadily (City of San Jose 1985, 54–55, 59).

The alternative involved the use of employee retirement funds to refinance several county properties (NCPE 1984, 44). Because two union representatives sit on the board overseeing these funds, and unanimity is required for fund allocations, labor had political leverage that they did not hesitate to use. The coalition threatened to tie up funds unless their contract proposals were accepted. As one respondent bluntly stated, "Our feeling was, if they don't use the money to help us, why give it to them?" The county responded by threatening bankruptcy, layoffs, and lawsuits (Rego 1984a, 1984b). In the end, the coalition relented and the financing went through; but shortly afterward, the county provided the "down payment" on comparable worth (Rego 1984c).[20]

Thus in round one, activists' willingness to intrude in complex financial as well as technical matters kept the pay equity issue alive. In fact, because the coalition was able to force action in a time of severe "fiscal stress," the National Committee on Pay Equity (1984, 40) has called the case a model for bargaining in times of declining revenues and "belt-tightening mood[s]."

Round Two: The Task Force

The second round of the Contra Costa comparable worth effort centered on the newly established labor-management task force. But just as the mandate for action in round one had been deliberately vague, so were the objectives of the task force. Round two, therefore, saw more jockeying over technical issues, as women again pushed for a piggyback job evaluation study while the county continued to avoid being pinned down.

The task force itself was divided into two information-gathering subcommittees, the Legal and Legislative Committee and the Benchmark Committee. From the start, though, the Benchmark Committee was *it*—the real center of the struggle. The Legal and

20. The fiscal crisis also tested the unity of the coalition. As in San Jose, the unions opposed taking comparable worth funds out of the general increase and felt strongly that any "down payment" should go across the board to all female-dominated classes. But the county offered the nurses a larger general increase (11 percent) with a lower comparable worth adjustment (2.5 percent)—an act that both the unions and the press saw as a "bad faith" effort to split the coalition (Rego 1984b). CNA, however, flatly rejected such offers, and the coalition won respect for its cohesion.

Legislative Committee, as one woman put it, "didn't have a whole lot to do." Most agreed it was primarily a vehicle the county used to dissipate the coalition's energy in a tiresome, redundant research endeavor.[21]

The mandate for the Benchmark Committee, as for the entire task force, was ambiguous, stating only that the committee should "analyze the County salary plan and recommend . . . which benchmark classifications should be included in addressing comparable worth in the meet and confer process" (NCPE 1984, 46).[22] Lee Finney, labor chair of the Benchmark Committee, explained that this vague directive was the best they could get: "The language creating the task force was somewhat vague and we were *not* real thrilled with it. But they would not agree to do a piggyback study; they would not agree to do a job evaluation study of any kind." Basically, all that was clear, according to Finney, was that "this task force would do all this research and look at ways to establish benchmarks to be used in better defining comparable worth for negotiations next time."

The union women, despite such limitations, tried to push the committee as far as possible toward their ultimate goal. Finney recounted how they edged closer and closer to a piggyback study:

The unions knew a whole lot more about some things than management did. We just had the expertise that they didn't have. . . . We talked a lot about how to look at the wage gap; whether we should be talking about entry-level jobs, minimum qualifications, [and so forth]. . . . And we

21. Excellent legal reviews were already available from advocacy groups, such as the NCPE or the California-based Comparable Worth Project (now a part of the Institute for Industrial Relations, University of California, Berkeley). The first labor chair of the Legal and Legislative Committee had hoped to review the county's budget for funding recommendations, originally a mandated objective of the task force (NCPE 1984, 46). She reasoned that if they had been "on top of" county finances, as in round one, they would have been able to evaluate management offers critically and to promote alternatives. However, the tenure of this sophisticated woman was cut short by illness, and the budget review was never conducted.

22. "Meet and confer" refers to the California law covering public agency employee relations. According to the Meyers-Milias-Brown Act, agencies are required to "meet and confer" with employee unions. Technically, only monetary agreements are considered binding under this law, but custom also serves to routinize bargaining over nonmonetary issues in many localities, and "contracts" have habitually been honored in both San Jose and Contra Costa County (Flammang 1986, 824).

talked to them about how do you decide where a classification belongs, and what your classification system looks like. . . . And then everybody's real frustrated. . . . And they're [management] all *terrified* of any kind of points!

So I said, okay . . . why don't we compare to see how many matches we can make between Washington and San Jose benchmarks and Contra Costa County classes, just to get some notion of rank and hierarchy. So we started doing this. And then we needed the job descriptions, so this personnel guy, he called Washington, he called San Jose. And each of us would take home an assignment and work on one class. . . . And management participated in this fully! We met every Thursday morning [for about six months]. . . . And we were just moving right along. And we were almost done.

Then the process came to an abrupt end:

[We] suggested that the next step was to draw the picture, "the DREADED TREND LINE!" It just freaked them [management] out! And the personnel guy felt he had been had. And he had let us develop something we weren't supposed to [i.e., a piggyback study], which was actually to develop something meaningful, that could be used against them.

So Cisterman [the director of personnel] went to the board [of supervisors]. And he took the county counsel and county administrator. The county counsel advised the board that they should *not* do anything that would be a comparison of one classification to another across occupational lines. And they shouldn't do any trend line. And the two master lists [comparing the county to] San Jose and Washington should be trashed. . . . Basically he told the politicians that their names would be individually and collectively carved in the tombstone of Contra Costa County if they let us do this![23]

At this time fears of litigation may have been at their high point, as the Washington decision had yet to be overturned. The *Contra Costa Times,* in fact, had just run a big article on a League of California Cities convention at which labor lawyers advised localities *not* to do job evaluation studies (Newbergh 1984d).

Any notion of doing a pay equity study in the county was now unrealistic. Under pressure, management women on the task force

23. The trend line, as explained in Chapter 3, refers to the "best fit" regression line expressing the relation between job evaluation (or factor) points and salaries. It is the central measure of wage disparities between male- and female-dominated job classes.

agreed to discard the lists matching county jobs to San Jose and Washington benchmarks, which they had painstakingly worked on for months. As an alternative, they suggested grouping male and female jobs into three wide bands, with wage gaps estimated in each. Labor women objected: this was far from the specification of wage inequities that they sought, and would go little further than the aggregate data presented in round one. Desperate for any positive movement, labor women took the notion of grouping jobs and presented a counterproposal containing six job groups based on the San Jose and Washington benchmarks. But as Lee Finney explained, while management agreed to use six groups to assess the wage gap, they refused to use the San Jose and Washington benchmarks and "proceeded to mess with" labor's groupings. According to Finney, this manipulation served to reduce the measures of wage disparity.

Ultimately, two reports were issued from the Benchmark Committee of the task force, one from labor and one from management, because the two sides could not agree on several points. Again, Lee Finney explained: "The recommendations, which we had thought would not be controversial, like a five-year plan should be developed—*No way!* . . . That a separate fund be established— *No*, they wouldn't agree to that. The only thing they would agree to is: 'there is a problem and it should be negotiated.' *Big deal!* And that's where we [finally] reached impasse."

Management's report was so hesitant and so qualified as to provide little further validation of comparable worth claims (Contra Costa County 1985b). In contrast, the labor report made clear that the job groupings were derived from the San Jose and Washington studies (Contra Costa County 1985a). Although it was unofficial, the Comparable Worth Coalition used their report in bargaining, feeling that it at least justified their demands for further down payments and underscored the need for a real study. But after months of further negotiations in which the county refused to budge, the women's unions finally gave up on the demand for a study, settling for another set of incremental equity adjustments. Feeling cynical after two exacting rounds of research and bargaining with so little concrete result, Lee Finney quipped sarcastically: "We didn't accomplish anything, but we sure looked tough going down!"

Other Tactics

The Comparable Worth Coalition also promoted activities outside their formal efforts in data collection and bargaining. For instance, they utilized the unruly or disruptive tactics that social movement scholars refer to as typical of subordinate movements (Jenkins 1983; Piven and Cloward 1977), though none was as dramatic as San Jose's strike. In round one, women picketed and held part-day walkouts (e.g., Cohen 1983). But in round two they became more inventive.

In the summer of 1985, while I was conducting interviews, the coalition held a "pink power" campaign to respond both to the disappointing outcome of the task force and to the start of contract negotiations. Members pinned pink ribbons to their chests and gathered pink postcards supporting comparable worth to mail to the supervisors. They also held a "pink power" rally, in which they all dressed in pink and sported pink balloons and buttons carrying the slogan "Smash the Pink Collar Ghetto!" At the rally, after a brief press conference, some two hundred women interrupted the Board of Supervisors' meeting, distributing pink carnations and congratulating the supervisors for their earlier support (Kidder 1985).[24]

Several months later, when negotiations had stalled over the issue of job evaluation, activists staged a mock funeral. They again interrupted a board meeting by marching in, dressed in black, carrying a coffin. This attracted the attention of at least the local press, which ran such headlines as "Workers 'Mourn' for Pay Equity Study" (Borenstein 1985). Unfortunately, four years after the San Jose strike, these actions and dragged-out efforts in Contra Costa County failed to capture the attention of even the larger regional newspapers.

Despite impressive grass-roots support, and "ruly" as well as unruly activity, by early 1986 the county was finally able to divide the unions in the Comparable Worth Coalition. Because the county

24. My impression, having been in the county offices at this time, was that involvement in this campaign was fairly broad. I saw many clerks wearing the pink ribbons (reminiscent of the red ribbons worn then by students at the University of California, Berkeley, supporting divestment from South Africa); several had pinned up balloons and buttons around their desks; there was excitement about the rally, and several higher-level employees made favorable comments to me about the campaign.

steadfastly refused to make any agreement on job evaluation but rather continued as one coalition leader put it, to "nickel and dime us to death," the clericals, nurses, and social workers were pushed into making separate settlements at the end of round two. The clericals settled first, in November 1985, while the two professional groups held out for job evaluation. The president of AFSCME Local 2700 explained that it was difficult for the clericals, the largest and lowest-paid group, to hold out on principle when they were being offered a good financial package (with an equity adjustment, general increase, and an increase in health coverage). She felt it was admirable that the group had held out as long as it did (nearly six months), because "our people really need the money."

The social workers finally settled early in the winter of 1986, when, they said, it became clear a study simply would not be approved (Borenstein 1986a). Both social workers and clericals settled for two comparable worth adjustments of 3 percent (on top of general increases), one in each contract year, 1986 and 1987.

Nurses also dropped their demand for a study, but took longer to settle. The county would offer them only the first of the two equity adjustments, citing the marketplace as justification. While clericals and social workers agreed that the county's use of market arguments threatened the validity of comparable worth, the nurses were left to fend for themselves. Representatives of the three female-dominated groups, however, stated emphatically that the pay equity issue in Contra Costa County was not dead (Borenstein 1986b).

Indeed, follow-up interviews with Lee Finney in 1988 and 1989 revealed that, as the women unionists had predicted, the issue did not die. Supervisor McPeak and unionist Finney have continued to press for full implementation. Although the coalition no longer exists, the female-dominated unions still cooperate to a limited extent. In 1987 contract negotiations, after continuing conflict over methodology, the county administration finally agreed to a pilot study conducted primarily in-house, but with the involvement of an outside consultant. The results of the pilot study, as well as the success of the process itself, at last persuaded the county to conduct a full study. (A series of court decisions against pay equity also helped by lessening fears of litigation.) Comparable worth proponents, however, had to abandon their preference for the faster piggyback approach—although the efforts of Finney and McPeak kept labor centrally involved. By 1989, a formal job evaluation study was under way (again, primarily in-house, with labor and management involvement), and a preliminary formula for implementation had been agreed upon.[25] The full study is scheduled to be completed by the spring of 1991, and implementation should begin later that year. As Finney concluded, "It is going to happen, but probably more watered-down than I personally would like" (personal communication 12/2/89).

Other Obstacles

Throughout the comparable worth effort in Contra Costa County, during the years of tedious meetings and arduous bargaining sessions, the Comparable Worth Coalition faced several obstacles to its success. The major ones have already been discussed: the county's fear of litigation and the severely constrained county budget. Lesser obstacles were present as well, ones that might have had little effect in an easier fiscal situation. These included the feared impact of comparable worth on local development and the attitude of the large, independent, male-dominated union, Contra Costa Employees Local 1.

Although the private sector exerted little direct pressure in this matter, county officials were concerned about the impact comparable worth might have on the local business climate. The National Committee on Pay Equity (1984, 48, 49), for example, noted that movement of "back office operations" to the area had created an "office job mecca," but "the county government is [still] the single largest employer in the county, and therefore, can have significant impact on the labor market. . . . [Thus] large companies are making their displeasure known." One labor official commented that he

25. The preliminary formula for implementation states that funds for equity adjustments be provided at fifty cents for every dollar in funds for general increases, as bargained for by the participating unions collectively (Contra Costa County 1987). This agreement does *not* resolve all conflicts, however; as Finney told me, there will be "squabbles" as the study nears completion. For example, she pointed out that no agreement had been reached on whether the regression line will be drawn as the average of male jobs or of all jobs or on the acceptable margin of error, or "equity corridor," surrounding the trend line. Yet she did comment that the study will stand up over time: "It has been such an organic process, in-house, with so much labor input" (personal communication, 12/2/89).

had heard many unsubstantiated rumors of such private sector "displeasure": "There's a great fear on the part of the oil companies in the county. I hear rumors that they were putting pressure on one of the supervisors not to go for comparable worth because that's going to raise the market value of clerical work. And Shell, Standard Oil, are going to have pay more down the line." Moreover, two women in personnel (a lower- and a middle-level manager) each told me of large businesses in the area making polite inquiries about the county's comparable worth policy. One woman said that she knew Standard Oil and Bechtel were paying attention and were nervous. Another explained that she had been invited to Pacific Bell to discuss how the county had managed to adopt a comparable worth policy avoiding both lawsuits and a job evaluation study.

Even Supervisor McPeak, a strong supporter of the Comparable Worth Coalition and possessive of the issue itself, was reported by the National Committee on Pay Equity as being troubled by the opposition of local business. While often in the minority on the board with her feminist stance, she was described as a friend to business and a promoter of county development (NCPE 1984, 48–49); and she was certainly concerned with her future political career (Diringer 1984).[26]

Interestingly, in the spring of 1984 a panel of women in local politics met to discuss the impact of the "office explosion" on county women. Although prodevelopment, these local politicians expressed strong support for comparable worth; yet their reasoning was somewhat contradictory. The panel emphasized that developers were not attracted to the county specifically because of cheaper labor. Rather, they relocate for the lower land costs and office rents. However, the *reliability* of the relatively untapped labor pool of suburban housewives was cited as a significant factor, as was the "generally lower cost of doing business."[27] Panelists ignored the fact that the touted reliability of these housewives likely would not include any collective push for comparable worth; they ignored as well the fact that the "generally lower cost of doing business" likely

26. Unfortunately, although I made many attempts, I was unable to interview Supervisor McPeak.
27. Studies have shown that of the San Francisco Bay Area counties, Contra Costa currently has the largest proportion of families with nonemployed wives (Herscher 1984).

included some consideration of wage levels. But instead of addressing the contradictory policy objectives (that is, on the one hand
promoting women's advancement and on the other hand promoting
development based on a low-paid female labor force), panel members simply urged county women to stop devaluing their own skills
(Newbergh 1984a).[28]

Although it is unlikely (and there is little evidence) that local
business became directly involved in the county's comparable worth
struggle, fears that large corporations might simply take their business elsewhere constituted indirect pressure to hold down women's
pay. By mid-decade, local politicians also had some reason to fear
an economic slowdown as office rents and developers' fees began to
rise, narrowing the differential with costs in downtown San Francisco (Newbergh 1985a). Furthermore, as a major developer stated,
a primary attraction of Contra Costa County, right after its lower
rents and taxes, was its "good secondary labor force of housewives
seeking work close to home" (Malaspina 1984).

In addition to the potential impact of comparable worth on local
business, the problematic relations between the female-dominated
coalition and Contra Costa Employees Local 1 presented another
obstacle to the activists' success. Like the conflicts with county officials, those with Local 1 were obscured by technical issues of job
evaluation. Unfortunately, my repeated attempts to interview a
representative of Local 1 were rebuffed; thus, I rely largely on
documentary evidence and the views of other informants.

At first Local 1 had actually been in the coalition: a very powerful group in the county, indeed the largest single union, it includes
such female-dominated occupational groups as librarians, voca-
tional and public health nurses, and medical attendants. Local 1
represented approximately 1,800 employees, with some 600 in
women's jobs, while the Comparable Worth Coalition represented
approximately 2,300, nearly all in female-dominated jobs (Cisterman 1983; Finney 1983). However, as one coalition activist explained, "the question for us was: *when* would they break, rather
than *would* they."

Local 1 did in fact break quite early from the Coalition—but not

28. This panel, ironically, appeared to confuse comparable worth with affirmative action policies, as they reportedly stated: "Unless we do something now,
we're not going to get the better jobs" (Newbergh 1984a).

with any open admission of opposition to comparable worth.[29] Rather, they obscured their opposition by insisting on a formal job evaluation study, to be conducted by outside consultants, before any other action was taken. They even went so far as to send letters supporting comparable worth to Supervisor McPeak.[30] However, a coalition leader explained what this actually meant: "I believe that Local One understands that the county is *not* going to do a study if they can possibly avoid it. And so it's real easy to be in favor of something that you know *isn't* going to happen. And therefore he [Clark, head of that union] doesn't have to deal with comparable worth and how it's going to affect his male classes." The director of personnel confirmed these suspicions with his comment in our 1985 interview: "I'll continue to recommend *not* to do a job evaluation study. Local One is screaming for a job evaluation study, but they know it'll lose. That's why they do it. If it happened, it'd be the last day they [the union's negotiators] work for that union!" Even after a compromise approach to job evaluation had been worked out between the county and the women's unions in 1989, Local 1 continued to object, though masking their opposition behind technical issues as Lee Finney pointed out—for example, objecting to questionnaire construction, interviewing procedures, and so forth.

Local 1's maneuvering, however, was fairly transparent to com-

29. One small male-dominated occupational group remained in the Comparable Worth Coalition, the engineering technicians. A group of about forty (approximately eight of whom were women), the engineering technicians are not part of Local 1; instead they are represented by a small AFSCME unit, Local 512, which includes their group and a female-dominated group of sixty eligibility work supervisors (Finney 1983). AFSCME 512 is of course closely allied with the clericals in AFSCME 2700, sharing the same business agent (it is also closely allied with SEIU 525, which represents the nonsupervisory staff in eligibility work). Thus, 512 strongly supported the comparable worth efforts, and much energy was put toward winning the support of the engineering techs. The task may have been made easier by the fact that 512's president at the time was one of the women technicians, who entered the field to escape years spent in underpaid female-dominated jobs and so identified with the comparable worth activists. Although their group is small, the support of the technicians was judged to have been significant, symbolic of male workers' support for a working woman's issue.

30. The local newspaper covered this story under the headline "Comparable Worth Gets Union Push." The technical difference between types of job evaluation again obscures actual political positions, as McPeak is reported here to be *against* an "exhaustive" study. In fact, she supported the coalition's call for a piggyback study, but this was not recognized by the local reporter (Rego 1982).

parable worth proponents. Henry Clark, the union's leader, was not seen as really interested in women's issues, despite a sizable female membership. Several respondents pointed out that the local had no women leaders. Others were angry that Clark had gained special market-based equity adjustments for several of his male job classes, subverting their efforts to narrow the wage gap. And Finney commented that, after publicly supporting comparable worth, "Clark asked his women to give up comparable worth to save some women's jobs in the hospital [threatened with layoffs in the budget crisis]. But he wasn't asking his *men* to give up *their* raises!" Finally, a longtime clerical pointed to what most believed was really behind Local 1's posturing: "Local One just feels comparable worth will come out of the men's pockets!"[31]

San Jose, with its strong liberal feminist community and presence in city government, may have been a particularly favorable environment in which to raise comparable worth. In contrast, the Contra Costa movement is notable for winning incremental gains in a relatively inhospitable local setting. Certainly the national context had changed by the mid 1980s; the Reagan administration's attacks on comparable worth and other civil rights issues, which had just begun at the time of the San Jose strike, were in full force several years later. Although federal government policies could not determine local outcomes, they provided good reason for Contra Costa officials to resist "the looniest idea since Looney Tunes" (*Contra Costa Times* 11/17/84).

Within the local contexts of these movements, clerical activism in Contra Costa was of a different character than in San Jose. Women clericals in the county had organized earlier than women in San Jose, and with a stronger sense of their particular class location. Although in both cases efforts to address low-paid women

31. Local 1 very likely saw its fears of comparable worth confirmed in the experience of the small city of Concord. Located in the central county district, Concord is a wealthy area of new development that contracted with a consulting firm to conduct a comparable worth study in 1984 (Newbergh 1984b, 1984c). When the results were revealed to the approximately three hundred city workers, men were angry that the consultant recommended pay cuts for jobs above the trend line. The city did not approve any cuts, but it did freeze wages in several male-dominated jobs in order to close the wage gap while bringing the female-dominated jobs up to trend (Ronningen 1985; Newbergh, 1985b).

were strengthened by committed women union staff, who introduced the notion of comparable worth, clerks in Contra Costa already had a strong labor identification and demonstrated a dual awareness of class and gender that anticipated comparable worth claims.

Clericals in Contra Costa were also influenced by affirmative action: it provided models for individual mobility out of clerical work into male-dominated fields as well as, for some, a sense of connection to a larger feminist movement. Affirmative action worked in several ways in the Contra Costa case. First, as in San Jose, it had a provocative effect on women's consciousness. By legitimating women's grievances and recasting them as moral issues of women's rights, affirmative action raised expectations that it could not meet. Because so few visibly benefited, women eagerly embraced the alternative of comparable worth, as they had in San Jose. This was particularly true for professional employees, who saw affirmative action as devaluing their occupational choices.

In contrast to the San Jose case, affirmative action also had an institutional impact in Contra Costa. At least in part because grand jury reviews of job integration had reported on the wage gap and recommended comparable worth, the county Board of Supervisors approved the policy in principle—thus practically inviting action by organized female employees.

Although I am drawing comparisons between two struggles for comparable worth, one in San Jose and one in Contra Costa, it is important to recognize that they are not independent, unrelated cases. The movement in Contra Costa followed that in San Jose, and both the proponents of comparable worth and county government were strongly influenced by what had happened in San Jose, as well as by notable cases such as that of Washington State. The political, legal, and fiscal climate had all shifted by mid-decade, but the most significant change between the early cases like San Jose and the "second string" of cases like Contra Costa may have involved attitudes about job evaluation. At first simply a technique to increase management control over wage setting, job evaluation had become a useful tool for comparable worth proponents. As I have illustrated, activists in Contra Costa had detailed knowledge of the techniques used in San Jose and Washington, and often demonstrated a more sophisticated understanding of methodological issues than county officials. Those officials, fearing litigation and budget crises, as well as further provocation of the female-dominated unions, were more opposed to job evaluation than officials in San Jose. Only the persistence of leading activists and the backing of the female unions over many years led the county finally to consent to put its fingerprints on the issue.

Still, one might consider the Contra Costa movement largely a failure. The coalition of female-dominated unions was broken in 1986, and so far proponents have been unable to resurrect it. Moreover, progress toward job evaluation has been painfully, almost ridiculously, slow—the study is still not complete nearly nine years later. Yet I believe this case may be judged a success on at least two counts. First, it is significant that any gains at all were made given the obstacles. As labor leader Lee Finney stated at a 1986 conference of comparable worth advocates, "We have not yet succeeded in getting a full comparable worth plan; but we have put real money in real people's pockets" (Berkeley Policy Notes 1986, 8).[32] Second, in addition to winning "real money" for "real people's pockets" while the struggle was dragging on, this case created a depth of conviction among those involved. As in San Jose, many of the Contra Costa comparable worth activists now see themselves as part of what one woman characterized as "a crusade." The notion that women have the right to decent economic conditions for their families, the right to be seen as valuable workers paid at a level commensurate with that of valuable male workers, and the right to challenge the marketplace when it infringes on these claims, is now seen as part of a larger struggle. My respondents equated the movement for comparable worth with the movement for women's suffrage, compared it to a religion, stated that it was one of their major purposes in life or that they were "passionately" committed to it. With this deep conviction, they now see themselves involved in a larger and lengthier struggle to bring together labor and feminist movements. On this count the Contra Costa case, despite the county's "nickel and dime" response, must be viewed as a success.

32. Finney (1987) found that the 9 percent in adjustments between 1983 and 1987 had closed the wage gap by 8 percent, leaving an aggregate wage gap of 23 percent. One press report stated: "By 1988, the county will have spent $17 million on negotiated comparable worth adjustments" (*Contra Costa Times* 11/21/85).

Five

Constrained Choices

Women's Interest in Women's Work

Should feminists take heart at the "passion" that the comparable worth issue inspires among women who in many cases did not consider themselves feminists? Or should it be a cause for discouragement that many of these women are unwilling to challenge the sex typing of occupations and prefer a strategy that leaves intact the barriers between men's work and women's work? In this chapter, I turn to such questions as I examine the possibly adverse consequences of job integration strategies.

Equality and Difference

Any evaluation of comparable worth is inextricably linked to a perspective on the existing sex segregation of the labor market. At one extreme is the position that women's choices of employment are constrained only by their own values and preferences, which differ from those of men. In this view, women are willing if unwitting victims of societal norms, as they are socialized to accept a marginal role in the workplace. At the other extreme is the position that large numbers of women are ready, willing, and able to enter male-dominated jobs but are prevented from doing so by the resistance of both employers and working men. In this view, low-paid women are unwilling victims of a coercive economic structure. The latter position, in its extreme, can lead to the conclusion that aggressive affirmative action policies are the key to eliminating gender in-

equality, while comparable worth may be less helpful, or even re-
gressive, because it reinforces the existing sex typing of work. The
former perspective, emphasizing female socialization, can lead either to the extreme free-market position that no intervention to
remedy gender inequality is needed, or to advocacy of comparable
worth on the grounds that the pressing economic needs of low-paid
women cannot wait for changes in deeply embedded societal norms.

These two perspectives were placed in stark opposition in the
sex discrimination suit against Sears, Roebuck. Historian Rosalind
Rosenberg, testifying as an expert witness on behalf of Sears, argued that the lack of women in high-paying sales jobs was due to
women's choices rather than to any discriminatory practices for
which Sears should be held responsible. She claimed that women,
having internalized family-centered values, possess different goals
and aspirations regarding paid work than men and are less concerned with maximizing their incomes (Freedman 1986; R. Rosenberg 1985, 1986; Wiener 1985a, 1985b).

Historian Alice Kessler-Harris testified for the EEOC against
Sears. She argued that Rosenberg's assumption of an unrestricted
labor market for women where free choice reigns is false; she also
argued that the historical evidence contradicts the determinacy
Rosenberg assigned to family socialization. Instead, according to
Kessler-Harris, women's location in the Sears organization, as in
the labor market in general, is due not to women's choices but to
discriminatory employment practices and coercive economic institutions (Kessler-Harris 1986, 66). The court, however, accepted
Rosenberg's argument and held that Sears was not liable.

Of course, less extreme intermediate positions explaining
women's position in the labor market are possible, and in fact are
favored by most analysts, including Kessler-Harris. In the Sears
case the adversarial nature of the legal process unfortunately prevented Kessler-Harris from presenting a more nuanced interpretation of women's location in the labor market that could still hold the
employer liable. Kessler-Harris's own views rely less on a simple
coercion model than on a view of women as active subjects who
make choices within constraints. Also, Kessler-Harris would very
likely agree that women do have extraeconomic reasons for traditional preferences, as Rosenberg insists. However, it is not at all

clear that female-dominated jobs *actually* better accommodate familial responsibilities than male-typed jobs (Kessler-Harris 1986, 66–68).[1] In any case, the fact that women often do have different priorities from men does not mean that they face unrestricted choices, or that employers should be free of responsibility for discriminatory practices. It is clear that the alternatives available to working women are highly constrained by the existing structural context, a context that includes the prevailing ideology about women as workers, resistance from employers and working men, a conservative national government, and an uncertain economic environment.

These structural obstacles, combined with a discomfort with "gender-inappropriate" positions (owing to gender socialization), tend to discourage many women from attempting to enter male-dominated fields despite the incentive of higher pay. Whether one emphasizes socialized preferences or structural obstacles, it is common nonetheless to view women as essentially passive victims in the labor market. Yet women are also making active choices, albeit among a set of limited alternatives, and some of their reasons for preferring to remain in "women's work" are valid—at least in the absence of larger social and economic change.

Two versions of feminist politics were placed in stark opposition during the Sears case as well. Rosenberg's testimony on behalf of Sears exemplifies a politics based on validating female difference. Such a politics can lead to advocacy of special benefits for women (including protective legislation, comparable worth, or maternity benefit policies), but it can also reinforce an inequitable status quo or, as in the Sears case, justify discriminatory practices. The politics represented by the EEOC position and the testimony of Kessler-Harris, in contrast, largely denies the relevance of gender difference and calls for equal treatment and policies of equal opportunity.

The tension between an emphasis on equality and an emphasis on difference underlies many feminist policy dilemmas, particularly the recent maternity disability issue. Existing U.S. policy, based on equal treatment, states that pregnancy cannot be a basis

---

1. In fact, Coser (1982) has argued that their rigid schedules make most women's jobs *less* able to accommodate family needs than many male jobs (also see Gutek 1988, 232).

for discrimination and thus protects women from being fired for pregnancy. At the same time, however, it limits maternity benefits to whatever temporary disability benefits an employer already provides. This policy falls drastically short of the substantive benefits provided in the other industrialized nations. Hence, feminist attorneys and legal theorists are currently engaged in a vigorous debate over whether to deviate from the principle of strict equal treatment in order to seek the special benefits many women need (see Kreiger and Cooney 1983; Vogel 1990; Williams 1982).

This same tension, to some extent, also underlies the difference between affirmative action and comparable worth strategies. Although affirmative action does single out certain groups for special treatment, it emphasizes only the selection of *equally* qualified candidates and generally does not impose quotas. Moreover, its logic is based on the assumption that moving women into male fields constitutes progress toward an ultimate ideal of an integrated, gender-blind labor market. Comparable worth, conversely, offers a vision of the labor market that valorizes women's work rather than moving women out. It accepts that women and men will continue to hold different jobs for the foreseeable future, so that a strict "equal treatment" standard offers little to most women. Although demanding equivalent pay, comparable worth is based on the acknowledgment of existing gender difference. For this reason, some arguments against comparable worth—that it will in the long run restrict women's opportunities or reinforce occupational segregation—parallel arguments against protective legislation earlier in the century (see my discussion in Chapter 2; and Blum forthcoming).

Policies based on valorizing difference certainly contain inherent dangers for feminists, as the EEOC's defeat in the Sears case indicates (Milkman 1986). However, demanding equal treatment within a context of existing inequality also poses problems for feminist politics (Kessler-Harris 1987, 1988; also see Ferree 1987). Equal treatment approaches may provide little for the majority of women who are not equally situated, as in the case of maternity disability. Even worse, equal treatment policies may pose potential harm for women. A case in point is the change in divorce laws mandating equal treatment of men and women by the courts; as Weitzman (1985) discovered, the financial consequences for women have been "catastrophic," largely because men and women are not equally situated in the labor market.

I argued in Chapter 2 that the substantive effects of affirmative action for women have been limited outside the elite professions. Here I suggest that job integration strategies, even if more successful, may have unintended adverse consequences for women workers within the present context. These consequences include the possibility of intraoccupational resegregation, increased job insecurity, and the loss of noneconomic rewards associated with some women's jobs.

In view of these risks and the limited benefits achieved by equal treatment approaches, I suggest that it may be neither irrational or antifeminist for working women to resist job integration in the present social, economic, and political climate. In embracing comparable worth, low-paid women do defend traditional preferences, but at the same time they also demand earnings and status on a par with men's. In this sense, they stake out a possibly dangerous but fertile middle ground between the positions exemplified in the Sears case: between choice and coercion, and between equality and difference. The logic of comparable worth suggests that women as social actors are neither misguided nor coerced into performing "marginal" work; the problem is rather with a system that defines whatever work women do as marginal.

Such a position does not necessarily reject the ideal of an integrated workplace, nor does it relieve employers and government of the obligation to remedy past and present discrimination. But in the absence of additional protections—which might include increased government enforcement efforts with attention to subtle forms of resegregation and harassment, full employment policies, and, most important, active labor-feminist alliances pressing for (and monitoring) workplace and state interventions—the comparable worth model may offer low-paid women more progress toward gender equality at the present time, with less risk of adverse consequences, than do policies of formal equal treatment.

Discussion of these issues is necessarily speculative. The negative consequences of job integration have only recently begun to receive serious attention, and a persuasive body of literature on the consequences of gender-integration approaches does not yet exist.

For the most part, these issues were raised only obliquely in my interviews. Nevertheless, such discussion is important for feminist discourse and politics.

Women's Entry into Male-Dominated Work: The Possibilities of Resegregation and Job Loss

Rosabeth Moss Kanter's classic work on gender and organizational behavior (1977) pointed out many of the problems women experience on entering male-dominated jobs. Subsequent research has looked in depth at these issues, which range from overt sexual harassment (MacKinnon 1979; Schneider 1982) to the hostile attitudes of male co-workers (O'Farrell and Harlan 1982) and the exclusion of women from social networks (Reskin and Hartmann 1986, 54–55; Roos and Reskin 1984, 245–246). This evidence suggests that rather than progressing incrementally toward gender balance in the workplace, we may in many cases be seeing the emergence of new divisions of labor within occupations and new areas of job resegregation; as the composition of particular subfields changes from being largely male to largely female, the sex typing of the field begins to shift, and integration may be in name only. Instead of asking about the extent of women's progress, researchers have begun to ask such questions as, "How can the newly integrated entry-level positions be kept from resegregating and becoming new female ghettos?" (O'Farrell and Harlan 1984, 276). In short, women's recent movement into male-dominated occupations, in part the result of affirmative action efforts, does not represent the wholesale progress once hoped for.

It is also important to bear in mind, as I emphasized in Chapter 2, that the extent of this movement has so far been very modest, and sex segregation in the workplace remains largely intact. Reskin and Hartmann (1986, 28–30), for example, point out that of all job growth between 1970 and 1980, that which resulted in increased representation of women in male-dominated occupations accounted for only 6.5 percent of the total growth in female employment. Growth in secretarial jobs alone created more employment than all such nominally integrated jobs combined. Furthermore, many prominent female-dominated jobs actually became more female-intensive during this period. Kanter and others consider this very low level of integration as itself the cause for many of the difficulties encountered by women crossing gender boundary lines. Such analysts assume that workplace interactions will cease to be problematic as more women enter, the proportion of men and women becomes more balanced, and the category of female "token" or "pioneer" becomes a historical artifact. Unfortunately, recent research into both historical and contemporary cases suggests that this view may be too simple and too optimistic.

Historically, the entry of women into previously male-monopolized fields is interrelated with the introduction of new technology, the reorganization of the labor process and restructuring of the occupation, and a subsequent decrease in status and rewards.[2] Clerical work, which changed from a male- to female-dominated occupation in the early part of this century, is the classic example of this feminization/degradation process: as demand increased and employers routinized the labor process, women entered the new de-skilled jobs at substantially lower rates of pay (Braverman 1974; Davies 1982; Strom 1987). Teachers, librarians, and bank tellers have followed similar patterns (Garrison 1974; Strober and Arnold 1987; Tyack and Strober 1981). This pattern is so prevalent historically that some argue women's recent progress in the elite male professions signals nothing more than the bifurcation of these fields into female-degraded and male-protected layers (Carter and Carter 1981).

Other researchers who have examined specific contemporary cases of occupational feminization in greater depth confirm a pessimistic interpretation of women's progress. Insurance examiners and adjusters (Phipps 1986; Reskin et al. 1990), computer systems analysts and operations researchers (Donato 1986; Reskin et al. 1990), and printing typesetters and compositors (Roos 1986; Reskin et al. 1990) are occupations with a disproportionately large number of women entrants in the past decade—in fact, in the insurance and printing job categories women have largely replaced men as the predominant sex, and some computer occupations at the bottom of the hierarchy also are increasingly female-dominated. In the

---

2. The causal order in this process is complex. Generally, increased demand and a changed labor process either precede or coincide with feminization, with loss in status seeming to follow (Reskin and Roos 1987; Reskin et al. 1990).

process of feminization these jobs have been degraded: automation has increased, job skills have eroded as the work has become more routine and narrow, and status and rewards have dropped (Reskin and Roos 1987; Reskin et al. 1990).

Organizational research focusing on specific firms has also suggested negative consequences from job integration. O'Farrell and Harlan (1982) found that, as a result of affirmative action efforts in a large electrical products firm, a small but significant number of women were hired for blue-collar jobs. However, these women were placed at the lowest level in the blue-collar hierarchy, with newly hired men placed above them. The women's job grouping had the lowest wage ceiling and the fewest highly skilled positions of the six blue-collar job "families." O'Farrell and Harlan (1984, 276–277) conclude that these nontraditional jobs are soon likely to become "traditional," as the women are not likely to move up and are forming a "bottleneck" at the entry level. Moreover, while the wages are better than those previously available to women, they are not likely to increase at the rate of the men's salaries.

My case studies of San Jose and Contra Costa suggest that women workers may be aware of the possibilities of resegregation or "bottlenecking." In San Jose two women suggested to me that the staff analyst classification, a bridge linking the clerical series to the personnel professional series, may have been the victim of this process. Located just below entry-level management, staff analysts are included in the union-represented classes; they handle the routine budgeting and staffing matters in different departments. The women, each in the job for several years, told me that it had changed from male- to female-dominated in the past decade, and now was thought of as a woman's job. They also claimed that the relative wages and status of the job had fallen, an issue discussed among union members.[3] For one of these women, resentment at this reputed loss in status and rewards was the major reason for joining the strike. In fact, according to the Hay job evaluation the pay for the female-dominated staff analyst I position was 31 percent below the average wage rate for its factor point score—one of the larger gaps indicated by the San Jose study (Van Beers 1981). Al-

---

3. I could not get independent validation of these claims, as EEO categories used by the city are too broad to trace feminization of specific job classifications.

though this disparity is not evidence of a comparative drop in pay over the past decade, it is consistent with the women's complaints.[4]

Examples of possible resegregation can also be found in Contra Costa County. Union clericals explained to me that the Sheriff's Department had always been an all-male preserve; sheriff's dispatcher had been one of the better-paying, male-dominated jobs that union leaders had encouraged their members to try for. Current figures indicate that this effort may have been all too successful, as the job may now be an example of a new female ghetto: in 1983, 89.2 percent of dispatchers were female (Finney 1983). It remains to be seen whether a comparative drop in wages or truncated career ladder will follow. The job was included in the category of female jobs covered by comparable worth, although it still appears to be somewhat better paid than clerical jobs (Contra Costa County 1985a).[5]

Although the comparable worth movement in San Jose helped women staff analysts reverse some of the reputed fall in relative status and earnings, and in Contra Costa it may protect women dispatchers from facing future losses, there may be other situations of "fallout" from affirmative action efforts in which comparable worth is of less help. In some instances women may have moved up only to dead-end in jobs that are classified as "managerial," and therefore ineligible for union representation and comparable worth raises.[6] Further, these women may come to identify themselves as managers who do not need representation of their interests. It may

4. This example of possible resegregation also reflects national trends: aggregate data for the personnel field show a disproportionately large increase in women between 1970 and 1980, from 33.4 to 47 percent female (Reskin and Roos 1987, table 1). Another possible case of resegregation in San Jose may emerge in the entry-level engineering technician position, a job women have just begun to enter. By 1984 the tech series was approximately 23 percent female (extrapolated from EEO categories listed by department in City of San Jose 1984). Whether a new female ghetto develops at the entry level will be revealed only by future research, but reported hostility of managers and rigged exams indicate a potential threat of bottlenecking. Also, whether wages will fall behind remains to be seen. At present, the entry-level technical jobs remain a better paying alternative for the small proportion of women that can be absorbed.

5. The pattern of high female entry into this field between 1970 and 1980 reflects national trends. Dispatchers increased from 14.6 to 31.5 percent female—as in personnel, a large, disproportionate gain (Reskin and Roos 1987, table 1).

6. In Contra Costa County managers in female-dominated job series that are deemed traditional areas of women's work were included in comparable worth ad-

even be that some women managers have been subject to job title inflation rather than genuine upward mobility, particularly if organizations need to create the appearance of increased integration (within broad EEOC categories). Baran (1987, 52) found evidence of this in one large insurance firm: the majority of female managers, promoted largely because of affirmative action pressures, actually earned less than white male clericals. The nominal promotion of some women out of union ranks also can undermine organizing efforts to promote women's interests, an effect that may likewise serve the interests of the organization. Regardless of the extent to which they become new female ghettos, low-level managerial positions, particularly within male-dominated categories, are not likely to be covered by comparable worth strategies negotiated through collective bargaining.[7]

Another occupation in which the pattern of feminization accompanied by degradation may be developing is accounting. Nationally, the number of women in accounting has increased; between 1970 and 1980, the field went from 24.6 percent female to 38.1 percent female (Reskin and Roos 1987, table 1). In both San Jose and Contra Costa, accounting was a male-dominated area into which some low-paid women had succeeded in gaining entry; indeed, in Contra Costa this mobility was considered the main affirmative action victory of clericals. The Contra Costa Comparable Worth Task Force estimated that the female accounting technician position—the bridge between the clerical and accounting series—was paid at a rate 40 percent below that for comparable male-dominated jobs (Contra Costa County 1985a). This provides indirect support for the suggestion that wages may have fallen behind with the feminization of low-level accounting positions. At the bridge level the position still has union representation, so comparable worth adjust-

---

justments, but this seems to be the exception rather than the rule. San Jose, following the more typical pattern, did not include managerial employees in any comparable worth adjustments.

7. An interesting counterexample may be a small group of female eligibility work supervisors in Contra Costa County. Although considered managerial-level workers, they had unionized over the comparable worth issue and were staunch members of the Comparable Worth Coalition. The county had punished them for unionizing by revoking some managerial benefits, but their identification remained as undervalued, pink-collar workers, in greater sympathy with the female-dominated group they supervised than with other county managers.

ments can help to narrow this gap. At the next step, however, the entry level to the professional accounting series, one is brought into a traditionally male-dominated and "managerial" category; here any lagging of rewards associated with feminization will be more difficult to address.

The resegregation tendency represents a "one step forward, two steps back" pattern for women of our era in that the hard-fought entry into male-dominated work has created the potential for new female job ghettos. Yet if even in the short run such newly integrated women benefit from higher wage levels, does this not signify at least some degree of incremental progress? It would be easier to evaluate such employment shifts more positively were it not for evidence of additional adverse consequences.

Several studies have found that affirmative action efforts tend to move women into jobs that are extremely vulnerable to elimination. These job cuts may be due to the introduction of new technology or other aspects of organizational restructuring stemming from economic contraction and an increasingly competitive world market (Baran 1987; Ginzburg 1987; S. Hacker 1982; Schreiber 1979). Moreover, some better-paying male-typed jobs appear to be far more vulnerable to recessionary cuts and layoffs than traditional clerical or service jobs—jobs in which many newly integrated women might otherwise have been employed (Baran 1987; Hunt and Hunt 1987; Reskin and Hartmann 1986, 14). Therefore, in return for a short-term gain in wages, some women may have to face the threat of displacement.

Affirmative action, moreover, can be used by management to obscure the displacement of workers and loss of jobs entailed in various strategies of organizational restructuring. Both S. Hacker (1982) and Schreiber (1979), for example, found that as a result of affirmative action women were moved into skilled craft positions that new technology was soon to eliminate. The firms they studied seemed to have manipulated affirmative action implementation to prevent employee resistance in situations where layoffs were already planned. In other blue-collar industries such as auto (Foner 1980, 522) and mining (Cowan 1987), newly integrated women with the least seniority have been the first fired when firms faced contraction. Some industries that were major targets of affirmative action efforts have since faced such severe contraction that they are

now virtually in crisis. Deaux and Ullman studied women's entrance into the steel industry following the signing of affirmative
action consent decrees in 1974; they found that progress made in
the five years following the settlement had been "totally wiped out
by recessionary effects" by the early 1980s (1983, 106).

The use of affirmative action to help rationalize internal labor
markets need not, however, indicate management's conspiratorial
plans to target women; perhaps affirmative action, in a time of generally increased competition, must function in a firm's plans to
streamline its work force if the policy is to be incorporated at all. In
white-collar industries, the fact that many firms today are poised
for contraction rather than expansion means that internal labor
markets only recently opened to women have been dramatically
weakened (Baran 1987; Appelbaum 1987; Noyelle 1987). Many
lower- and mid-level managerial positions in which women had
made large gains—in such industries as insurance, banking, and
financial services—are the first to be targeted in organizational restructuring and firms' attempts to become "lean and mean" (Smith
1988). Moreover, with the introduction of office automation apparently it is the middle-level white-collar positions that become redundant (in contrast to the once-predicted massive elimination
of clerical jobs); the information-gathering and synthesizing functions of these mid to lower managerial levels can be taken over by
cheaper skilled clericals, for whom demand is expected to continue
(Appelbaum 1987; Baran 1987; Deborah Bell 1985). If, on balance,
the results of affirmative action and women's entry into better-
paying male jobs in fact do fit Hacker's description of the process at
AT&T (she wrote: "While some women moved up, more moved
out"; 1982, 250), it may be less risky, particularly in the current
economic climate, for women to remain in pink-collar work.[8]

Women Staying in Women's Work:
Extraeconomic Benefits

In much of the literature on sex segregation, with its emphasis on
job integration strategies, a subtle bias against women's work has

8. But see Reskin and Hartmann (1986, 13–14), who are guardedly optimistic.
They conclude that while reducing segregation will place women in more "cy-
clically sensitive sectors," short-run problems will be outweighed by the long-run
gains.

been too rarely questioned.[9] Although the male-dominated occupations pay more, comparable worth proponents dispute the assumption that men's jobs are inherently more desirable. For some of my respondents, particularly the professionals, extraeconomic factors in the workplace, such as intrinsic job satisfaction, were important reasons for choosing female-dominated occupations—as well as for resisting the suggestion that they must change jobs to achieve higher earnings. This does not mean, as R. Rosenberg (1985, 1986) has suggested, that women are not concerned with their low earnings. As Chapters 3 and 4 have shown, low-paid women are becoming angry, frustrated, and deeply dissatisfied with the marginal wages they receive for what they consider valuable work.

The female-dominated professions are, of course, a better example of jobs high in intrinsic satisfaction than clerical work; these professions have long been viewed as desirable jobs for women of both working- and middle-class backgrounds (Gamarnikow 1978; Melosh 1982). Occupations such as nursing, librarianship, social work, and teaching offer, as Feree (1985) has pointed out, the sense of direct human contact, care, and personal involvement so often lacking in the paid work environment. Several feminist theorists, notably Chodorow (1978) and Gilligan (1982), have suggested that under current gender arrangements women often have a less instrumental moral orientation and stronger preference for nurturant, humane work than men. Empirical studies of occupational values tend to confirm the persistence of such gender differences (Marini and Brinton 1984, 206–207).

Both the San Jose and Contra Costa case studies suggest that many women professionals embrace comparable worth because they would like to remain in their chosen fields—but at the same time, they are not willing to sacrifice extrinsic rewards for intrinsic satisfactions.[10] Although this preference reflects an element of economic rationality (in terms of the human capital investment made

9. But see Phillips and Taylor 1980.

10. Of course, as the current national nursing shortage and regional teacher shortages both indicate, women will not always prefer traditional fields. Studies of women teachers suggest that the sense of intrinsic and extrinsic reward often becomes intertwined. For example, Spencer (1988, 174) found that job frustrations combined with low pay led many to have "difficulty determining whether there are rewards at all in teaching" (also see Stromberg 1988, 216–217). Nevertheless,

in education, credentials, and experience), it also reflects extra-economic concerns, namely, the desire to retain the satisfactions found in traditional work. Traditional preferences, however, certainly also derive in part from an aversion to gender-inappropriate behavior, well documented in studies of occupational socialization (Ireson and Gill 1988; Marini and Brinton 1984). As Mason (1984) comments, to work in a job of the opposite gender can be considered degrading, as it may unconsciously violate cherished norms of identity. Nevertheless, it would be a mistake to dismiss the preference for staying in a female profession as mere acquiescence to traditional gender ideology.

Excerpts from my data illustrate these points. For example, several nurses explained why they found their jobs fulfilling. A public health nurse explained her employment preference in this manner:

I work out of Riverdale Hospital. I do discharge planning for the elderly on Medicare and set up arrangements so they can go to their own homes. I also work with new mothers . . . and I make home visits.

I had wanted to get a master's degree in public health [MPH] . . . but I don't like administrative work. . . . I work for my own satisfaction, not just to climb up. Anyway, MPH's used to get program director jobs, epidemiology jobs. Now they're just more money-oriented, like kicking patients out of hospitals. So I'll stay in this work. . . . I really like it and I'm good at it.

While other women professionals also described the positive features of their jobs, they went on to point out the accompanying negative stereotypes that often are used to justify low pay. A woman who runs a neighborhood recreation center providing programs for children and senior citizens explained why she likes her job: "There's a lot of satisfaction in the participants that come and take part in the things that we put together. When it's all over they come up and say: 'Hey, this was really great, a really enjoyable experience. My children really liked the program. I was really glad I was a part of it.' You know, that's neat! I always like that." At the same time, she spoke of the negative image her field has as paid work. As is typical of work involving the care of children, her job is often seen as such a natural activity for a woman that it hardly

national surveys of nurses and librarians reveal that, despite many frustrations, intrinsic job satisfaction persists among a fairly high proportion (Corley and Mauksch 1988, 142–146; Stromberg 1988, 222).

deserves significant economic return. In fact, in social situations she had become accustomed to hearing such sarcastic remarks as, "What do you do all day—throw basketballs around?"[11]

Another nurse, whom I met at a conference for comparable worth activists, made a comment that expresses particularly well the notion of constrained choices, the idea that preferences should be respected even though they develop within certain limits. She was angered by the argument that activists should stop complaining and change jobs if they want more money: "I am insulted by that! I *like* the profession I'm in. But we also need to address where people are and where the jobs are. Not everyone *can* just change jobs."

The popularity of comparable worth among clericals, as among women professionals, clearly indicates deep dissatisfaction with the economic rewards of clerical work. Yet some clericals do enjoy their work and may feel, within the existing range of possibilities, it is their best employment alternative. Even given the opportunity to change fields, some may prefer not to for a complex array of reasons. One longtime secretary I interviewed had had the opportunity to go into a better-paying, male-dominated field, but she decided against it. Although she was older and may therefore have felt a stronger "pull" to remain in a gender-appropriate situation,[12] she explained: "I like being a secretary. I really enjoy doing it. It has variety. It's not a boring job. . . . This commission in Washington has their heads in the sand. Our positions *are* underpaid, and we make a contribution. Without the women, the offices would go down the tubes!"[13]

11. These comments, regardless of the negative sex typing, may indicate a degree of resentment. Some men, too, may sense that such "feminine" job satisfactions are not available in many male-dominated jobs. One engineering technician, whose "gray-collar" desk job involves drafting and computer mapping, explained resentfully (see Chapter 3) that he considered working in a library or recreation center "a cushy job, all fun and games."

12. Some evidence indicates that occupational preferences are becoming less sex-typed among younger women and girls (Ireson and Gill 1988; Marini and Brinton 1984, 205–206). Yet O'Farrell (1988, 267) suggests that women who actually seek nontraditional jobs tend to be experienced workers, particularly single mothers who have tried to support their families with traditional jobs. Therefore, in addition to this woman's age, the fact that she remained married throughout her working life may be significant; that is, she was able to "afford" her preference for a clerical job.

13. This interview occurred just after the U.S. Civil Rights Commission had issued a highly negative report on comparable worth (Pear 1985a). The comments of this clerical worker also indicate the extent to which local women felt personally involved and followed the issue nationally.

The experiences of women who do change fields, while not entirely negative, may partly reinforce the basis for this reluctance.
Another longtime clerical did decide to enter a male-dominated
field, primarily in order to increase her earnings after all efforts to
gain a job upgrade for her clerk's position had failed (this was in
1975, before the emergence of the comparable worth issue).[14] Although she entered the technician series at the entry, trainee level,
she earned more than she had as an experienced clerical. Looking
back, she explained that a major drawback of the change was the
loss of contact with people; many clericals, according to surveys,
consider the extent of social contact to be a primary benefit of their
jobs (Gutek 1988, 233). In her present job my respondent tends to
work alone, but she finds satisfaction in "careful, accurate work
with figures." Although she had succeeded over time in advancing
several steps up the technician series, she had failed to gain the job
she desired most (working outdoors), owing, in her view, to sexist
attitudes on the part of managers. When asked what she thought of
comparable worth for clericals, she stated emphatically: "It's about
time!" "It's long overdue!"

Rosabeth Moss Kanter, in her classic analysis of the organization
of office work (1977), notes that many clerical workers find a sense
of fulfillment from the close, one-on-one relationships they develop
with their bosses. Such relations, which are more characteristic of
traditional secretarial positions than of newer forms of office organization, can be far more humane than other authority relations in
the workplace. While probably less so than for female professionals, for secretaries the quality of personal interactions may be
what makes the job intrinsically satisfying. Several of my respondents confirmed this point. One middle-aged woman who had
worked her way up to the position of executive secretary explained
that she really likes her work; she described her job as mainly involving "keeping track of my boss and his calendar . . . filling in for
him because he is gone a lot, and speaking for him." This woman
had gotten to know her boss well, and she considered their one-on-
one relationship the best part of her job.

We should not, however, confuse these women's enjoyment

14. Interestingly, this move coincided with her divorce and change in status to
single head of household (see note 12 above).

of aspects of their jobs or job content and possible reluctance to change fields with satisfaction with the recognition they are accorded. Kanter (1977) has noted the negative side of such "patrimonial" relations; the "office wife" stereotype invites a range of negative responses, from overt sexual harassment to more subtle forms of exploitation.[15] As we have seen, when the executive secretary quoted above was taking the test for her current position and encountered the question "Would you run errands for the boss's wife?" she and twelve other women stormed up to the personnel office to protest. Expressing the desire for the "intimacy of the office" without its abuses, this woman also strongly supports comparable worth.[16]

A similar desire for increased recognition was expressed by many of my respondents, clericals and professionals alike. For such women, comparable worth seemed very different from other advancement strategies in that it also offers intangible recognition of their contributions. Establishing the principle that women's work must be given respect and recognition was nearly as important as the issue of money.[17] One woman, a former clerical, exemplified this perspective. When I asked her to define comparable worth,

15. Kanter does not, however, discuss an additional negative effect of this structure of social relations: the inhibition of women's labor identification and ability to organize because of personal ties of loyalty to the boss (see Chapter 7 below).

16. Popular response to the portrayal of secretaries in the television series "L.A. Law" indicates the appeal of comparable worth rhetoric to clerical women, and the potential challenge to popular discourse concerning women and work. Initially the character Roxie, a legal secretary, was portrayed as madly in love with her boss, attentive to his every need, a "pure doormat." During the series' first season, however, the character was transformed, largely in response to a huge influx of mail from clericals. According to the actress who plays Roxie, women wrote in that they are "sick and tired of seeing secretaries represented as always in love with their boss, [and thus] of being faintly stupid" (Kort 1987). By the season's end, a decisive scene depicted Roxie demanding a raise from her boss. Using the language of comparable worth, Roxie indicated that she was not being paid for the actual value of her work, and she listed the many unrecognized extra services she performed. "I'm worth what I'm worth," she said, and "if I can't get it here, I'll go somewhere else!" This episode alone generated a large response. On a syndicated national talk show ("The Oprah Winfrey Show," April 28, 1987), the actress claimed that she received a lot of mail and was frequently stopped on the street by women clericals telling her that they took Roxie's advice, that they have asked for raises, and even that they have used the character's words.

17. The number I spoke with was neither large enough nor sufficiently representative to allow generalizations to be drawn. Some large clerical surveys, how-

she said: "Well, I see it as about being equal. Equal pay, but also being *treated* equal. I don't feel that the majority of low-paid women are treated the same as even a low-paid man. He has more status. . . . I feel that a maintenance worker or a laborer . . . they have more status than a typist or clerical person does. Because for some reason, clericals are viewed *low*, low in people's esteem." Another clerical woman explained the desire for more explicit acknowledgment: "We take something with poor grammar and no punctuation, and we make it into something wonderful. We make them look good, and they know it!"

Of course, many clericals today work not in situations of close one-on-one relationships, but in word and data-processing pools and centers or less-centralized minipools (Murphree 1987). Such work organization can bear a closer resemblance to industrial production work than to traditional secretarial positions. With office automation on the increase, many have predicted that jobs "pushing paper" will soon all resemble assembly line jobs, with extreme task fragmentation and deskilled work (Braverman 1974; Marschall and Gregory 1983).

Others argue that this prediction has not been simply borne out, that the responses to new technology and changes in work organization are in fact quite varied (Attewell and Rule 1987; Baran 1987). Still, it would be foolish to suggest that production-clerical jobs are as desirable or intrinsically satisfying as the women's professions, or that large sacrifices in satisfaction would be the cost of moving out of such work. Production-clerical jobs may also be less enjoyable, on the whole, than traditional secretarial positions. Baran (1987) has shown that the changing labor process can benefit clerical jobs. Many jobs now entail wider task variety, increased decision making and responsibility, and higher levels of training (Baran 1987, 47). Yet pay is typically not commensurate with the new skill requirements; women complain of physical problems such as eyestrain, fatigue, even radiation exposure (Gutek 1988, 236), and jobs that are skill-enriched owing to the introduction of computer technology become more vulnerable to exacting control and monitoring (Attewell and Rule 1987; Baran 1987; Deborah Bell 1985).

---

ever, do provide evidence of clericals' concern with both lack of recognition and low pay, although these studies are not specifically concerned with comparable worth (Murphree 1987, 108–110).

To generalize about the extraeconomic rewards afforded by such jobs is difficult; work organization varies significantly according to industrial sector and product market as well as to managerial discretion (Baran 1987). The changes are perhaps least pronounced in the public sector, where comparable worth has been most prominent; the implementation of costly computer equipment, for example, is occurring at a slower pace and to a lesser extent than in the private sector, where productivity is more at issue (Deborah Bell 1985). The women I spoke with who worked in positions with new computer-linked tasks claimed to enjoy their jobs and to have gained skills that were highly satisfying (although one women was also very concerned with health and safety issues). Assessment of such comments is not easy. The novelty of new tasks or the "hype" surrounding computers as the wave of the future could account for women's positive feelings toward their jobs. Yet evidence from several surveys indicates that clericals do tend to experience the new technology positively, and that automation improves their jobs despite the complaints mentioned above (Form and McMillen 1983; Gallant 1984; Hartmann, Kraut, and Tilly 1986, 127–150).

In any case, the employment preferences of women workers depend not only on their qualitative experiences in clerical jobs, but also on their perceptions of the available alternatives. The present and future of good white-collar or blue-collar alternatives are not promising. Moreover, although there has been much discussion of massive job loss in the clerical occupation due to office automation, in fact this does not appear to be occurring. The extremely rapid growth of clerical employment in the post–World War II period has slowed, but moderate growth is expected to continue, with some shifting internal demand between clerical subfields (Deborah Bell 1985; Hunt and Hunt 1987; Hartmann, Kraut, and Tilly 1986, 87–126). Clerical jobs will likely continue to be widely available and easily accessible for women entering the labor market. With a shrinking of the middle levels of white-collar employment, upskilled clerical jobs will represent good job choices for women, particularly those with less privileged educational backgrounds (Gutek 1988).[18]

18. There is concern in the literature for the fate of minority women, who are concentrated in relatively declining clerical subfields. In addition, as firms continue to relocate outside of urban centers, displacement of many minority employees occurs (Baran 1987, 54–59; Harmann, Kraut, and Tilly 1986, 126).

In terms of blue-collar employment, it is clear that the availability of good skilled and semiskilled work is very limited owing to structural shifts in the economy (Bluestone and Harrison 1982; Kuhn and Bluestone 1987). Also, because what nontraditional blue-collar work is available may not seem worth the efforts required to gain entry (Reskin and Hartmann 1986, 98; Roos and Reskin 1984)—or worth the sacrifice of satisfying but lower-paying pink-collar jobs—women today should not be expected to have strong preferences to enter male blue-collar jobs.[19] Rather than concluding, however, that women simply desire "marginal" employment, we may see traditional preferences, at least in part, as a rational response to the existing, problematic employment context (O'Farrell 1988).

Male Entry into Female-Dominated Work: Economic and Extraeconomic Consequences

Job integration is usually discussed in terms of female entry into male-dominated occupations. It is important, however, to consider the reverse process as well—for if women are to move into men's jobs in significant numbers, men will have to enter women's jobs to find employment (Remick and Steinberg 1984, 293–294).

As Blau and Hendricks (1979) have shown, some men did enter

19. In general, it has been more difficult to recruit women for nontraditional blue-collar than nontraditional white-collar work (Reskin and Hartmann 1986, 97–98). O'Farrell and Harlan (1984, 273) have explained this phenomenon by women's unfamiliarity with such work. Padavic and Reskin (1987), however, found that women office workers who had worked temporarily in men's plant jobs were actually *less* likely to desire transfers to those better-paying jobs than women who had never left the office. The prevalence of sexual harassment may be partly to blame. According to O'Farrell (1988, 267–268), about 30 percent of women entering men's blue-collar jobs report harassment. Sex-typed job assignments may be another factor. Both Padavic and Reskin (1986) and Deaux and Ullman (1983) found that women entering plant jobs became concentrated in plant cleaning and janitorial work, certainly some of the least skilled, least challenging, least pleasant jobs in the plants. Another reason for this reluctance may be that some women wrongly believe they will be stuck for good in the unpleasant jobs to which they are initially assigned. Reskin and Hartmann (1986, 98) maintain that this misperception arises because dead-end career paths are realistic for female occupations. Yet, as was discussed above, with resegregation and bottlenecking occurring, women's perceptions of their odds for gaining skilled blue-collar jobs may not be misplaced.

female-dominated work between 1960 and 1970, primarily in the professions. In this period occupations such as elementary school teaching and social work saw large increases in demand. (Evidence for the following decade, 1970–1980, indicates minimal changes in this direction, as well as in clerical work; Reskin and Hartman 1986, 30.) Although the small shift in sex composition in the female professions has not even begun to change the entrenched sex typing, it has been enough to create a noticeable pocket of men in these jobs. It is, therefore, important to ask what consequences this process has had for women.

Some studies suggest that the entry of men into female-dominated job sectors may have had adverse consequences. Both Grim and Stern (1974) and Stromberg (1988) find increasing intra-occupational segregation in the women's professions; the entry of even small numbers of men leads to the replication of gender-based status hierarchies in which "men [are] disproportionately employed in positions involving supervision, direction, and planning" (Grimm and Stern 1974, 693). In other words, when men enter these fields, they tend to move into the elite positions at the top of the occupations, quickly moving into dominant and directive jobs.

My case studies suggest that women professionals may suspect such patterns, which in turn contributes to ambivalence toward job integration. Expression of such ambivalence is not, of course, a popular approach to the problem of sex segregation. Most people applaud men's entrance into women's work as a means of breaking down oppressive sex stereotypes and, quite possibly, improving the status and rewards for the women's professions in the long run. Indeed, most of the women I interviewed gave almost as a reflex or rote response, "Yes, it's good to have men become nurses, social workers, and so forth. People should choose the jobs they want, not go by any set rules." Further probing, however, often revealed a hesitancy that respondents felt uncomfortable discussing but that should not be completely dismissed.

Some women with whom I spoke admitted that they simply could not imagine men in their jobs. One nurse practitioner, for example, concluded that her image of nurses was female, and she really couldn't imagine male nurses. Others went further, describing their negative experiences with male co-workers. A public health nurse recounted perhaps the most negative view, saying that she would prefer it if men would "just stay out of nursing altogether" and let the current sex segregation continue. She explained that the male nurses she had known acted just like "little doctors," and she had always hated dealing with doctors. In fact, she had entered public health primarily to escape dealing with physicians and their negative treatment of nurses. She added emphatically: "I don't want to compete with men. I just don't want them to be around!"

In addition to her job experiences with male nurses, this woman had known several men in nursing school. She explained that while the women were choosing such specializations as public health, obstetrics/gynecology, pediatrics, or psychiatric nursing, the men she knew had chosen anesthesiology—a narrow, highly paid, "high-tech" pocket within the field. In fact, a recent national survey confirms this nurse's observations: men in nursing do gravitate to particular specialties, including nurse anesthetist, which pay far higher than the average nursing salary (Stromberg 1988, 210–212).[20] Internal stratification due to the increasing division of labor in health care is already a political concern in the nursing profession. Thus, my respondent's resentment that men's entry has coincided with, and likely contributed to, the development of a more hierarchical occupation may be well placed.

A librarian in one of my case studies was not as explicitly anti-male as this public health nurse, but she discussed similar developments in her field. She had been a children's librarian, whereas two male co-workers had worked in the business reference department. She indicated that business reference was viewed as more important in subtle ways, although there were no overt distinctions such as different job titles. (Incidentally, by the time of our interview this woman had left librarianship for a male-dominated, technical job, which she described as far more satisfying than her previous "gender-appropriate" profession). Also, a male librarian explained how he had gravitated to particular kinds of projects within the workplace, specializing in audiovisual equipment, instructional cable TV, and the development of a computerized database on regional businesses. Some of these projects had brought in outside

20. In 1984, the average salary for a nurse anesthetist was $37,000, while the average registered nurse made only $23,500 (Stromberg 1988, 212). Grimm and Stern (1974), moreover, find men disproportionately located in such higher-paying positions as administrator, supervisor, and head nurse.

grants, generating additional funds for library services in the local-ity. By developing such male-stereotyped projects, this man was able to distinguish himself and gain status within a largely female workplace.[21] As with nurses, national-level data on librarians tend to confirm such patterns of intraoccupational segregation (Grimm and Stern 1974; Stromberg 1988); furthermore, men in this field earned on average 21 percent more than women in the 1980s (Stromberg 1988, 221).

These examples, together with the national-level data, suggest that gender-based hierarchies of power, expertise, and status that are irrelevant in an all-female work site will be replicated with the entry of even a few men. It is likely that men seek out and are channeled by management and embedded organizational practices into different tasks, job assignments, and areas of specialization, or are otherwise distinguished from female co-workers when enter-ing a female-typed field. In addition, deeply rooted social patterns may lead women to acquiesce, at times, in this process. As several of my female respondents suggested, new hierarchies of more and less valuable work would then emerge, with women again in subor-dinate positions. In fact, one analysis of librarianship has suggested that a dual-career structure is developing, with "those more ag-gressive and ambitious students"—who tend to be male—directed toward the new, higher-paying subfields in information manage-ment, and women directed toward traditional positions emphasiz-ing direct client or user services (Estabrook 1984; Stromberg 1988, 223). But even where such gender differentiation is more subtle and not validated by job title or salary differentials, women may become vulnerable to overt differentiation in the future unless ex-plicit protections or monitoring exists.

Wharton and Baron (1986, 1987) present evidence that lends credence to suspicions of the replication of gender hierarchy in women's work. Examining men's experience of job integration and segregation through survey data, they found that male entrants into female-dominated work were as satisfied as those remaining in male-dominated jobs *despite substantially lower pay.* In contrast to women crossing gender boundaries, men entering women's work "are likely to receive superior treatment" and to "enjoy the privi-

---

21. Indeed, he had become a leading political spokesman for the librarians, as well as for the other female-dominated fields represented by the union local.

leges . . . associated with the master status of being male" (1986, 11). It is fair to ask whether comparable worth might inadvertently further or hasten the entry of those with "the master status" into women's work. Raising status and rewards might make women's work an acceptable option to larger numbers of men, thus subjecting more women to these new gender hierarchies. Research on the Depression (Milkman 1976; Strom 1985) suggests that, in the past, social barriers to job integration based on gender ideology have resisted even the strongest economic pressures. But is this still true today, nearly sixty years later? If it is, then the number of men entering these "inappropriate" jobs will likely remain quite small in spite of comparable worth. But if not, there may be additional adverse consequences to consider alongside the positive challenge to the sexual division of labor.

In addition to the possible formation of new gendered job hierarchies, another potential adverse consequence of men's entry into women's work should be explored. Without other protections, might women have a stake in maintaining the monopoly over women's work simply to preserve their right to paid employment in times of economic retrenchment? Research on the Depression suggests that sex typing, because it becomes institutionalized, may protect against job loss under such conditions (Milkman 1976; Strom 1985). Milkman explains that labor market inflexibility, or the "caste-like" character of sex segregation, protected women in the 1930s. Women were not simply pushed out of their jobs by men, despite an ideology that exhorted women to leave the paid labor force, sacrifice their jobs to displaced male workers, and return to home and hearth. In fact, there is little evidence of mobility from male to female labor markets during the period, despite the severity of the times (Milkman 1976, 80). Of course, while such labor market inflexibility protected women's jobs, it did nothing to promote greater gender equality.

In the context of today's economic climate, with contractions in the sectors that provide good male jobs, women might justifiably feel defensive about their jobs and their right to paid employment. Economic evidence indicates that clerical and service occupations and industries, the major female employers, are more recession-proof or less vulnerable to the "vagaries of the business cycle" than major male employers such as manufacturing or construction (Hunt and Hunt 1987, 241). Indeed, a favorable industry mix is a benefit for women, as it leads to employment that "does not ordinarily retreat during recessionary periods, but continues to expand" (Hunt and Hunt 1987, 243). Several researchers have found that women's occupational and industrial distribution contributes to substantially lower layoff rates and less cyclical unemployment than men experience (see Reskin and Hartmann 1986, 13–14).[22]

Recent case studies (S. Hacker 1982; Kelley 1982) support the suspicion that when gender boundaries are forcibly relaxed (in these cases, largely as a result of affirmative action settlements) women's employment share may drop. Hacker's study of AT&T and Kelley's study of a large electrical products firm each discovered that, with legally mandated job integration, men entered female-dominated jobs to a greater extent than women entered male-dominated jobs. Thus a policy ostensibly intended to promote women's interests resulted in a proportional loss in female employment within these organizations. Kelley (1982, 55) explains this ironic outcome: "Affirmative action hiring meant in large measure the substitution of white men for white women in traditionally female job classifications. This hiring policy did not improve the position of women in the plant; it only served to mask the severity of the sex segregation problem to the casual observer."

The tenacity and persistence of some aspects of traditional gender ideology may play a large part in allowing such results to occur. Although the majority of adult women now participate in the paid labor force, the right of women to paid employment is still often viewed as contingent, and women's earnings are still considered secondary or less than essential. Attacks on women workers in several newly deregulated industries, for example, have explicitly stated that women should bear the brunt of concessions because they *do not* support families (*National NOW Times* 1986b; Moore and Marsis 1983a; Rozen 1986).[23] And recruitment of women work-

22. But as Reskin and Hartmann note, the relationship between sex segregation and unemployment is not straightforward. Until 1981, men's aggregate unemployment rate was lower than women's; since 1981 the women's rate has been slightly below that for men. Women in female-dominated manufacturing and blue-collar jobs have fared badly in recessionary periods, and women who work in female-dominated occupations tend to be unemployed for longer periods than women who work in male sectors (Reskin and Hartmann 1986, 13–14).

23. AT&T and the regional Bell companies have not been so blatant. While not explicitly arguing that women work only for "pin money," they have nonetheless attempted to slash wages by as much as 40 percent for women's work (Sacks 1986).

ers in expanding areas is still explicitly discussed in terms of the housewife's desire to provide *supplemental* income (Peterson 1987). One of my younger respondents was careful to point out how little dominant beliefs have changed: "I had this college instructor who used to always say that if only *all the women* would just stay home then we wouldn't have any economic problems. There'd be enough jobs for everyone who needs to work. Like women don't really need to work—they're all just bored housewives." And *Ms.* magazine recently noted in an article on working mothers: "Instead of being praised for their efforts, working mothers today are likely to be condemned for being selfish. In spite of the economics forcing women to work, in spite of the fact that 80% of women are still tied to traditional female jobs . . . the feeling that working mothers are 'getting away with something' is so strong, it is almost palpable" (Berg 1987, 73). The "something" these working women are "getting away with" is not merely the neglect of home and family, but also the assertion of the right to paid employment.

Certainly, other aspects of gender ideology have changed. Milkman (1987b), for example, points out that despite the persistence of occupational sex segregation, public opinion polls show broad agreement with the notion of equal treatment of men and women in the labor force. Furthermore, exhortations for married women to return to the home have not met with the wide acceptance they found in the 1930s. Milkman therefore concludes that the increasing number of women in the labor force, combined with the presence of a feminist movement, "ensure that women workers [today] will *not* be faced with an assault on their employment rights" (1987b, 127; emphasis added).

Although people may endorse equal treatment in the abstract, evidence strongly suggests that women's employment rights are not yet considered fully on a par with men's. In the existing difficult economic climate, working women might well prefer to maintain an occupational arena in which they do not have to compete directly with men. Indeed, without other political changes they may be at a dangerous disadvantage in such a competition. As in the Depression, the protection of women's jobs through the reinforcement of gender boundaries offers little prospect of furthering women's equality; at most it may allow women to "hold the line" in a highly problematic conjucture. But as O'Farrell (1988, 272) suggests,

truly integrating the workplace—and avoiding negative consequences for women—will require careful planning and a great deal
of government intervention. Whether this will happen will very
likely depend on the future success of labor and feminist alliances
in both advocating and implementing positive changes for low-paid
women (also see Needleman and Nelson 1988). Meanwhile, it may
not be unreasonable for many workers to risk what security they
have only with the greatest reluctance.

I have discussed the possibility that women may at present have
an interest in maintaining their monopoly over particular jobs and
working to improve those jobs rather than entering into direct job
competition with men. By making this admittedly provocative suggestion, I do not mean to imply that women are better off if they
simply embrace job segregation. Obviously this would do little to
advance feminist goals of diversity or equality. But it is a tricky
matter to promote gender equality within a context of persistent
inequality. As in recent discussions of the "mommy-track" issues of
flexible and part-time career options (*Business Week* 1989; Lewin
1989a; F. Schwartz 1989), policies that are in many respects desirable will likely only reinforce women's secondary status in the labor
market. Of course, policies like flextime and part-time work can be
implemented as formally gender-neutral and available to parents of
either sex, and this may be an important principle to establish. But
it is unlikely that these options will be gender-neutral in practice or
in employers' perceptions at present, given women's continuing
primary responsibility for child rearing. We need ways to address
the situation facing low-paid women that do not further entrench
their subordinate position. But we also need ways to protect women
from the possible "fallout" of apparently progressive policies that
ignore their existing position.

As examples of such "fallout," I have discussed suggestive evidence that unintended negative consequences are emerging as a
result of even the limited occupational integration achieved in recent years. The possibility that newly integrated women are actually moving into new female ghettos, in which jobs have been deskilled and wages have fallen behind, leads one to question the
effectiveness of affirmative action strategies. Moreover, the generally worsening employment climate of the past decade has cut

deeply into what gains were made initially. Some research even suggests that affirmative action policies may be used by firms to obscure or assist in the rationalization of an internal labor force, possibly to the detriment of women workers.

I have also suggested that there are qualitative reasons for women to prefer women's work, although this preference may involve a degree of acquiescence to existing sex role prescriptions. Changing to a nontraditional field can require the sacrifice of intrinsic job satisfaction, particularly for those in the female professions. Also, given the relative instability in many areas of traditional male employment, some areas of female employment may offer greater security. In view of the difficulty of gaining and retaining a nontraditional job, even less satisfying pink-collar jobs may represent the best available employment alternative under the present situation.

Finally, I have suggested that men's entrance into traditionally female work may threaten women in that gender hierarchies may be replicated; even in subtle forms, such distinctions leave women vulnerable to devaluation. Furthermore, in cases where gender boundaries are forcibly relaxed, as long as women are still seen as a contingent labor force, men's entrance into female-dominated occupations may cause a loss in women's employment share—although with proper government, labor, or feminist monitoring, this outcome could perhaps be prevented.

While this discussion is merely exploratory, the evidence does suggest that women today may have valid reasons for remaining in sex-segregated work. Between the views of choice versus coercion voiced in the Sears trial, this preference should be understood as a reasonable "choice" made within existing constraints. The questions posed in this chapter present a dilemma for feminists as to how to make further progress toward gender equality. In view of the current contracting economy, several successive conservative and antilabor administrations, and the tenacity of an ideology that treats women's labor force participation as secondary, perhaps limited progress can best be made by improving conditions within the pink-collar sector.

Bianca Becalli, an Italian feminist responding to a similar debate on traditional preferences versus androgynous objectives, has perceptively asked: "Why should women struggle to get into heavy, dirty and risky jobs?" (1984, 47). An obvious answer is that they will earn much higher pay; but when the odds of entering such jobs are quite low and initial advantages may erode, we can hardly blame women who prefer not to take the gamble or pay the price for moving into "inappropriate" gender positions. Without broader economic interventions, one must ask what jobs are available that traditional women workers ought to be choosing, as well as what adverse consequences may arise from making gender boundaries more fluid. As comparable worth activists in San Jose and Contra Costa County have pointed out, the assumption that women should enter male fields implies that low-paid women in traditional jobs either fundamentally misperceive their interests or make choices on irrational grounds.

The comparable worth issue enlarges the terms of this discourse by challenging the systematic devaluation of the work women do and rejecting the assumption that men's work is inherently better. As Remick and Steinberg (1984, 295) have observed, rather than question individuals' job preferences, we should question a system that says a clerical woman must "promote" to a position such as custodian or delivery truck driver in order to earn a decent living.

To conclude, I suggest that improving pink-collar pay may represent the best available strategy for promoting the class and gender interests of low-paid women, at the present time. Moreover, affirmative action or job integration strategies, if they are to advance the interests of low-paid women, require serious rethinking. As many proponents now acknowledge, these approaches will have to be more carefully designed and implemented, including more effective enforcement efforts and sanctions against employers, before they will be truly successful. However, I would add that such policies must also be seen in a larger context; without other efforts to guarantee the right to paid employment and a full family wage, integration may be disadvantageous to low-wage women. The most significant of such efforts would certainly be the building of active labor-feminist alliances, ensuring that the interests of low-paid women are represented.

Six

Limits of the
Comparable Worth Movement

In this work I emphasize the radical potential of comparable worth and the ways it moves beyond affirmative action strategies to address low-paid women and to challenge the marketplace. In this chapter, however, I focus on comparable worth's limitations, for, like affirmative action, comparable worth contains critical ambiguities that hamper its effectiveness in practice. These contradictory tendencies include (1) universalization of women's gender-based interest in comparable worth, (2) universalization of a class-based interest in comparable worth, (3) reification of the legitimacy of occupational hierarchy, and (4) enhancement of technocratic control rather than grass-roots participation. The manner in which these tendencies are handled not only shapes the outcome of local comparable worth cases; it also determines the extent to which the issue's radical possibilities are realized and cumulatively shapes the future direction of the movement.

Gender-based Interests

Although comparable worth goes beyond affirmative action in the extent of change called for, it imports much of affirmative action's vocabulary. Within this liberal, equal-treatment framework, comparable worth is often described as being in the interests of all women *as* women, regardless of class differences. While the claim of a universal gender interest is enormously appealing in the abstract, in practice all women do not have the same stake in the success of comparable worth. As a result, the policy can become distorted, and success can come to be defined in ways less beneficial to low-paid women.

In both of my case studies, low-paid women looked to women in influential positions, either in mid to upper management or in elective office, as their natural allies. They expected such women to lead the way, or at least to substantially smooth the way for implementation. Yet in each case comparable worth activists met with frustration and disappointment: What initially appeared to be a natural alliance based on the assumption that all women have a common interest in pay equity turned out to be unreliable and problematic.

In San Jose, the "feminist capital of the world," the female mayor, council majority, and assistant city manager opposed the union's attempts to study and implement comparable worth. While professing agreement with the principle of pay equity, women officials initially opposed having the Hay study conducted for nonmanagerial employees, resisted bargaining over implementation, and threatened the jobs of those who participated in the 1981 strike. As a result, low-paid women questioned the feminist convictions of these officials, realizing that elite women had their own conflicting agendas. The low-paid women's resentment was expressed in several slogans displayed in the picket lines. One read: "If I hear the mayor say this is the feminist capital of the world just once more, I'll puke!" while another gibed: "Promise her anything, but give her nothing."

Although some journalists noted the irony of women opposing a women's reform (Beyette 1981; Keppel 1981), the image of the "feminist capital" has persisted (e.g., Flammang 1985; Mueller 1985). Women officials used this image to enhance both their individual careers and the city's reputation. For example, Mayor Janet Gray Hayes continually stated that as a woman she sympathized with those on strike, but merely disagreed with their impatience (Tong 1981). She also strongly implied that city officials deserved the primary credit for advancing the pay equity issue, while the union's actions, in her words, constituted "a giant step backwards" for women's rights (Keppel 1981). Mayor Hayes was likely sincere in her feminist convictions; her opposition to the union was primarily the result of her divergent class and institutional location.

Sally Reed, assistant city manager for personnel and labor relations in San Jose, handled all the negotiations surrounding comparable worth.[1] As a woman in this influential position, her views were, not surprisingly, similar to those of Mayor Hayes, and may illuminate the perspective of elite women. In our interview, she stated that:

My position, I think one everyone [in city administration] felt comfortable with, is that comparable worth is a legitimate, proper issue to be addressed by employers generally. [But] while the city might be a leader in trying to address the issue, the city should not get too far ahead of the rest of the world in terms of employers. . . . [It] would be going too far with the taxpayers' money. . . .

We had a view of ourselves as one employer among many. We could not solve the problem on our own, either economically or philosophically.

Additionally, . . . to imply that the employer is somehow responsible for the equity in salaries when salaries are negotiated, and we have lost the ability to set them unilaterally, is inappropriate. The issue is one of negotiation, rather than one of "what is right." We don't necessarily pay any of our employees what we "think is right." [quotes stated by Reed.]

I probed further for her views of the union's actions, asking: "Where did the consensus on comparable worth break down?" She explained:

I have not been anxious to share this in the past. But the issue was so volatile that I don't think there was any way of avoiding the strike, simply because, as a part of the labor movement, it was seen as the right place for the issue to surface, and it had to surface in a visible way. . . . Maybe it was not deliberate. It was the feminist capital, it was the place to do it. They emotionalized the issue, and it *can be* emotionalized, beyond the point [at] which you can deal with it rationally.

The reality is, *no one* employer is going to change this. You have to have a very long-term perspective.

For those whose paychecks are the object of contention, however, it is difficult to share the "very long-term perspective." In

1. She was in this position until autumn of 1981, at which point she left the city system to become the county executive of Santa Clara County.

statements made to the media, union leaders could not have been more blunt in expressing their antagonism toward San Jose's feminist officials. One union activist commented: "The city wanted tokenism. The city didn't do anything. It was dragged kicking and screaming along the path to equality by the union" (Johnston 1981, 165). When asked what difference it had made to have women in power, another activist said flatly: "I'd say none. . . . If San Jose is the feminist capital of the world, it's because the men and women of this union make it that way" (Fischer 1982, 2085).

In my interviews with low-paid women, the contradictions inherent in trying to retain the common gender-based interest in comparable worth also emerged. For example, a recreation worker explained to me that because Sally Reed had come up through the ranks of city employment

a lot of the older gals out on the picket line were [saying]: "And where in the hell did you come from?" It's like all of a sudden you got up there, and now you have to play the game that there just wasn't enough money, and that's all it [city opposition] was.

So, it's funny because there were women with the power at that time. It wasn't a real male trip. So, on the one hand, they couldn't be putting down the plight of women's jobs, but yet they have the dollars and cents of the city budget to look out for. So there wasn't a lot of bad-mouthing of the issue . . . and nobody ever came out and said "Hey, that's all you should get paid."

Just recently the *This Week* [Sunday *San Jose Mercury News* feature magazine] had a thing on Sally Reed, and I read it. She was the cover article, and now she's the top [Santa Clara] county executive. I guess I expected just plain old empathy, a little bit more empathy. From the mayor, and from her. . . . Wouldn't you just naturally assume that there'd be a little bit more empathy? I mean, *was she* born with a silver spoon in her mouth?

In Contra Costa County, tensions also emerged between elite and low-paid women. Proportionally fewer women were at top levels than in San Jose, however, and the county could hardly be considered a feminist capital. Two of the five members of the Board of Supervisors were women, but no women worked at the highest levels of management; only a scattered few were at middle strata, and these were primarily assistant department heads and middle-level managers within the female-typed departments, particularly social services. Not only were fewer women in power to disappoint low-paid women, but, in striking contrast with San Jose's liberal milieu, the conservative, even blatantly sexist men in county government were a more obvious problem.[2] Nonetheless, diverging interests did emerge where it had been assumed or hoped that shared gender would take precedence.

One of the two women supervisors in Contra Costa, Sunne Wright McPeak, has been a stronger ally, willing to take more political risks, than female officials in San Jose. The other woman supervisor, Nancy Fahden, wavered initially and later opposed the Comparable Worth Coalition. Low-paid, labor-identified women particularly resented Fahden's stance. At a regional conference of comparable worth activists, when one speaker optimistically declared that "women in political office are our friends," a Contra Costa activist snorted and whispered to me: "Not Nancy Fahden!"

Even in dealing with Sunne McPeak, a strong backer of comparable worth, tensions lay just beneath a surface appearance of solidarity with the women's labor coalition. McPeak had made comparable worth "her issue" on the heels of the San Jose strike, and she became very visible statewide as an advocate of pay equity (see, e.g., *Contra Costa Times* 1/27/84). It was probably no coincidence that McPeak was seen as an up-and-coming voice in the state's Democratic party at that time (Diringer 1984).[3] In a lengthy interview with a labor activist, however, the ambivalence toward McPeak as an elite ally was strikingly revealed. Lee Finney (heard from at length in Chapter 4) became quite explicit on the class-based conflicts of interest between women, and on her views of McPeak:

It's real interesting to me that, on the one hand, unions are the ones doing it [comparable worth]. On the other hand, there's a lot of a sense of ownership of the comparable worth issue among women in management and political leadership. [But] they feel they're special, and they don't ac-

2. The gossip reported to me on this score was very consistent. As I mentioned in Chapter 4 it was rumored that the director of personnel had never hired women until forced to by the affirmative action settlement, and that he would then hire women only if they were young and attractive. Also, his chief negotiator on the comparable worth task force was described by the women as the type who puts *Playboy* calendars up in his office.
3. Indeed, she ran for the state senate in 1988 but was defeated.

cept collective action. They don't want to be contaminated with a labor association.

I think some women in politics see their own political futures in comparable worth. Sunne McPeak has gone around the country claiming *her* success on this issue, when by the County's own figures there's still a 33 percent wage gap!

We've been real willing to let Sunne take a lot of the credit; she deserves it. But, on the other hand, if you want to make history, you have to *do* something. You can't just talk about it! If we indeed had solved the problem, we could *all* talk about how great we are, how we all *cooperated* and solved it. Until somebody comes along and says: "Wait a minute—the Emperor's not wearing any clothes!"

But several years after this interview took place, when significant progress had finally occurred, Finney had changed her view of McPeak. Writing to me in 1988, she emphasized McPeak's importance as a strategically placed ally and played down their differences: "At this point, I no longer care whether her [McPeak's] interest in the issue is because it is politically correct in the pragmatic sense or because of a heartfelt passion; she has delivered over and over and insisted that we were going to do this even when I was not so sure" (personal communication, May 18, 1988). (In fact, by 1989 Finney and McPeak had together gone on to address other gender issues in the county, including family leave and video display terminal safety standards; personal communication, 12/2/89).

Although I was unable to gain an interview with McPeak, I did speak with one of her close circle of supporters, a woman in a midmanagerial position in the county. She implied (in 1986) that McPeak deserved much of the credit for bringing comparable worth to the county and portrayed the effort as harmonious and cooperative. However, the success that McPeak claimed was the "no fingerprints" strategy, which at the time had so infuriated low-paid women such as Finney. In the words of her supporter:

After the San Jose strike, Sunne felt the issue was coming up and called a meeting of the unions to talk about it. And this started the coalition and the effort. . . . We've done comparable worth without a lawsuit, and without a study. And we've avoided any budget problems also. I just went over to Pacific Bell, who asked us for information on our comparable worth approach. We've found a way which is salable to the private sector.

This is the most important thing we've done. You get on with it while you work with the pieces. And no lawsuits and no studies.

Other women in midmanagerial positions in the county were also supportive of comparable worth and the labor coalition. As discussed in Chapter 4, some were selected to work in the joint labor-management task force. Yet for labor women, relations on the task force were not as harmonious as they have been described by the elite women. Again, Lee Finney explains:

I think women in management in the county are angry, but they are just not conscious enough of the idea of any kind of collective action. They see themselves as vulnerable. The attitude is: "I am special. Not special enough—I should be director and I'm only an assistant. But I don't have to sit at that typewriter, and I don't want to be contaminated by those people who do still sit at the typewriter when I have escaped *those* ranks."

I have this friend, a woman manager who was on the task force. After one of our big confrontations, I was really angry. And we had lunch. And I said: "*Listen,* are you *a woman*—or are you *management?*" And she said: "Is that a choice?" And I said: "Well, it may be!"

Finney's friend, a woman with many years of experience in the social services field, is, however, sincere in her feminist convictions and support of comparable worth. In our interview she summed up her position: "I really *am* management. But, I really believe this county should do something about comparable worth!"

The San Jose and Contra Costa cases illustrate that not all women have the same interest in gaining comparable worth despite its promulgation as a women's reform. As in the history of conflicts between the elite Woman's Party and unionist Women's Bureau summarized in Chapter 2, conflicts often develop over *which* women will be best served by feminist efforts. Alliances across class and institutional location can become strained with the difficult realities of pay equity implementation (particularly if "ownership" of the issue is contested). Yet in much analysis of pay equity, elite women are credited with the policy's success, and the significance of their distinct class location is overlooked. In contrast to the labor women of San Jose heard from above, Janet Flammang (1985) and Carol Mueller (1985) have specifically argued that without a network of

women in elite leadership positions, the comparable worth contract in that city would not have been possible. Similarly, Elaine
Johansen (1984) claims that a core of elite women has been instrumental in comparable worth's success in other cases. Although
women managers and politicians may truly support the principle of
pay equity and be better placed to get the issue onto political agendas, the "elite female network" explanation ignores one critical
problem: namely, once comparable worth is on the agenda, the
sides may not agree on what actually ought to be done.

As we saw in Contra Costa and San Jose, competing definitions
of success can emerge, representing the different needs of elite as
opposed to low-paid women. Women who have "escaped from the
ranks" and no longer sit at the typewriters obviously do not have
the same stake in comparable worth as those who remain in the
pink-collar ghetto. One danger for low-paid women is that too
much will be given up, compromised, or put aside so that elite
women can claim a quick and easy success. Women public-sector
officials like Sally Reed or Sunne McPeak may feel pressures to
demonstrate that they are capable administrators and that they do
not support bloated budgets, yet still have a sincere interest in as-
sisting low-paid women. Precisely as Steinberg (1987a) describes in
the New York State case, however, this ambivalence leads to a redefinition of comparable worth, a minimizing of its objectives, and
implementation of a "reasonable" reform more palatable to the
business community, the taxpayers, and the male officials with
whom elite women must work. As my case studies show, even with
strong alliances to low-paid women, the result of elite women's differing interests may be that a token amount of money is allocated,
much rhetoric heard, and the issue too quickly deemed solved.

Evans and Nelson, studying implementation in Minnesota localities, found evidence on both sides of this issue. On the one hand,
elite women at the state level were crucial for the initial passage of
pay equity legislation; and on the local level, women in decision-
making positions were both more sympathetic to pay equity and
more committed to the implementation process. On the other
hand, female managers, like their male counterparts, "tended to
emphasize technique and cost-containment" and managerial control of wage-setting (Evans and Nelson 1989, 147). What this meant

for many localities was the use of techniques that minimized measures of wage inequities and, thus, the size of wage adjustments
(Evans and Nelson 1989, 155). Because the state mandated local
implementation, these were basically top-down cases in which
grass-roots groups had little initial involvement. Furthermore, the
technocratic handling of the issue by female and male political
elites and public managers ensured that it remained less politicized, isolated from employees and their organizations, and that
"contested ownership" of comparable worth did not arise (Evans
and Nelson 1989, 163–165).

From the point of view of low-paid women, such domestica-
tion of comparable worth (that is, its "ownership" as an elite, or
management-controlled, policy) may mean not only smaller wage
adjustments due to cost-containment measures but also, and more
importantly, a loss of the mobilization or empowerment that occurs
in grass-roots cases. The tendency of elite women to emphasize
cost containment may itself make mobilization of low-paid women
more difficult. In my case studies, the magnitude of the wage inequities often came as a revelation to the workers. Emphasis on an
inexpensive or easily corrected problem is not what had mobilized
the clerical or professional workers in San Jose and Contra Costa.
In fact, the sense of an unmanageable and expensive demand may
actually have provided greater validation to their sense of injustice
and moral outrage.

In my case studies, as well as in notable cases such as those
at Yale and Columbia Universities, the politicization of low-paid
women has been the most striking accomplishment of comparable
worth efforts (Amott and Matthaei 1984; Frank 1986; Gross 1985;
Ladd-Taylor 1985; *New York Times* 1985; Serrin 1984a, 1984b,
1984c, 1985). While many elite women are likely to support the
ideal of pay parity, and are better placed to help implement top-
down approaches, as in Minnesota or New York, such approaches
can reduce the notion of comparable worth to merely an additional
bureaucratic procedure (although still providing at least some wage
increases for pink-collar women). But the radical potential of comparable worth—the creation of labor-feminist alliances, the mobilization of low-paid women, and the transformation of political discourse—is thwarted when control is by elite women.

Class-based Interests

Another contradiction within the comparable worth movement involves the attempt to construe pay equity as simply a labor issue, to claim that it is of equal interest to men, and to draw a classlike alliance in contrast to a solely gender-based alliance. Comparable worth activists in both San Jose and Contra Costa County tried to build alliances with men in male-dominated jobs, maintaining that comparable worth constituted no threat to them and that they should support it as a labor issue. As one feminist politician has declared: "Men, don't be frightened, be enlightened" (*Contra Costa Times* 6/14/84). However, while no one advocates cutting wages for men's jobs, comparable worth can lower the overall "pie" unless special supplementary funds are made available.[4] Furthermore, much of the women's anger in my case studies was directed against these same men, with whom they compared their jobs and wages. As a result, men may well react defensively, feeling that they are the targets, making the issue divisive for labor.

The anger of many women at men of a similar class location came across strongly in my interviews. For example, when I asked a San Jose secretary her opinion of comparable worth, she fiercely seized her classification handbook and proceeded to read the specifications for concrete finishers to me. Then she read the specifications for executive secretary, and their respective wages. When she was through reading she nearly screamed: "If this is comparable worth, someone's not doing their job!" She accused all men of trying to undermine existing policies and saw the union, because it represented both men and women, as a weak ally at best. Only women, she maintained, could be expected to really work for pay equity.

A Contra Costa woman who over twenty years had worked her way up from a clerk typist to a supervisor position expressed similar hostility toward working-class men. She told me that she had had no idea what men were actually being paid until she joined the negotiating team for her union. Then she said, "It really gets to you!" She continued vehemently:

4. Even then, as Evans and Nelson (1989, 93–94) point out, it is a political question whether such funds are considered truly supplementary.

Window washers for the county make more than I do! A second line supervisor of men makes $600 a month more than I do! There's no excuse
that a janitor makes more than an eligibility worker! Local One [the union
for most men's jobs in Contra Costa] owns this county. And they are real
male chauvinist pigs! And they've been kissed royally this year. They've
been fed from *my* trough, mine and every other female-dominated job.

This woman also went on to tell me approvingly of the comparable
worth effort in the small city of Concord (in the wealthy central area of the county), where the wages of male-dominated jobs
deemed overpaid were frozen for a three-year period. She noted
with much regret that this would never happen in the county
system.

Generally, comparable worth advocates reject any suggestion to
cut men's wages. Certainly one reason for this is the desire to preserve labor unity. Yet the suggestion is also rejected on principle:
low-paid women want to have the full extent of their underpayment
measured. The key "scientific" or technical question here is
whether the trend line used to establish "equity" is determined by
the average wages of the male-dominated jobs only or by averaging
male and female wages together. Clearly, averaging the male- and
female-dominated jobs together produces a lower measure of wage
inequity: it understates the wage gap for female-dominated jobs
and at the same time represents male-dominated jobs as "above
trend" or overpaid. As in the San Jose case, the drawing of a single
trend line showing the average of male and female wages can be a
dangerous political compromise—one that management has a distinct interest in promoting.[5] Sally Reed, the San Jose official heard
from above, stated the management position emphatically:

What comparable worth really says is that half the people are overpaid by
the marketplace and half of the people are underpaid. . . .

As a union issue it's always a problem to take on the cause of one portion of the membership. . . . So [comparable worth] can become very divisive because it *is* saying, "We ought to get more money and you ought

5. Evans and Nelson (1989, 151, also 93–94) discuss how this occurred in
many Minnesota localities; as I mentioned in Chapter 3, this was unfortunately
based on the precedent set in San Jose. Acker (1989, 120–124) also discusses how
trend line questions threatened to divide the interests of men and women in the
Oregon State case.

to get less." They don't say the "you ought to get less" very often, but it is in fact what it means.

In contrast to this perspective, union activists in Contra Costa and San Jose did not see comparable worth as meaning that men were overpaid. In San Jose, labor accused management of exacerbating union divisiveness by insisting on the overpayment/underpayment definition and its accompanying methodology—that is, with the trend line pulled down by inclusion of women's low wages. As one activist complained, "All these women's salaries clustered at the bottom are going to drag that average down!" Neither low-paid women nor working-class men are likely to be best served by this form of measurement, yet this crucial point can be easily obscured by its overly technical character (a point I return to in the final section of this chapter).

A more accessible argument, and one more often voiced, as to why men should support comparable worth is based on men's interests in family betterment. Proponents claim that comparable worth is really a "working person's issue" because, as one male union representative often explained to the press, it takes two *full* paychecks to support a family today; with women's work so underpaid, families are getting only one and one-half paychecks, and this hurts men as well as women (Beyette 1981; *Newsweek* 1981, 59). Since nearly all men have working wives, daughters, sisters, or mothers, advocates felt it should not be difficult for working men to grasp this argument and see pay equity as being directly in their interest.

The family-based argument assumes that class interests can and ought to take precedence over men's gender-based interest in maintaining dominance, both at work and at home. However, while the solidary, egalitarian working-class family may be an appealing image, the argument does not seem to be as persuasive as proponents hope. In Minnesota, for example, where male snowplow drivers, street maintenance workers, and firefighters all objected to pay equity, Evans and Nelson (1989, 167) conclude: "The link between [gendered] work hierarchies and familial patriarchy remained an implicit but ever-present subtext to many local debates." In my interviews, rather than hearing of husbands' enthusiasm over their wives' bringing home larger paychecks, I heard stories of marital strife provoked by wives' union involvement. In the workplace, too, men in male-dominated jobs were often at odds with those in pink-collar jobs, despite images to the contrary.

In San Jose, the comparable worth effort did create an image of a class-solidary movement (see, e.g., Moore and Marsis 1983a)—in contrast to the more apparent lack of gender-based unity. Union membership was close to half male and half female, a proportion that the 1981 strike participation reflected. Moreover, the most prominent union spokesperson during the strike was a man, while the most visible opponents were women officials. I repeat the apt comment that one San Jose activist made: "If San Jose is the feminist capital of the world, it's because *the men and women* of this union make it that way!" (Fischer 1981, 2085; emphasis added).

The tension between men and women workers in San Jose emerged primarily after the strike. As one man employed in a male-dominated job explained,

Comparable worth is an issue of fairness, and I don't feel it hurts me. It was the most public issue in the strike. But I believe in unions, and I support the union. I'll go on strike if we vote for it. But to me, the strike was on the whole contract as a package, the general increase too. A union has to work for all its members. It can be comparable worth at times, but this total focus on comparable worth [even after the strike] is divisive.[6]

Another man put it this way: "I have no argument with women 'going for Number One.' Hey, get as much as you can! But give-and-take is required, and they want always to only give to the female-dominated. This is not fair."

While supporting the image of solidarity during the strike, one of the primary male-dominated groups affected, the engineering technicians, demonstrated their resentment of comparable worth later by attempting to split off from the union local. I was told that 93 out of 115 technicians signed petitions requesting their own organization; the city, however, refused to charter another bargaining unit. More recently, the technicians have demonstrated their resentment by trying to show that they are underpaid according to marketplace criteria. Documenting that their wages are 10–20 percent below those in other municipalities, they bypassed the union and appealed to the city administration for market-based raises.

6. As we saw in Chapter 3, initially the city intended to fund comparable worth adjustments out of the amount allocated for general increases; the union demanded that equity adjustments be in addition to cost-of-living increases.

It may be that these men experienced "status anxiety" as a result of comparable worth efforts by women. As one technician explained to me, these were nondegree positions, occupied by men who often felt they should have done more, such as finished college and taken the engineering exams. What this man did not say, but was suggested by his resentment, was that the men's shaky sense of status was bolstered by women's subordination and by the fact that "techs" were paid more than women with bachelor's and even master's degrees. Because comparable worth erodes the relative advantage of men in male-dominated jobs, threatening their position in the culturally prescribed gender hierarchy, they may react defensively regardless of the real extent of the economic threat posed.[7] As several feminist analysts observe, much of what male workers perceive as a threat is psychological; because skill itself is associated with masculinity, men's very gender identity, in addition to their dominant status, may seem under attack by job comparisons that, relatively speaking, devalue their work (Acker 1989, 159; Steinberg 1986, 124).

In Contra Costa County the dynamic between men and women workers differed from that in the San Jose experience. The movement was closer to, and appeared as, a gender-based and gender-solidary movement. The union coalition represented the heavily female-dominated jobs, and the primary spokespersons for comparable worth were women from the coalition. The opposition, conversely, was made up primarily of male county officials and male blue-collar workers represented by their separate union, Local 1.

Owing to the recalcitrance of most of the male-dominated groups in Local 1, the very small group of engineering technicians in Contra Costa played a somewhat similar role to that played by the technicians in the San Jose strike—providing an important symbol of the possibility for a class alliance behind the women's demand. The Contra Costa technicians were, if anything, more supportive than those in San Jose, but they represented a far smaller proportion of the male-dominated jobholders. One of the few women technicians may also have had an important influence, for she served as the union representative during much of the comparable worth effort.

---

7. Recall that this attitude was demonstrated by the San Jose engineering technician who remarked that women's jobs are really "all fun and games" and don't deserve higher pay.

Unlike those who distance themselves from the pink-collar ghetto once they have left it behind, this woman maintained a strong identification with gender issues and the comparable worth issue in particular. She explained how she tried to influence her co-workers:

We tried to get the men to understand that it's a new issue, *a cause*. We're not just talking about pantyhose allowance! We tried to get men to defer their needs, and they did. But they're not exuberant. But they did picket for comparable worth. And in secretaries' week events, they handed out balloons with the clericals' union. Their support enhanced the strength of the issue, and it probably contributed to the respect of the women's coalition in the eyes of management.

Another woman, an AFSCME organizer who had worked with the male-dominated engineering technicians, commented on gaining the men's support: "We tried to prepare them for comparable worth. We pointed out that they had a real decent wage level, and that women had been waiting a long time. We tried to make it a *workers'* issue. And they [the technicians] were a good group, with very progressive values. The problems were with Local One. They fostered the male/female split."

Both the San Jose and Contra Costa experiences illustrate that attempts to establish a general class-based interest in comparable worth are riddled with tensions. Although some might feel that the potential for divisiveness between men and women workers is so great that organized labor should not pursue comparable worth, I suggest that there is reason for hope in building such problematic alliances. In both cases, some male-dominated groups, at some points in time, were supportive of the women's demands. Attempts at education or consciousness-raising with male groups did seem to make a difference.[8] In addition, employers' actions often exacer-

8. Evans and Nelson's finding in the Minnesota case (1989, 123–124) is therefore disconcerting. Evidently Minnesota AFSCME leaders decided to publicize pay equity only in the female-dominated units, and to "respond quietly" in the male units in order to quell possible opposition. Thus, male workers were no source of support. In addition, AFSCME decided to make no announcement when raises were actually paid for the same reason. As a consequence, many low-paid women were ignorant of the policy, with the paradoxical result that strategies that damped opposition also damped support. In contrast, Kautzer (1989) finds in the Yale case that men in the male-dominated union were able to support women's demands, and the two groups worked together during the women's strike. Although she concludes that unions will remain imperfect vehicles for gender-based

bate the conflicting gender-based interests between working men and women and may be held partly responsible for problems of labor divisiveness (as for example in San Jose, with management's use of all jobs rather than male-dominated jobs to construct their trend line). Unions could do more to focus attention on this issue (as occurred at Yale, where blue-collar men did come to support comparable worth; Kautzer 1989).

Ultimately, however, the accusation that comparable worth is divisive of working-class unity may be true to some extent. Perhaps any strategy useful for low-paid women will be divisive, requiring the placing of gender before class interests; the crucial issue is the extent to which such conflicts can be minimized. Yet I suggest that comparable worth is likely to be less divisive than other strategies intended to assist women workers. Affirmative action, for example, because it contravenes unions' hard-fought seniority rights, may be much harder for labor organizations to uphold and still maintain internal cohesion. Although comparable worth threatens men's sense of relative status, their position in the hierarchy of rewards, and their relative share of the wage bill, it may still be less threatening than affirmative action, which, if pursued fully, would directly threaten men's jobs. Like the class interests dividing low-paid and elite women in comparable worth efforts, the gender-based interests dividing working men and women will continue to be problematic. And where such conflicts become exacerbated, the radical possibilities of comparable worth, particularly for labor-feminist alliances, will very likely be severely compromised.

Hierarchy

As we saw in the discussion of gender-based interests in comparable worth, some analysts have viewed the issue primarily as a reform "from above" implemented by networks of elite women. Others have argued that comparable worth has more radical possibilities, because it involves significant collective activity by labor and low-paid women (Amott and Matthaei 1984; Feldberg 1984;

---

demands, Kautzer still sees possibilities, as do I, for working men and women to form alliances for pay equity. Also see Acker's analysis of intraclass gender conflict in the Oregon State case (1989).

Moore and Marsis 1983a). Yet these radical possibilities have been limited by comparable worth's liberal, equal-treatment vocabulary, as well as by contradictory conceptions of the issue as one fundamentally of gender or of class. Moreover, as Feldberg (1984) points out, although comparable worth questions the legitimacy of the market and the value of male and female labor, it is not an attack on occupational inequality; in fact, it reinforces the legitimacy of skill-based hierarchies of rewards. The movement raises the idea that the judgment of skill is politically and ideologically based (Feldberg 1984, 321–324), but its objective is a new hierarchy built on a gender-neutral evaluation of work.

In this respect, comparable worth contrasts strikingly with truly egalitarian strategies like the solidary wage policies pursued by Swedish labor unions. Such policies, by implementing either flat rather than percentage raises or higher increases to the lowest paid, aim explicitly at narrowing the spread between the highest- and lowest-paid workers (Cook 1980). Although in both of my case studies concern was voiced for those with very low earnings, in Contra Costa County the Comparable Worth Coalition refused to accept offers that included adjustments only to the lowest end of the wage scale, and in San Jose adjustments were based primarily on the amount of discrepancy within each factor-point grouping rather than on a job's location in the overall wage hierarchy. Evans and Nelson (1989, 74–75) consider the states of New Mexico and New Jersey to have pay equity policies resembling solidary wage approaches, for there increases went only to the lowest paid. However, such one-time changes were more likely implemented to avoid full-blown job evaluation, minimize the extent of overall wage increases, and obscure the entire question of how work is valued, rather than to satisfy egalitarian impulses—indeed, this is precisely how Acker (1989) depicts the change from "true" comparable worth to "poverty relief" in the Oregon state case. Such a redefinition of comparable worth, masked by an ostensibly egalitarian concern, was what Contra Costa activists feared. These states, however, are not typical of most, where comparable worth has involved the hierarchical implementation of "pay for points" (Evans and Nelson 1989, 74–75).

When I conducted my interviews, although perceptions varied, most respondents did not question the legitimacy of hierarchy or income inequality itself. It was rather the existing gender hierarchy that stood out as unjust. When I asked for their definitions of comparable worth, most emphasized the extent to which women's work is undervalued and stated that comparable worth is a way to remedy this situation through recognition of the skills, complexity, or value of this work. One woman, a clerical union activist, best expresses the contradictions inherent in comparable worth—of equity versus equality—as well as those of class versus gender identifications:

I'm not a women's libber. I don't believe women should all have men's jobs. I don't believe women should all be single and working. *But* I do believe that you have to have some education to be a clerical worker! Comparable worth means paying for what you had to have learned for a job. You take the qualifications and rate them somehow. But there's the rub—who does the rating?

Comparable worth is *not* socialistic. It's not everybody getting the same thing. I'm not for *that*. But [pondered the issue]—then I do hear of doctors getting $70,000 a year. Are they *worth* it? It does seem like they have a lot of schooling and so forth. But then, more are probably in it for the $70,000 than for the care of people.

While to this clerical woman comparable worth is not an egalitarian demand, it has provoked her to question why she has assumed some instances of inequality to be just and others unjust. Another respondent, interestingly, described comparable worth in opposite terms; nevertheless, their views are not very different in substance.

I think comparable worth is really very socialistic. You revalue everything you've got in society. It's a real threat. . . . It undercuts the people who traditionally have been thought to be more valuable—a manager over a social worker, or a policeman over a teacher, or seeing clericals as now doing critical work. It makes you think: What *are* the difficult jobs? What are we willing to pay for? What *is* most important to us as a society?

Both of these women reveal that comparable worth can provide a point of critique of existing hierarchies; it provokes questions of how we form normative evaluations of existing inequalities. Comparable worth is based on the assumption that the structure of rewards ought to be based on merit, yet by making the merit of women's work an object of struggle comparable worth reveals that evaluating achievement *is* an inherently political process. What is

considered deserving of reward is shown to be part of a field of social conflict (that may or may not be clearly articulated) in which
outcomes are determined by power relations rather than by any
values that naturally inhere in tasks. The clerical woman above expressed her sense of the politicized character of occupational hierarchies when she commented, "There's the rub—who does the
rating?"

Finally, while comparable worth represents redistributive objectives, it does not provide an argument for equality per se, as the
very use of the term *equity* makes clear. In other words, the demand is for *just*, not leveled wages. Therefore, to some extent
comparable worth does reify notions of the liberal meritocratic
marketplace and a "natural" hierarchy of rewards. It goes further,
however, when proponents succeed in making the just recognition
of merit and allocation of rewards a directly politicized process.[9]

Science and Politics: Grass-Roots Movement
Versus Technical Reform

Since the moral legitimacy of the comparable worth movement depends on the claim that women are underpaid because of their gender, it also depends inescapably on the technical methods used to
validate this claim. As a result, the success of the movement hinges
on its handling of technical measurement issues. Because the politics of comparable worth must be played out within this context,
there is an ever-present threat that managerial control of the job
evaluation methodology will compromise the interests of low-paid
women while at the same time obscuring this fact. Activists, though
aware of the risk involved, often feel a need for tangible results,
which leads them to accept existing evaluation systems with little
challenge. Moreover, the preoccupation with job evaluation issues
itself leads to the danger that opportunities to mobilize low-paid
women will be lost.

9. This more critical potential is often noticed by conservatives. One conservative analyst, for example, has written: "[Feminists] declare that they simply want
. . . to encourage employers to focus solely on the worker's individual qualifications. The actual philosophy of most feminists, however, is precisely the opposite.
Underlying their view . . . is a thoroughgoing anti-merit, anti-individualistic
egalitarianism" (Schwartz 1982, 42). For an astute feminist analysis of how this
critical potential in comparable worth was lost and hierarchy reproduced in the
Oregon State case, see Acker 1989, esp. chap. 3.

Social theorists have seen the contradiction between bureaucratic and technical expertise and broader democratic participation as characteristic of politics in modern society in general. Max Weber, in his classic analysis of the modern bureaucratic state, emphasized that technical expertise inevitably comes to dominate and shape decisions in governmental action and policy making, even in the most democratic of societies. According to Weber (1975, 129–158, 215–216, 350–358), industrial society's need for specialization, rationalization, and calculability in the conduct of affairs demands the trained expert; and science, the formal sphere of specialized technical knowledge, legitimates the expert as the objective arbiter of this knowledge. More recently, Daniel Bell, following Weber's characterization of modern society, has noted the increasingly technical character of politics and the way this precludes participation by nonexperts. He writes: "*The central question* of postindustrial society, therefore, is the relation of the technocratic decision to politics" (1973, 337; emphasis added).[10] Finally, Jürgen Habermas (1971), working in a critical Marxist tradition, adds that technocratic policy making aids in the reproduction of class domination by both excluding participation and obscuring class power and politics behind the neutral veil of scientific decision making. This analysis can be extended to explain the interrelated gender and class domination confronting low-paid women. Moreover, the contradiction between technocratic and democratic impulses poses a crucial issue for any subordinate group attempting to gain state action in support of their interests.

Evans and Nelson (1989) have also identified this contradiction, which they call "the paradox of technocratic reform," as a central dynamic in the politics of pay equity. They document how in Minnesota comparable worth fostered increased managerial control of job classification and wage setting rather than mobilization of low-paid women and grass-roots participation. Although pay equity did increase women's wages somewhat, it became a largely bureaucratized procedure handled by specialists and lost much of its transfor-

---

10. For Bell (1973, 1976), however, this question is answered by placing sufficient faith in the meritocratic functioning of the labor market to view the intellectual elite as those most capable of making decisions for the whole society. In his view, moreover, some loss of participation is not too steep a price to pay for the high standard of living and social stability we enjoy.

mative or radical potential to further democratic impulses. Some policy analysts have argued that technocratic reforms, because they *appear* narrow, specialized, and uncontroversial, often achieve greater success than more democratic or participatory efforts, which are liable to provoke opposition (Gelb and Palley 1987). Evans and Nelson point out that this may have been true with comparable worth in Minnesota, where implementation was achieved fairly quickly and easily. Yet they also acknowledge that this occurred at a cost far beyond that of the smaller wage adjustments and restricted measures of the wage gap: the opportunity was lost to build a grass-roots movement that might then demand an ongoing role in workplace and gender politics.

Whether primarily a technocratic reform or a grass-roots movement, it is still notable that comparable worth has not degenerated into a sterile debate over methodological or measurement issues. There are two reasons for this. First, the underpayment of women's work is so systematic that even the existing, gender-biased techniques reveal substantial disparities. While job evaluation methods like the Hay system used in San Jose do not recognize culturally devalued aspects of women's work, nonetheless sizable inequities appear when employers are forced to rate women's jobs *as if* they were men's jobs, measuring them on the same set of "masculine" compensable factors (Acker 1989, 68; also Remick 1984; Steinberg and Haignere 1987). As a result, employers are now unlikely to be able to neutralize the claims of low-paid women, or with any methodological sleight of hand to wholly undermine the documentation of wage disparities.[11]

Second, organized women have, as in San Jose, recognized the political nature of the evaluation process. My case studies (in contrast to Evans and Nelson's findings) indicate that the need for "objective" documentation of the wage gap does not preclude the par-

11. Whether job evaluation techniques can be further politicized and pushed to validate "feminine" job traits will depend on the extent to which proponents take up this issue and amass the power and expertise to counter managerial control of the technical arena. In the Oregon state case, "feminizing" the compensable factors to eliminate gender bias became an issue of political contention. But proponents, lacking both a mobilized base of support and control over the methodology, were largely unsuccessful. Token changes in compensable factors won by feminists were undermined by renewed managerial control in the evaluation process (Acker 1987; 1989, 68–76).

ticipation and mobilization of low-paid women. The local efforts in San Jose and Contra Costa County may be atypical, but as at least partly successful efforts by grass-roots groups to handle the "paradox of a technocratic reform," they offer instructive examples of attempts to balance the need for technical expertise against the abdication of all control and participation. In San Jose in particular, the union insisted on participating in the job evaluation process. From the writing of job descriptions to membership on the evaluation committee, activists demonstrated that it is not necessary to surrender all control to management. Also, aspects of the process such as the writing of job descriptions became tools for involving women and furthering their politicization.

But even in such grass-roots movements there is the risk that comparable worth may be co-opted over time and, like affirmative action, become increasingly bureaucratized after an initial victory. Employers can adapt existing job structures and classification systems to erode initial material benefits and diffuse women's mobilization, whether actual or potential. In much the same spirit as personnel professionals took up affirmative action, consultants advise that comparable worth too can be a good management strategy (Sape 1986); they recommend upgrading a small number of female employees (see Remick 1982) or granting broad but very small pay adjustments in order to avoid litigation and "improve morale" (*Contra Costa Times* 5/21/85). As Evans and Nelson (1989, 147, 172) point out, constant vigilance is needed to prevent comparable worth from degenerating into a "kind of managerial revolution" that rationalizes pay practices and extends the control of personnel professionals. Although such degeneration threatens all pay equity cases, the necessary vigilance is more likely to be sustained where broad-based mobilization has occurred than in cases where elite-controlled legislative strategies have been adopted. And to the extent that comparable worth can be used more effectively than affirmative action to promote mobilization and collective action, low-paid women will stand a better chance over the long run of resisting managerial manipulation.

It is indeed possible that submitting the pay equity issue to managerial control, as in Minnesota, may lead to quicker results. Yet the potential of building a larger movement for economic justice— one that may grapple toward a less hierarchical, more egalitarian

workplace or effect broad changes in gender and class ideology—
lies with grass-roots efforts like those in San Jose and Contra Costa
County.

In this chapter I have discussed four contradictory tendencies in
the politics of comparable worth, each of which poses problems for
the issue's radical or transformative potential. These tendencies
arise from the complex intertwining of the class and gender interests of low-paid women, as well as from the movement's need
to operate and gain legitimacy within bureaucratic organizational
settings. As Acker (1989) argues, comparable worth attempts to
change the way gender is incorporated into the class structure;
therefore, political alliances favoring and opposing the policy are
complex. Moreover, because the technical context in which job
comparability is determined, as well as the attendant hierarchical
notion of organizations, effectively blunts the issue's radical potential, comparable worth too often becomes a managerially controlled
addition to bureaucratized wage-setting procedures.

In the next and final chapter I explore a more exciting possible
outcome for pay equity: the transformation of consciousness and
political discourse while bringing economic gain to women workers.

Seven

Radical Possibilities of a Class and Gender Movement

In this final chapter I return to the question that has motivated this endeavor: Does comparable worth contain radical possibilities? Can it mobilize low-paid women, contribute to the building of feminist-labor alliances, and provoke changes in the ideology supporting an unjust class/gender system? In this chapter I show that it can by focusing on the low-paid women I have studied, on their understandings of gender and class interests and their politicization. Changes in the consciousness of women workers have not been evident in other major studies of comparable worth; such research has largely neglected the grass roots and focused on levels of elite action (Acker 1989; Evans and Nelson 1989; Steinberg 1987a). In addition, I place comparable worth in the larger social context of economic reconfiguration and the rise of the service economy, and the need for changing agendas in both labor and feminist movements—for the most radical possibility of comparable worth may be its linkage to a broad agenda of social change.

Discourse and Mobilization

Although often overlooked by social movement theory (e.g., Jenkins 1983), the initial construction of a sense of collective interest and group solidarity is crucial to political mobilization. And the vocabulary or discourse invoked in political debate plays an important role in this process. In this respect comparable worth creates new possibilities for both feminist and labor movements in the United States. The issue moves beyond the predominant vision of each movement, shifting the terms of debate surrounding women's status away from both the feminist agenda, which has ignored social class, and the traditional labor agenda, which has ignored gender. By incorporating vocabulary and tactics from each movement, comparable worth has enlarged the available discourse and may therefore mobilize new constituencies.

The two comparable worth efforts considered in this study began, however, with very different vocabularies. Despite some oversimplification, it is fair to say that in San Jose the women workers initially identified primarily as women, while in Contra Costa they identified primarily as workers. In each case, the movement developed by incorporating the originally excluded vocabulary; that is, in Contra Costa County low-paid women moved from class to gender terms, and in San Jose they moved from gender to a class-based vocabulary (of course, this represents a relative shift, for the issue itself always involved both gender and class politics). Each case therefore represents a convergence. Each drew strength from an identification with both the feminist and labor movements, and each came to articulate the class- and gender-based interests of pink-collar workers.

As Chapter 3 illustrates, in San Jose low-paid women originally organized and articulated grievances *as women*, both in the librarians' group, Concerned Library Active Workers, and in the clericals' group, City Women for Advancement. Although some of these women were union members, they did not at first consider the union an organization in which their gender-based interests could be expressed. Directing their early efforts at forming alliances with officials, many of whom were women, they framed their demands in the existing "top-down" model of affirmative action rather than with any sense of class-based antagonism or confrontation. Frustration with this approach, the realization that power in collective bargaining would be very useful, and the presence of a dynamic female AFSCME organizer led the women to make comparable worth a union issue. The process culminated in a strike—the classic tactic of the labor movement—and the presentation of a class solidary image.

In Contra Costa County, in contrast, clerical women in particular were highly class conscious, as can be seen in their early organizing efforts and 1972 strike. Unlike San Jose women, they felt little tie to feminism and originally had little concern for issues central to the feminist agenda. Their organizing efforts largely followed traditional union models, although they used a language, innovative for that time, of "breadwinning mothers." Also, they saw their demands and interests as antagonistic to the interests of their employer, the county. Certainly, as I have shown in Chapter 4, affirmative action played an important role in promoting gender-based identification and new expectations of upward mobility among low-paid women, as well as in providing the political opportunity to raise the wage gap problem. Yet only after the clericals became involved with the San Jose strike (and after considerable efforts by a feminist-oriented labor organizer) did a stronger connection to feminist ideology emerge. At that time, the female-dominated unions of clericals and social workers joined with the nurses' association in forming the Comparable Worth Coalition.

Several excerpts from my interviews highlight the convergence of class and gender interests that developed among many women in each case.

San Jose—Gender to Class and Gender:

It's bullshit that comparable worth is a middle-class women's issue! The only ones saying that are men—professional, white men!

In general, there's not enough recognition and respect for clericals. That's been my experience. And its true for all the working people. This country should respect the working people.

Contra Costa—Class to Gender and Class:

Say, if you belong to NOW, you don't even need comparable worth. They're all upper middle class, and mostly single. They don't have much to do with the day-to-day things of life, like whether you have any health insurance, or what to do if your husband leaves you with three kids.

We need comparable worth, but more important are education and jobs policies. . . . I mean, most of the new jobs are those low-level kind of jobs that really exploit women.

I never considered myself a feminist until I discovered I was one.

Comparable worth is a labor issue *and* it is a feminist issue.

These trajectories are of course oversimplifications of a complex, textured political reality. In each case the originally dominant vocabulary remained the more important discourse invoked throughout, and convergence of the two was not complete. Nevertheless, regardless of women's initial sense of group identification, the politics of comparable worth revealed how both class and gender led to their low pay. For it was San Jose's feminist-identified activists who stated that the major lesson to be learned from their experience was that unions are valid for women; and it was Contra Costa's class-identified activists who marched, all in pink, displaying the slogan "Smash the pink-collar ghetto!"

It is simpler to describe the differing class and gender relations in these two comparable worth cases than to explain them. A number of factors, however, can be identified that contribute to the differences, including the local economy and political culture, the shape of previous workplace conflicts and organization, and the type of opposition encountered by low-paid women. San Jose was the more liberal area, with an integrated ethnic milieu and high-tech industrial base. The area had a prominent local feminist movement, reflected in the number of women in elite positions. Contra Costa County had a strong working-class, labor-identified local culture, as the area has been dominated by a traditional industrial base of steel and oil and the new affluent bedroom communities have developed as largely distinct enclaves. Low-paid women in each case thus began framing their issues within the more familiar, available context—or, to use classic sociological terms, each group used the "vocabulary of motives" that was the norm in their community (Gerth and Mills 1953).

The type of opposition encountered in each case, and the manner in which the opposition interpreted and responded to the pink-collar women's efforts, also affected women's gender and class identification. In San Jose, low-paid women did not generally receive a sexist or antifeminist response, but rather a response based on the divergent interests of elite women. But in Contra Costa County, women who saw themselves primarily as members of a labor organization consistently received a sexist response from management—even during their earliest efforts, when a management representative accused clericals of having "sugar daddies" at home to support them. It is not surprising that these responses would have some effect on the "vocabulary of motives" of low-paid women.

To evaluate the ultimate promise of comparable worth, we must consider whether this development of the consciousness of women workers, toward a dual, class and gender, identification, is likely to be typical. I suggest that the trajectory of gender to class-gender consciousness exemplified by the San Jose case is very likely the more generalizable to other comparable worth cases (at least to other grass-roots cases), and to other cases of working women's organizing. Gender may be a more resonant or salient category than class for most working women, if not in terms of group solidarity and collective action, then at least in terms of group identification.[1] Simply put, most working women identify more readily as women than as workers and may find it easier, initially, to organize as women (although, as I showed in Chapters 1 and 2, neither gender nor class has by itself provided a good basis for organizing working women). Even in Contra Costa County, where clericals had a strong sense of class solidarity, the label *union* was originally rejected because of its overly masculine connotation. The first union president discussed this point with me in an extensive interview:

Women don't really go for unions anyway. And then the leader of the only union at that time [Local 1]—the women hated him. He comes off like some 1920s gangster type, yelling, screaming, like a big blowhard. . . . And women just don't go for that. . . .

So we couldn't use the term *union*. It was a dirty word. It was the United Clericals *Association*. . . . I couldn't really figure it out. My dad believed in unions, my husband believed in unions. Unions were positive, they had done some good in this country. But the women in my day [unlike younger women today] weren't changing or questioning their role in the home.

It is beyond the scope of this study to account for the unusual level of labor organization among the Contra Costa clerical women. But the low level of unionization among clericals in general is best explained by the social relations of the office, in addition to the sexism of many labor organizations. The patrimonial, personalistic relations of the office create a strong sense of loyalty between women and their bosses that generally inhibits collective organizing (Kanter 1977; Massachusetts History Workshop 1985). To examine why, in this case, these intimate relations proved less prohibitive to

---

1. Research by social psychologist Patricia Gurin (1982) suggests that group identification among women increased dramatically through the 1970s, although endorsement of collective action remained low (also Gurin 1985).

organizing would require a detailed comparative study of relations in the workplace. I can only observe that the double identification of comparable worth with both class and gender appears to be more successful than traditional labor union strategies in overcoming this obstacle to mobilizing women. One San Jose secretary's story captures the willingness to risk "disloyalty" in the gendered office hierarchy that came with the comparable worth effort: "Personal loyalty was an issue. . . . My boss was very cold to me after we had the one-day comparable worth sick-out [prior to the strike]. Finally I just took him aside and I said: 'I'm not management and you are, and that's all. It's nothing personal!' But he tried to get me to take it personally and tell him if we were going to strike and give him other inside dope."

In contrast to my suggestion that gender is more meaningful to working women than class, evidence from other grass-roots cases might support a somewhat different interpretation. Cases like those at Yale, Columbia, Harvard, and New York Universities (Frank 1986; Gross 1985; Kautzer 1989; Serrin 1984a, 1984b, 1984c, 1985), in which pay equity was a secondary issue in pink-collar unionizing efforts, suggest that in some communities initial class identification is at least as strong as gender identification. In such cases, which follow a trajectory more like Contra Costa's than San Jose's, dual identification may be important right from the start for successful organizing. Even though women in such unionizing efforts may identify strongly as *women* workers, identification with the feminist movement appears to be low, at least initially.[2] Comparable worth is not the primary impetus to action in such "dual" cases, but it adds an important moral basis to unions' economic demands: it becomes a tool and a symbol providing women with a greater sense of legitimacy and solidary purpose, and struggling unions with better ammunition to use in public relations battles against recalcitrant employers.

Whichever trajectory is more typical, however, the most difficult problem is still how to organize a previously unorganized group and how to build a sense of solidarity that can support collective action. Several analysts contend that in the past the labor move-

2. But Kautzer (1989, 43) notes that some Yale activists, like the Contra Costa activists, credited the union effort with "expanding their allegiance to the women's movement."

ment has failed in this because it has not honored women's distinct experience or addressed gender issues specifically (Feldberg 1987b; Strom 1983). At least one contemporary study confirms this suspicion by showing that where women's issues have been emphasized, labor has won a significantly higher proportion of representation elections (Moore and Marsis 1983b). This evidence and my findings suggest that working women, whether they explicitly identify with feminism or not, respond more immediately to a gender-based vocabulary than to a purely class-based discourse.[3]

Women's subjective identification with gender versus class categories and the ability of such identifications to mobilize women has been seriously debated by feminists. While some argue that traditional gender identification precludes class militancy and unionization because it reinforces women's subordinance and passivity (Benston 1969; Hartmann 1979; Matthaei 1982; Mitchell 1971; Tilly and Scott 1978), others maintain that women's cultures, which valorize women's traditional experiences, form the basis for class militance and resistance to capitalist domination (Benson 1978; Costello 1985; di Leonardo 1985; Lamphere 1985; Melosh 1982; Zavella 1985). Examination of the comparable worth movement suggests that the relation of class and gender interests is both more complicated and more variable than either of these positions indicates (also see Feldberg 1980; Hyman 1985; Nussbaum 1980; Strom 1985). On the one hand, my case studies show that honoring women's distinct experiences is a crucial part of mobilization, and involvement with the issue may, for some, reflect the desire to defend traditional gender boundaries. On the other hand, attention to class location and the manner in which gender is built into the class structure seems just as important.

The greater accessibility of gender discourse and group identification was not lost on the union activists whom I interviewed. Diana Doughtie conjectured that the clerical union in Contra Costa succeeded early on because it was led by the women themselves;

3. Jane Mansbridge (1986, 189) has also noted the high initial salience of gender and its significance for progressive class politics. She explains: "There is no chapter of the Democratic Socialists of America in Peoria, Illinois, but there is a chapter of NOW. The same is true in many other towns and small cities where NOW provides the only organized group more radical than the local Democratic Party." But, as I explained earlier, this feminist organizing was successful primarily with middle-class women.

working among their peers, she observed, they ran the group with the same commitment as women run their own families or do church work. San Jose labor activists Joan Godard and Bill Callahan, discussing why they felt it was so hard to organize women, concluded that the major lesson from their efforts was to be found not in the actual wage adjustments but rather in the demonstration that unions are valid for women workers.

The potential impact of initially gender-based identification and its threat for workplace politics have also been noted by the business community. A *New York Times* article on working mothers' support groups (Machlowitz 1987) noted that many companies have "nixed" such groups (just as they often "nix" attempts at union organizing). Employers realize that these women are unlikely to be satisfied with simply providing emotional support and may begin "clamoring for a whole host of things," which could easily become a prelude to collective action. In fact, such a trajectory in the creation and articulation of group interests would be very similar to that of the women in San Jose, who ultimately did turn to union activity and confrontation with their employer.

Even as I completed final revisions of this book, I kept encountering examples of the way in which gender identification leads to involvement with comparable worth and culminates in labor militancy. One of the most apt comes from a *New York Times* account of the six-week-long comparable worth strike at Hofstra University. The *Times* reports: "What truly galls the clerical workers is that the custodians, grounds workers, guards, and painters, drivers and locksmiths, most of them men, earn considerably more than they do. 'That's what started the whole thing,' said Anne Noonan, the strike coordinator, who conceded that *before her feminist epiphany she used to walk across picket lines blithely*" (King 1989; emphasis added).

Finally, I must add a more personal note. It seems to be particularly easy to dismiss participants' own understandings of their interests when those participants are primarily women. I often met with this type of response when presenting this research. Many people had trouble accepting the centrality of gender and gender identification for the participants, maintaining that comparable worth really ought to be just a union issue or just a class issue. Yet low-paid women *have mobilized* around a dual class and gender construction of their issue. And because gender is often the more resonant category of group identification, they represent themselves and articulate their demands as working *women*. As Tilly (1981, 61) has warned, "It takes confidence, even arrogance, to override a group's own vision of its interests in life."

The Continuing Significance of Class

Despite the greater prominence of gender-based discourse, in both of my case studies low-paid women came to realize that they could neither wholly ally themselves nor identify with *all* women. Involvement with comparable worth tends to heighten this awareness of difference even where initial gender identification is strong, as it was in San Jose. I suggest that this tendency to highlight differences dividing working women may develop because comparable worth itself represents part of a larger trend: it may be both an expression and a result of a continuing, or perhaps renewed, significance of class among women. I also suggest that this divergence in life chances has important implications for feminist discourse and politics, and for the question of whether comparable worth will realize its radical possibilities.

In a similar vein, Wilson argued in *The Declining Significance of Race* (1978) that economic and political changes stemming from the civil rights movement led to greater class division in the black population. The black middle class, which had the resources to benefit from increased opportunities, now faces conditions very different from those encountered by the black underclass, which remain difficult and impoverished. Wilson therefore maintains that class has become increasingly more critical than race in determining individual life chances; to be effective, then, the black political agenda must address class issues. Although this analysis is instructive, it has been criticized for its reductive or zero-sum treatment of race and class. For example, Marable (1986) contends that the growth of class stratification in the black community has not made race any less central in social and economic life; it only indicates that the shape of institutional racism has changed.

I suggest that a somewhat similar process of class differentiation to that described by Wilson may be occurring among working women: as a result of feminist gains and recent economic shifts, increasing (though small) numbers of women are moving into elite managerial and professional positions, and their interests tend to diverge from those of low-paid women. In earlier writings I have referred to this phenomenon as the "declining significance of gender" (Blum 1987), for which I received criticisms parallel to those directed at Wilson. Indeed, the term is misleading. As my discussion of the resilience of sex-segregated labor markets and of the prominence of gender identification makes clear, the significance of gender in determining women's experiences and perceptions shows no sign of declining, and there has been little reduction in gender asymmetries within social classes. There is also no question that the sexual division of labor is as intertwined with the class structure as in the past; my argument concerns only the changing relationship of these two structures.

The history of women's movements in America (see Chapter 2) makes it clear that class differences among women have long been both pronounced and politically significant. I suggest that this continuing significance of class is taking on a renewed importance. Two decades of "second wave" feminism—in the context of contracting economic opportunities and a rising service economy—have intensified the divergence of women's life experiences, a divergence that economists predict will likely grow.[4] Furthermore, the exacerbation of class difference is now widely attributed to the feminist movement and its uneven distribution of benefits (in that it expanded the female "middle class" while neglecting the "underclass"; e.g., Dionne 1989).

Two notable political expressions of the continuing significance of class and the inability to unite women with universalistic gender-based appeals may be pointed to. Both the Equal Rights Amendment movement and the abortion rights movement have strikingly illustrated that not all women feel they have the same stake in women's reforms. As Luker's analysis of the pro- and antiabortion movements (1984) reveals, and Mansbridge's analysis of the ERA (1986) confirms less directly, much of the difference in worldview that leads women to embrace or reject feminist reforms stems from class differences. Women who feel threatened by reproductive rights and the constitutional guarantee of equality tend to be women

---

4. Economic researchers Noyelle (1987) and Appelbaum (1987) emphasize that outcomes for women are likely to become even more stratified by class, although no less sex-segregated, as the service sector continues to be the predominant location of new jobs and economic growth. (Also see Baran and Teegarden 1987.)

with lower family and personal incomes and less education who are either full-time homemakers or have lower-status paid occupations than those who support the reforms (Luker 1984, 194–195; Mansbridge 1986, 90–117). Furthermore, both sides on the ERA and abortion issues present their claims universalistically as being in the best interests of all women; the result, however, has been the emergence of sharp political antagonism. Although on one level this antagonism reflects the division between homemakers and career women, much of the divergence between traditional and nontraditional women is also due to class differences and differences in the distribution of feminist gains and employment opportunities (Gelb and Palley 1987, 149–157; Luker 1984; Skerry 1978; Skocpol et al. 1986–1987).

Ever since early industrial times some women, typically working-class women, have sought paid employment outside the home. Nonetheless, normative assumptions of "a woman's place" changed little, and a consensus on female domesticity remained in place across social classes despite its restriction in practice to the affluent (Kessler-Harris 1982). But economic changes in the last thirty years, which "pushed" and "pulled" women of all classes into the paid labor force, have led both to the breakdown of the old normative consensus and to the new pejorative stereotype of being "just a housewife."

The ideology of the resurgent feminist movement certainly played a role in changing norms, but as Mansbridge (1986, 105) points out, the decline in the status of homemaking was *not* caused by feminist attacks. Rather, feminism has brought increased opportunities for some women, with greater chances for middle-class women in particular to enter high-status employment; and increased workplace opportunities tend to lessen women's exclusive identification with the domestic sphere (Gerson 1985). Thus, the traditional class basis behind the ideal of women's full-time homemaking has changed, and its status has consequently dropped. Whereas formerly domesticity was associated with affluence, the new affluent ideal of the dressed-for-success woman who "has it all" (rather than abandons family life) implicitly denigrates the full-time homemaker. The homemaker is now a role associated with working-class traditionalism and as an occupation is perhaps most desirable to those women with less workplace opportunity (Gerson 1985).

The growth of the postindustrial, service-based economy contributes to the renewed significance of class differences among women in several additional ways. Because economic resources determine the extent to which families can purchase services that free women from domesticity, the class divergence in women's experiences, even among employed women, is intensified. Such services, which replace women's work in cleaning, child care, and food preparation, are certainly not new, but as a result of women's increased labor force participation as well as feminist ideology they are more acceptable than in the past. Furthermore, the increase in women working outside the home itself leads to the increased demand that has made these very low paid, female-typed services such growth industries—ironically creating even more "opportunities" for women's employment. Yet for low-paid women who cannot afford to purchase these services, the often-discussed "double day" has become the new norm. In addition, when fast-food meals and franchise child care are the only affordable alternatives, full-time homemaking may appear very attractive, even if it is not a practical possibility. Nostalgia for traditional domesticity can be strong given a loss in the quality of family life. These are precisely the sentiments, and the audience, to which antifeminist arguments appeal.

Both Mansbridge (1986) and Luker (1984) contend that underlying the vehement opposition to the ERA and legalized abortion is the threatened loss of women's claim on men's earnings and of men's "natural" obligations to their families. This threat expressed by feminist reforms is underscored by class antagonism, as the women who promulgate these reforms appear to be free of economic worries, to "have it all." This sentiment was exemplified by the Contra Costa woman quoted previously who said that women in NOW did not know what it is like to worry about health insurance or supporting one's children. She also expressed the low-paid woman's dilemma in worrying about her family's quality of care, explaining: "I'd really rather work part-time and care for my family in a better way. It's really not healthy, having to go so fast, and using Pampers and eating take-out food."[5]

5. A similar statement of the significance of class differences among women is suggested by Ferree (1985). She has pointed out that it is incorrect to posit a simple dichotomy in which middle-class women *want* to work, while others, of the working class, *must*, for even the most degraded of paying jobs offers some satisfaction, if only the social ties with co-workers. Ferree maintains that working-

nothing

It may be quite important that comparable worth has not, to date, led to a grass-roots, antifeminist backlash movement of the type induced by the ERA or legalized abortion. In fact, this is not for lack of effort on the part of conservative leaders. Phyllis Schlafly and the Eagle Forum have had a task force on comparable worth, which attempted to paint the issue as an attack on the family, much as the campaign against the ERA did (Schlafly 1984). They argue that comparable worth threatens married men of average education with well-paid blue-collar jobs. According to Schlafly, pay equity will just take money from these men, who will then be unable to support their families[6]—ultimately, in other words, it only hurts working-class women, the wives of such men. The themes sounded are identical to those underlying other backlash movements—namely, the need to maintain women's claim to men's protection and support on the one hand and to stop the erosion of men's duty and obligation to their families on the other.

While sounding the same themes as the anti-ERA and antiabortion movements, the anti–comparable worth rhetoric has not found a receptive audience. I suggest that this is because comparable worth speaks as well, or better, to the interests of working-class women, perhaps even addressing their fears more directly—for women *are* losing their claims, whether natural or not, to men's support. Working-class and even middle-class wives are likely aware that divorce rapidly "turns gender into class."[7] But even among married women, a husband's paycheck is less likely to suffice as traditional union jobs are replaced with nonunionized service-sector employment. Rather than desperately attempting to grasp at

---

class women are deeply ambivalent about working outside the home, as both home and work roles entail particular rewards and costs. Although she suggests (following German feminist theory) that *all* women experience this ambivalence more acutely than men, she contends that middle-class, professional women are relatively better protected from the costs of combining family and paid work than are working-class women.

6. As I suggested in the last chapter, there is a bit of truth in Schlafly's attack. Comparable worth *can* be implemented in ways that cast men's jobs as overpaid and, thus, at risk of being pulled down. However, as I also pointed out, this outcome is not inevitable; other approaches to implementation can be pursued, particularly if it is made clear that *employers* benefit most by arguing that men's jobs are overpaid.

7. I borrow this phrase from Arlie Hochschild (private communication, 1986). Also see Arendell 1986; Weitzman 1985.

an idealized verison of traditional marital rights and obligations, comparable worth acknowledges the changed reality. Forthrightly, the issue admits that men can no longer be relied on to be the sole breadwinners; therefore women, who work just as hard, must be able to earn decent incomes in return for their efforts. As the two case studies here indicate, this acknowledgment appeals to low-paid women, many of whom feel precariously situated. The case studies suggest that, in general, low-paid women do not consider comparable worth antifamily, or an issue for affluent, single-career women; rather, they see it as very much *their* issue. As one woman union activist explained: "My female members are very strong on comparable worth. One told me: 'I'm doing this for my grand-daughters.' It's a crusade—like women gaining the vote. Even some I least expected are strong supporters, some who were not strong union people before. It's the comparable worth issue, they are emphatic on that. Because it's a woman's issue, and it really comes close to your heart."

Of course, I may be wrong about comparable worth's appeal. It may be that no backlash has developed only because under the Reagan and Bush administrations no nationwide success on the scale of the *Roe v. Wade* decision or the initial ERA passage made a large-scale opposition movement necessary. However, sufficient national attention has, I believe, been focused on comparable worth to make my explanation for the lack of a backlash plausible (also see Evans and Nelson 1989, 64).

Just as some labor organizers have noted the importance of gen-der identification to their mobilizing efforts, many in the feminist movement have begun to take note of the continuing significance of class among women and to speak to the distinct concerns of work-ing-class pink- and blue-collar women. As I discussed in Chapters 1 and 2, this shift is both altruistic and pragmatic for these move-ments. Certainly it stems from needs to acquire new constituen-cies, build movement strength, and further individual political careers, but it also represents a new commitment to address subor-dinate women.

In the labor movement this concern is most explicitly advocated by such groups as the Coalition of Labor Union Women and 9 to 5, which work to push gender issues on to the labor agenda (Milkman 1985). As pink-collar women come to make up a larger proportion of the constituency for organized labor, both actual and potential, this activity is beginning to have some effect, though clearly it is not overwhelming. In public-sector unions such as AFSCME and SEIU, where pink-collar workers already make up about half the membership, comparable worth has become a priority issue. Other unions, such as the UAW, have lately tried to organize office workers, dedicating more resources to this effort than in the past (Prial 1987).

Evidence that the continuing significance of class is becoming a feminist concern has also emerged. The *New York Times*, in its coverage of the 1987 NOW convention, noted that some feminists take seriously the reality that "economic and social forces have widened the gap between the concerns of middle-class and poor women" (Chavez 1987). Articles in *Ms.* magazine sound similar themes. Walsh (1987, 70), for example, explains: "One shortcoming of the Women's Movement that even most feminists will acknowledge is its tendency to speak to, and for, mainly white, middle-class women." And Ehrenreich (1987, 166) concurs: "Of all the charges leveled against feminism . . . probably nothing rankles more than the well-worn accusation that it is 'just a middle class movement.' I used to have a half-dozen rebuttals ready at hand. . . . But I have begun to think that it does matter." Both these authors go on to explain that this narrow base is broadening in part because of the action of subordinate women, a primary example of which is the comparable worth movement. In addition, each author finds evidence of a potential for working-class feminism in the emergence of what Walsh (1987, 70) generously terms the women's economic justice "movement." This hybrid label refers to the half-dozen or so small regional and state organizations that developed in response to the feminization of poverty issue, hoping initially to build momentum through the reputed gender gap in voting.[8] These groups include the Women's Economic Agenda Project in California, the Women's Agenda in Pennsylvania, and the Women's Lobbyist Fund of Montana; they held their first national conference in 1987.

Although such groups may have some low-income participants,

8. As with my argument regarding the continuing significance of class, some object to the "feminization of poverty" discourse (see Chapter 2) because the term both minimizes race and class as continuing causes of poverty and treats all women as equally vulnerable (Burnham 1985; Malveaux 1985; Sparr 1984).

for the most part they seem to be led by middle-class activists and are more oriented toward lobbying state legislatures than grass-roots organizing. Nevertheless, the targets of these lobbying efforts are the needs of low-income women: welfare reforms, increased budgets for social programs, comparable worth, and the combating of teen pregnancy. The number of such women's economic justice organizations (or, as Ehrenreich calls them, "low-income women's rights groups") is still very small. But along with the comparable worth movement and the shifting concerns in organized labor and feminist groups, all honor the divergent class and gender position (or gendered class position) of low-paid women. And all indicate the possibly important effects that attention to the continuing significance of class can have for building labor-feminist alliances and promoting a progressive agenda.

Although Ehrenreich (1987) is optimistic that working-class women will form the next wave of feminism, the anti-ERA and antiabortion movements illustrate that class-based divisions among women can also fuel reactionary movements. These issues, however, were articulated in ways that overlooked the separate interests and experiences of working-class women. Comparable worth provides one indication that if low-paid women's distinct interests are addressed and class differences not ignored, gender and class issues might be linked in a progressive manner.

An Ironic Consequence

Although comparable worth expresses the continuing significance of class and therefore has radical possibilities, it may have the unintended effect of further accentuating class divisions among women by increasing the sense that some women subsidize the affluence of others, an impression already strengthened by previous feminist gains and the growth of the service economy. Economic research indicates several ways in which comparable worth may actually push some women down while pulling others up.[9]

9. Economists debate the extent to which comparable worth will induce disemployment effects, but all agree it will produce some negative consequences. The issue provokes the ongoing debates over the consequences of market interventions between those favoring neoclassical versus institutional models. Predictably, neoclassical economists, who favor an unimpeded labor market, predict

By forcing employers to raise wage levels, comparable worth creates incentives to cut labor costs; in so doing, it may unwittingly promote already-existing threats to women's employment. First, employers might turn to increased subcontracting of work and use of part-time and temporary workers in order to substitute workers whose positions are excluded from comparable worth settlements. This practice is already common where companies wish to reduce

---

larger disemployment effects. Institutional economists and those utilizing segmented labor market approaches predict smaller effects, contending that the rigidities of sex-segregated labor markets, and the sectoral differences in oligopolistic industries and public employment, function to protect women somewhat (summarized in Evans and Nelson 1989, 53).

Many refer to the Australian case, a large national experiment with pay equity in which miminum wage levels are established by federal and state tribunals. Since 1972 these minimums have been set equivalently for male and female occupations, and the female-to-male wage ratio has increased from .61 to .77 (Gregory and Duncan 1981, 409). Considering the magnitude of this increase, some view any negative results for female employment as trivial (e.g., Gregory and Duncan 1981). Others, however, argue that while women's employment was increasing in the period studied, pay equity reduced the rate of growth and raised the level of unemployment relative to what they would have been (Killingsworth 1985; also see Aldrich and Buchele 1986, 160). In addition, research shows that while comparable worth did not directly reduce the number of women employed, it did reduce the number of hours they worked (McGavin 1983). (Interestingly, the large shift in relative wages did little to reduce occupational sex segregation; Gregory and Duncan 1981, 427).

Although researchers do not concur in their assessment of the Australian experiment, American proponents of comparable worth interpret it in a positive light (Bergmann 1985, 1986; Steinberg 1986). Evidence from this country is limited. In Minnesota, the National Committee on Pay Equity (1985b) notes that since initial wage adjustments the number of female employees has increased 6 percent. But Evans and Nelson (1989, 54) warn that local officials "do not rule out the possibility of cutting female-dominated jobs or the overall work force" in the future. Others have constructed estimates of effects if pay equity were to be adopted nationwide. One finds that for adjustments between 10 and 20 percent to female-dominated occupations, employment would decline by 1 percent (Aldrich and Buchele 1986); another finds that a 20 percent increase in women's wages in state and local governments would result in a 2–3 percent decline in female employment (Ehrenberg and Smith 1984; but see Sorenson 1987); and finally, another predicts that were comparable worth to be implemented throughout the U.S. private sector, it would lead to a 1.6 percent decline in the GNP, and a 2.5 percent drop in total employment (*New York Times* 1987c).

Taken together these studies illustrate that the economic impact of comparable worth would be much less damaging than the cataclysmic effects conservative opponents often invoke. But at the same time, the possibility of negative consequences cannot be dismissed.

wage bills and avoid union contracts. Even the public sector is now
using large numbers of temporary workers (Deborah Bell 1985),
and temporary agencies are experiencing rapidly increasing demand (Appelbaum 1987). Second, employers might opt for job cuts
and layoffs, thus displacing women workers. In the public sector
this may be a particular hazard, as services can be reorganized or
cut back to eliminate jobs if taxpayers insist. In the private sector,
some types of women's service work can be transferred to cheaper
offshore production (as bank credit processing, for example, has
been transferred to Barbados). Other jobs may be made redundant
by increased use of office automation; new technology becomes a
more attractive investment if labor costs are pushed up.

In the current context of economic retrenchment, subcontracting, underemployment, and unemployment are all likely to continue, with or without comparable worth. Yet to the extent that
comparable worth intensifies these trends, some women will gain
from others' losses. On a strictly practical level, pay equity is likely
to pull some women up closer to middle-income levels; this group
may eventually include a substantial portion of public-sector clerical and "semiprofessional" employees, and some number of those
employed in core or oligopoly firms. Pulling up these women may
mean that others will find only part-time jobs, or jobs with subcontracting, peripheral firms or temporary agencies, while some
will find no employment at all. It may also increase the number
of women working in low-paid domestic labor for higher-wage
women, as day care providers, babysitters, housecleaners, and so
forth. For feminists this would be a most ironic outcome.

Some observers dismiss comparable worth as having little political significance if it remains confined—as it largely has been so
far—to public-sector employment.[10] But ultimately comparable

10. Comparable worth has been successful primarily for public-sector workers
for several reasons. First, pink-collar workers are more highly unionized in the
state sector owing to the more protected environment for labor there (Deborah
Bell 1985). Second, the public sector is not subject to the market-based constraints that face the private sector; instead it depends on the health of the economy in general and on the direct political negotiation of budgets. Finally, more
specifically, information on wages and job classifications, a matter of public record
in the state sector, is often unavilable in private firms, so the right to knowledge of
the wage distribution would have to be established before raising pay equity con-

worth, like affirmative action, will make a larger contribution on the level of political discourse than on the immediately practical level. Just as affirmative action, with all its limitations, laid the basis for more far-reaching demands by legitimating women's gender-based claims, so comparable worth can contribute to change by providing a vocabulary to address class and gender inequality. Moreover, because the state plays a central institutional role in organizing class power and gender relations, a public-sector movement may actually be better placed to transform political discourse.[11]

In addition to regulating the private labor market, the state functions as a large employer of female labor; as such, its actions provide important validation of comparable worth (as they did for affirmative action), leading to its direct inclusion in formal policy and electoral debates. State action also shapes discourse indirectly, both by providing subordinate groups the space to articulate new claims and by focusing public attention on these issues. Through state sponsorship comparable worth may, like affirmative action, also lead to the emergence of new strategies to address the needs of those to whom it does not directly apply.

Although material benefits can be eroded, the larger contribution of comparable worth to an extended or enlarged discourse of class and gender will be less easily turned back. The moral claims established—that working-class women are entitled to earn decent incomes for their families, to have their jobs reevaluated as equivalent to men's jobs, and to challenge the market when it infringes on these rights—raise new questions of the justice of current work and family arrangements. As Karen Nussbaum, head of the clerical rights organization 9 to 5, has stated, although comparable worth is not a model for women in the private sector, it has an important "demonstration effect" (cited in Milkman 1985, 317). Indeed, many comparable worth activists sense that their efforts are part of a larger effort—one like 9 to 5's linking labor and feminist concerns, an effort necessary to improve the quality of life for working women and their families.

cerns (Kelly and Bayes 1986). While comparable worth has also been a successful strategy at several private universities, conditions there may be closer to the public sector rather than to private industry (e.g., Kautzer 1989).

11. For a similar conclusion about the relation of gender politics and the state, see Piven 1987.

This larger agenda of class and gender includes other gender issues honoring women's distinct familial experience, such as guaranteed maternity/parental leave, public funding for child care, and better enforcement of child support awards; most optimistically, it might come to include renewed job integration efforts, carefully constructed and monitored. It might also be extended to include alliances with working men around such issues as plant-closing protections and full employment legislation. The fact that child support, parental leave, and child care subsidies are now seen as possible areas for state action indicates the potential for women's new moral claims to influence debates of class and gender justice (Noble 1988; Passell 1988; S. Taylor 1988). Also, by uniting women and men around traditional labor concerns and new family issues, an enlarged class and gender agenda may help to reinvigorate the labor movement and renew its public support (Bohlen 1989; Totten, Totten, and Rostan 1988).

Many conservatives have been quick to sense the radical potential inherent in the political and moral claims of comparable worth. For example, one author provides an apt description of what is new in comparable worth as compared to affirmative action, and how this radically extends the feminist agenda:

For comparable worth is more than an intervention in the free market—it is a denial of the *possibility* of a free market. . . . [Comparable worth] represents a major leap from the idea of "affirmative action." The latter restricts itself to the field of ethics. . . . Comparable worth, however, is an argument from metaphysics. . . . The one is a demand for charity; the other, a call for the restructuring of reality. . . . All that women need is the political freedom to demonstrate their value—not the political power to compel recognition (P. Schwartz 1982, 40–41).

As Lee Finney, feminist and labor activist from Contra Costa County, asserted in 1986: "It may not be the issue of the eighties. But it's the issue of the nineties. Comparable worth is here to stay!"

Appendix A

Overview of Women's Position in the Labor Force

TABLE A-1. *Women as a Percentage of the Total Labor Force, 1950–1987*

1950	27.8
1960	32.1
1970	37.2
1980	42.5
1987	44.8

Sources: U.S. Bureau of the Census, cited in Diamond 1984; 1987 figure from U.S. Bureau of the Census 1989, table 642.

TABLE A-2. *Occupational Distribution of Female Labor Force, 1950–1987 (in percentages)*

	1950	1960	1970	1980	1987[a]
Professional	12.2	13.3	15.5	15.9	15.6
Managerial	4.3	3.8	3.6	6.8	12.2
Clerical	27.4	30.9	34.8	33.8	33.0
Sales	8.6	8.3	7.4	7.0	9.1
Crafts	1.5	1.3	1.8	1.8	2.6
Operative	20.0	17.2	14.8	10.7	9.3
Laborer	0.9	0.6	1.0	1.3	1.7
Private Household	8.9	8.4	3.9	3.0	0.9

TABLE A-2. (*continued*)

	1950	1960	1970	1980	1987[a]
Other Services	12.6	14.4	16.3	18.8	15.2
Farm	3.7	1.9	0.8	1.0	0.4

Sources: U.S. Bureau of the Census, cited in Bianchi and Spain 1983, 20; 1987 figures calculated from U.S. Bureau of the Census 1989, table 666.

[a]There are some inconsistencies between 1987 figures and earlier figures. First, some changes were made in the detailed occupations included in each major occupational category (for which I have only very crudely corrected). Second, 1987 data are based on Current Population Surveys, which display greater sampling variability than census data. I include 1987 only for purposes of rough comparison.

TABLE A-3. *Women's Share of Selected Professional Degrees,*
1956–1987 (percentage of total degrees to women)

	1956	1967	1971–1972	1978–1979	1986–1987
Law	5.0		7.3	28.5	32
Medicine	3.5		9.2	23.0	32
MBA		2			33

Sources: U.S. Department of Labor, Women's Bureau, 1983, Bulletin 298, table IV-16; 1956 figures from U.S. Bureau of Census, cited in Diamond 1984; 1986 figures for law and medicine cited in Greer 1986; MBA figures from Center for Education Statistics, U.S. Education Department, cited in *Business Week* 1987.

TABLE A-4. *Women as a Percentage of the Total in Law and Medical*
Professions, 1972–1985

	1972	1981	1985
Law	4.0	14.2	18.1
Medicine	10.1	13.7	17.2

Sources: U.S. Department of Labor, Women's Bureau, 1983 Bulletin 298, table II-4; 1985 figures cited in Greer 1986.

TABLE A-5. *Median Income of Year-round, Full-Time Nonfarm Workers, 1960–1987 (ratio of female to male)*

	1960	1970	1980	1987
Professional	.64	.67	.66	.68
Managerial	.58	.56	.55	.59
Clerical	.68	.64	.60	.68
Sales	.49	.43	.42	.51
Crafts	—	.55	.63	.70
Operative	.60	.59	.60	.63

Sources: U.S. Bureau of the Census, cited in Bianchi and Spain 1983, 23; 1987 figures from Bureau of Labor Statistics 1989, table 54.

TABLE A-6. *1987 Median Earnings of Year-round, Full-Time Workers, by Sex and Race*

	Women (in dollars)	Men (in dollars)	Ratio
White	17,034	26,677	.64
Black	16,002	19,014	.60[a]
Hispanic	14,569	17,487	.55[a]
All races	16,909	26,008	.65[a]

Source: NCPE 1989a, 6.
[a] As a proportion of white male earnings.

TABLE A-7. *1984 Median Earnings of Year-round, Full-Time Workers, by Sex and Education (in dollars)*

	Women	Men
Fewer than 8 years	9,828	14,624
1–3 years high school	11,843	19,120
High school graduate	14,569	23,269
1–3 years college	17,007	25,831
College graduate	20,257	31,487
1+ years postgraduate training	25,076	36,836

Source: U.S. Bureau of the Census, cited in *New York Times* 1987b.

TABLE A-8.   *1987 Ratio of Earnings of Year-round, Full-Time Workers, by Sex, Education, and Race*

	Male	Female
High school graduate		
White	1	.64
Black	.7	.63
Hispanic	.77	.61
College graduate		
White	1	.72
Black	.84	.66
Hispanic	.84	.70

Source: NCPE 1989b, 10.

TABLE A-9.   *1983 Extremes of Income Distribution, by Sex (in percentages)*

	Men	Women
$10,000 or less per year	36	66
$25,000 or more per year	26	5

Source: U.S. Bureau of the Census, cited in National Organization for Women 1985.

Appendix B

San Jose Interview
and Documentary Material

Interviews

Thirty in-depth interviews were conducted for the San Jose case study during 1984 and 1985. These were distributed as follows:

1. City Management: 3

The (former) assistant city manager, the affirmative action officer, and the employee relations representative (who was also a past president of the San Jose chapter of NOW).

2. Female Professions: 7

Four librarians, including one man and three women; three women recreation professionals (including one who left after the strike to work for AFSCME). Within this group, one librarian served as the president of AFSCME Local 101; the second had served as MEF president; the third had participated on the negotiating committee; and both the fourth librarian and one of the recreation professionals had served on the job evaluation committee.

3. Clerical: 12

This all-female group includes two women who had worked for many years as city clericals but recently had won promotions to professional positions in accounting. It also includes two women in staff analyst positions, the first step above a clerical rank in the city system but still represented by the union. One of these women had been a clerical. The other, a long-time city employee at a professional level and former women's coordinator, took this position after having children; although a demotion, it was the best job available on a part-time basis.

4. Engineering Technicians: 6

Three women and three men. Of the women, two had worked as city

clericals, one briefly, the other for many years. The third woman had
been a city librarian.

5. Union Staff: 2
One man and one woman, former and present bargaining agents with
AFSCME Local 101.

This sample was generated by a snowball sampling method. I began by
calling the local AFSCME office, where I obtained the names of the three
women librarians, all leaders in the effort for comparable worth. I then
asked these and all other respondents whom else I should talk with in
order to understand the comparable worth compaign in the city. I spent
approximately one to two hours interviewing each respondent, usually
meeting them on their lunch hour or after work. I followed a loosely struc-
tured interview schedule, typically spending about half the time inves-
tigating their job history and job experiences, educational background, and
work aspirations, and the other half discussing their feelings about and involvement with comparable worth, the union, affirmative action, and
feminist or other groups. In addition, I attended two conferences of local
pay equity activists, for whom the San Jose case figured prominently, as a
participant observer: the Comparable Worth Project Leadership Training
Conference, held at Laney College, Oakland, California, on April 12,
1986; and a conference entitled "Comparable Worth in California, Dilemmas of Policy and Implementation," held at the University of California,
Berkeley, on May 2, 1986.

Finally, I recontacted three key respondents during the revision process in 1988 and 1989. I circulated a draft chapter, solicited their comments, and spoke to two on the phone about their continuing work for
comparable worth.

Documentary Materials

The primary qualitative information was supplemented by documentary
and archival materials, including extensive newspaper and magazine coverage, as well as by published and unpublished reports and accounts of
this case, detailed in the following references.

Signed Articles

Achenbach, Joel. 1981. "Union's Negotiator: Callahan Stays in Control
    While Operating at a Breakneck Pace." *San Jose Mercury News*,
    July 8, 1B.
Acuna, Armando. 1978. "Bias in Hiring Women, Hispanics, Threatens
    S.J. Revenue Sharing." *San Jose Mercury News*, November 21, 2B.

———. 1980. "San Jose Declares Impasse in Labor Negotiations. *San Jose Mercury News*, July 26, 7B.

Acuna, Armando, and Bill Romano. 1980. "San Jose Continues Talks with Unions." *San Jose Mercury News*, July 12, 1B.

Beyette, Beverly. 1981. "Dispute in San Jose: Equal Pay for Comparable Worth—Study of Salary Inequities Fuels City Strike." *Los Angeles Times*, July 13, V1.

Blum, Linda M. 1983. "Politics and Policy-Making: The Comparable Worth Debate." *Berkeley Journal of Sociology* 28: 39–67.

Calvert, Cathie. 1981. "International Lends Strike Support." *San Jose News*, July 9, 1B.

Farnquist, R. L., D. R. Armstrong, and R. P. Strausbaugh. 1983. "Pandora's Worth: The San Jose Experience." *Public Personnel Management* 12, no. 4: 358–368.

Fischer, Russell G. 1981. "Pay Equity and the San Jose Strike: An Interview with Patt Curia." *Library Journal*, November 1, 2079–2085.

Flammang, Janet A. 1985. "Female Officials in the Feminist Capital: The Case of Santa Clara County." *Western Political Quarterly* 38, no. 1: 94–117.

———. 1986. "Effective Implementation: The Case of Comparable Worth in San Jose." *Policy Studies Review* 5, no. 4: 815–837.

———. 1987. "Women Made a Difference: Comparable Worth in San Jose." In *The Women's Movements of the United States and Western Europe*, edited by M. F. Katzenstein and C. M. Mueller. Philadelphia: Temple University Press.

Goligoski, Bob. 1981. "Eye on the City: A Day with the 'Generals' on Both Sides of Strike." *San Jose News*, July 7, 1B.

Gruber, Stephen. 1977. "Women Demand City Job Parity." *San Jose Mercury News*, April 8, 1B.

Hay Group. 1982. *The Hay Guide Chart-Profile Method of Job Evaluation*. San Francisco: Hay Group.

Heinsen, Arthur, Jr. 1981. "San Jose Can Set an Example for the Nation" (letter to the editor). *San Jose News*, July 14, 6B.

Herhold, Scott. 1981. "S.J. Workers Walk off Jobs in Pay Protest." *San Jose Mercury News*, March 28, 1B.

Howard, Robert. 1982. "The Way in San Jose." *Working Papers* 9, no. 1: 34.

Johnston, David. 1981. "Will They Lead the Way in San Jose?" *Working Women*, November, 163–165.

Keppel, Bruce. 1981. "San Jose on New Ground in Women's Wage Debate." *Los Angeles Times*, June 30, 1.

McGuire, Mike. 1982. "A New Way to Equal Pay: Women Win in San Jose." *Dollars and Sense* 76 (April): 12–17.

McMillian, Penelope. 1981. "Council Rejects San Jose City Strike Accord." *Los Angeles Times*, July 13, 3.

Miller, Darla. 1981. "On the Way to Equitable Pay." *San Jose News*, July 15, 1C.

Mueller, Carol. 1985. "Comparable Worth in Santa Clara County." *Radcliffe Quarterly*, March, 14–15.

Pifarre, Juan (Assistant City Manager, Human Relations, City of San Jose). 1984. "Affirmative Action Plan." December 6.

———. 1985. "City of San Jose Memorandum: Affirmative Action Progress Report, June 1980 to July 1985." October 9.

Rannells, Jackson. 1981a. "The New Equal Pay Concept Behind the Strike in San Jose." *San Francisco Chronicle*, July 9, 6.

———. 1981b. "San Jose Strike Talks Set Today." *San Francisco Chronicle*, July 10, 7.

Silva, Barbara. 1981. "Supply and Demand at Work" (letter to the editor). *San Jose Mercury News*, July 20, 6B.

Swan, Gary E. 1981a. "The Report That Started S.J. Strike." *San Jose Mercury News*, July 7, 1A.

———. 1981b. "Change in City's Offer May Get Sides Talking Again— City Softens Stand, Talks May Resume." *San Jose Mercury News*, July 9, 1A.

Sweeney, Frank, and Phillip J. Trounstine. 1981. "Council, Union Bargainers Reach Tentative Agreement." *San Jose Mercury News*, July 14, 1A.

Tong, David. 1981. "San Jose Mayor, Union Chief, to Address Issues on TV." *Oakland Tribune*, July 7, A7.

Trounstine, Phillip J. 1981a. "San Jose, Union to Resume Negotiations on Pay Parity." *San Jose News*, May 6, 1B.

———. 1981b. "City's Equal Pay Talks Falter." *San Jose News*, July 3, 1B.

———. 1981c. "Both Sides Claim Victory in Strike." *San Jose Mercury News*, July 7, 1A.

———. 1981d. "City Strike: Talks, but No Yielding." *San Jose Mercury News*, July 10, 1B.

———. 1981e. "Strike Over: City Workers Accept Pact; $1.45 Million Pledged to Attain Pay Equity for Women." *San Jose News*, July 14, 1A.

———. 1981f. "Eye on City Hall." *San Jose Mercury News*, July 20, 1B.

Trounstine, Phillip J., and Cathie Calvert. 1981. "Talks Resume After S.J. Council Rejects Pact." *San Jose News*, July 13, 1B.

Trounstine, Phillip J., and Gary E. Swan. 1981. "Behind the Explosive Hay Report." *San Jose News*, July 8, 1B.

Van Beers, Lois B. 1981. "The Effects of Implementing Comparable Worth Pay Criteria in the City of San Jose." Master's thesis, Graduate School of Public Policy, University of California, Berkeley.

Miscellaneous Newspaper and Magazine Articles

Comparable Worth Project Newsletter. 1981. "San Jose Strike Gains." 1, no. 4: 2.

Labor Notes. 1981a. "San Jose City Workers Vote Strike for 'Comparable Worth.'" April 28, 7.

————. 1981b. "San Jose City Workers Win Strike for 'Comparable Worth.'" July 28, 5.

Los Angeles Times. 7/6/81. "City Workers in San Jose Strike." 1.

Ms. 1982. "Pay Equity: The Job Issue of the Eighties." February, 162–165.

New York Times. 7/6/81. "San Jose Employees Strike over Equal Pay for Women." 1.

Newsweek. 1981. "Women's Issue of the '80's." June 22, 58–59.

Oakland Tribune. 7/7/81. "Pandora's Box in San Jose" (editorial). A8.

San Francisco Chronicle. 7/9/81a. "Bay Area Pay Patterns." 7.

————. 7/9/81b. "Striking Workers Hamper San Jose Airport Buses." 9.

————. 7/14/81. "San Jose Delays Firing of Striking City Workers; Deadline Passes—Talks Go On." 17.

San Jose Mercury News. 1/21/74. "Rights Panel Says City Snubs Minorities for Top Positions." 4A.

————. 9/26/74. "NOW Chapter Files Sex Bias Suit Against Philco-Ford Co." 1A.

————. 10/27/74. "NOW Convention Draws 800." 1A.

————. 2/13/76. "Minority Job Plan Lagging." 1A.

————. 12/22/76. "S.J. Minority Hiring Plan Works—With a Few Buts." 1B.

————. 8/2/80. "City Employee Union Sets a Settlement Deadline." 4B.

————. 7/8/81. "What Women's Work Is Worth" (editorial). 8B.

————. 7/17/81. "Comparable Worth—Finding a Middle Ground" (editorial). 10B.

San Jose News. 8/1/80. "Largest City Worker Union Sets Negotiations Deadline." 4F.

————. 9/25/81. "Comparable Pay Bill Is Signed." 3F.

Time. 1981. "Upping the Ante: Over Equal Pay in San Jose." July 20, 28.

Appendix C

Contra Costa County Interview and Documentary Material

Interviews

Thirty in-depth interviews were conducted for the Contra Costa County case study in 1985. These were distributed as follows:

1. County Management: 7

Four top county officials: the male director of personnel, and the female affirmative action officer, director of nursing, and chief of special operations for social services (these three women were also management members of the Comparable Worth Task Force); also, three female managers from middle and lower managerial ranks, who bargain with and supervise many low-paid women in both health and social service departments.

2. Female Professions: 8

Four nurses, all women, and four employees in the social work group, including one male. Of the latter, two were considered eligibility workers, and one woman (a former clerical activist) had progressed to eligibility work supervisor.

3. Clerical: 12

Eleven women and one man, all in clerical positions with the exception of one woman who had recently been promoted to office manager after some thirty years as a clerk.

4. Engineering Technician: 1

I interviewed one member of this small group of forty. This woman, formerly in a female profession, had served as president of AFSCME Local 512 (which represents the techs and some forty-five eligibility work supervisors) when the first comparable worth contract was negotiated.

5. Union Staff: 2
One man and one woman, the former and current (1985–1986) bargaining agents for AFSCME Locals 2700 and 512.

This sample was also generated by a snowball sampling method. As in San Jose, I began by calling the local AFSCME office, which provided the name of the current bargaining agent, who in turn referred me to others involved in the comparable worth effort. Other details are similar to those recounted in Appendix B.

Finally, I recontacted two key respondents during the revision process in 1988 and 1989. I circulated a draft chapter, solicited comments, and received updates on events in the county through December 1989.

Documentary Materials

As in the San Jose case study, I supplemented interview data with documentary and archival materials, including extensive local press coverage and county documents.

Signed Articles

Bachman, Marcy. 1981. "San Jose Strike." *Contra Costa Times*, July 8, 3B.
Berkeley Policy Notes. 1986. "Comparable Worth in California: Dilemmas of Policy and Implementation." Conference Report 2, no. 2 (Fall). University of California, Berkeley, Graduate School of Public Policy.
Borenstein, Daniel. 1985. "Workers 'Mourn' for Pay Equity Study." *Contra Costa Times*, October 30, 3A.
———. 1986a. "Coalition's Equal Pay Fight Ends in Defeat." *Contra Costa Times*, February 6, 1A.
———. 1986b. "CC Endorses Wage Parity: Talks with Nurses Will Prove Intent, Union Leaders Say." *Contra Costa Times*, April 14, 3A.
Cisterman, Harry (Director of Personnel, Contra Costa County). 1983. "Report of Information Relevant to Comparable Worth." May.
City of San Jose. 1985. "Sixty-ninth Annual Financial Report" (for year ending June 30).
Cohen, Barbara. 1983. "Women County Workers Picket over Alleged Pay Inequities." *Contra Costa Times*, December 2, 3A.
Contra Costa County. 1981–1982, 1982–1983, 1983–1984. Comprehensive Annual Financial Reports.
———. 1984. "Affirmative Action Program, Annual Report" (presented to the Board of Supervisors).

————. 1985a. "Comparable Worth Task Force Report, Benchmark Sub-committee. Labor Report."

————. 1985b. "Comparable Worth Task Force Report, Benchmark Sub-committee. Management Report."

————. 1987. "Memorandum of Understanding Between SEIU Local 535 and Contra Costa County, 1987–1989." November.

Croskey et al. v. County of Contra Costa (C-73-0906); *Burt et al. v. County of Contra Costa* (C-73-1967). Consent Decree of U.S. District Court, Northern California. October 14, 1975.

Diringer, Elliot. 1984. "Sunne Wright McPeak: Bright, Hard-working, Charismatic; But Some Say She's Out for Herself." *California Journal* 15, no. 10: 386–387.

Feder, Shirley Sloan. 1979. "Successful Working Women Tell How They Got There." *Contra Costa Times* (Sunday Magazine), January 21, 24.

Finney, Lee. 1983. "Closing the Wage Gap in Contra Costa County: Strategies for Action." Report of the Comparable Worth Coalition, September 20.

————. 1987. "Progress Report: Closing the Wage Gap in Contra Costa County, 1983–1987."

Ghent, Janet. 1978. "'The Militant Period Has Passed' Says Editor: Working Women Need a Game Plan." *Contra Costa Times*, September 23, 23.

Grossman, Ellie. 1978. "Women Succeed in Sales." *Contra Costa Times*, November 29, 31.

Hartson, Merrill. 1981. "Equal Pay Drive Strengthened by S.J. Victory." *Contra Costa Times*, July 26, 1A.

Herscher, Elaine. 1984. "CC Reports Fewer Working Women, Bigger Families, ABAG [Association of Bay Area Governments] Says." *Contra Costa Times*, October 19, 1B.

Hollis, John R. 1972a. "Public Hearing on County Pay Today: Major Employee Unions Unhappy over Proposals." *Martinez Morning News-Gazette*, June 21, 1.

————. 1972b. "Supervisors to Meet Under Strike Threat." *Martinez Morning News-Gazette*, June 24, 5.

————. 1972c. "Supervisors Adopt Hard Line on Strike: Acting Chairman Declares Board Decision Final; Clerical Employees Turn out to Picket Most County Offices." *Martinez Morning News-Gazette*, June 28, 1.

————. 1972d. "Public Urged to Put Heat on Strikers: Supervisors to Hold Special Meeting Today." *Martinez Morning News-Gazette*, June 29, 1.

———. 1972e. "County Strike: No Settlement Yet in Sight." *Martinez Morning News-Gazette*, July 12, 1.

———. 1972f. "Injunction Use Voted in Strike." *Martinez Morning News-Gazette*, July 13, 1.

Keeble, Pat. 1972a. "Strikers Pinpoint Problems." *Contra Costa Times*, June 29, 1.

———. 1972b. "Strike Talks Begin: Meeting Relations Key Issue." *Contra Costa Times*, July 2, 1.

———. 1972c. "County Services Ebb; Strikers Seek Mediator." *Contra Costa Times*, July 6, 1.

———. 1972d. "Angry CC Strikers Halt Food Stops at Hospital." *Contra Costa Times*, July 13, 1.

Kidder, Lynn. 1985. "County Workers Rally for Pay Equity." *Contra Costa Times*, July 24, 3A.

Malaspina, Rick. 1984. "Lowering the Boom on Boom Town: Walnut Creek Aches with Growing Pains." *San Francisco Examiner*, September 30, B1.

Newbergh, Carolyn. 1984a. "Panelists See Job Bonanza for Many Women in County: SR [San Ramon] Mayor Suggests 'Equal Pay for Equal Work' Push." *Contra Costa Times*, April 27, 3A.

———. 1984b. "Equal Pay: Comparable Worth Study for Concord." *Contra Costa Times*, September 13, 1A.

———. 1984c. "Concord Promises to Study Gender Pay Bias." *Contra Costa Times*, September 22, 3A.

———. 1984d. "Comparable Worth Implications Weighed: Officials Warned That Sex Bias Studies Could Lead to Lawsuits." *Contra Costa Times*, September 26, 3A.

———. 1985a. "PGE Re-Evaluation of Concord Move Is No Shock to Officials" and "The Exodus: A Who's Who." *Oakland Tribune*, July 24, B2.

———. 1985b. "Concord Comparable Worth Pay Move Gains Mostly Favorable Reaction." *Oakland Tribune*, August 2, A1.

Rego, Nilda. 1979. "County Employment—Report: Few Women, Minorities, in County Hierarchy." *Contra Costa Times*, July 3, 6.

———. 1981. "Report Criticizes CC Hiring of Women, Handicapped." *Contra Costa Times*, January 28, 1A.

———. 1982. "Comparable Worth Issue Gets Union Push." *Contra Costa Times*, December 13, 3A.

———. 1983. "Board Says New Study Superfluous." *Contra Costa Times*, March 16, 7A.

———. 1984a. "Union Women Threaten County's Deficit Plan." *Contra Costa Times*, March 28, 1A.

———. 1984b. "Union Fight Could Cut 1,850 Jobs in County." *Contra Costa Times*, March 31, 1A.

———. 1984c. "CC Nurses Comparable Worth Pact May Be Among First in Nation." *Contra Costa Times*, April 13, 2A.

Ronningen, Judy. 1985. "Study Advises Pay Changes in Concord." *Contra Costa Times*, May 22, 1E.

Security Pacific National Bank. 1983. *Monthly Summary: Northern Coastal Counties of California* 15, no. 3 (March).

Sestanovich, Molly. 1979. "The League Speaks: Women's Tough Search for Employment." *Contra Costa Times*, June 15, 20.

Vogt, Rick. 1972a. "CC Employees' Talks at Impasse." *Contra Costa Times*, June 22, 1.

———. 1972b. "Women Cite Principles, Not Money, in Continuing County Clerks' Strike." *Contra Costa Times*, July 14, 1.

———. 1972c. "CC Board Action Expected Today on Strike Negotiators' Package." *Contra Costa Times*, July 19, 1.

———. 1972d. "County Employees Plan Return to Work as Accord Reached." *Contra Costa Times*, July 22, 1.

———. 1978. "Women in Accounting." *Contra Costa Times*, November 1, 47.

Witt, Matt. 1978. "Women Seek Better Futures in Mines." *Contra Costa Times*, December 21, 21.

Miscellaneous Newspaper Articles

Contra Costa Times, 6/20/72. "CCC Clerical Employees Ponder Strike over Wage, Benefit Offer." 1.

———. 6/25/72. "County Employees Talk Strike Awaiting Union Results." 1.

———. 6/28/72. "County Workers Strike over Pay." 1.

———. 6/29/72. "County Strike Spreads: Clerks Double Salary Demand over 3.4% Grant." 1.

———. 7/4/72. "CC, Strikers, Plan New Negotiations." 1.

———. 7/11/72. "Strike Continues: 'Bricks' Aid Start 3rd Week." 1.

———. 7/20/72. "Friday Deadline Set by CCC Board on Final Wage Plan." 1.

———. 7/21/72. "Labor-County Maneuver for Progress: Strike Talks Fail." 1.

———. 9/6/80. "County Jobs Give Less to Minorities, Women." 3A.

———. 7/9/81. "Strike Is Beside the Main Point" (editorial). 14A.

———. 8/20/81. "Prejudice Against Women Remains" (editorial). 14A.

———. 11/5/81. "Comparable Worth Gets Cool Reception." 7B.

———. 11/18/81. "CC Meets Minority Job Goals." 4A.

———. 9/1/82. "Supervisors to Insist on Equal Pay for Equal Work." 1A.

———. 12/16/82. "Comparable Worth—County Can Take Next Step Toward Equality" (editorial). 16A.

———. 1/27/84. "McPeak: Equity Fund for Women." 12B.

———. 6/14/84. "'Comparable Worth Is a Job and a Women's Issue.'" 6A.

———. 11/17/84. "Comparable Pay Ridiculed by Civil Rights Chairman." 2A.

———. 5/21/85. "Comparable Worth Advice: 'Go Easy.'" 1B.

———. 11/21/85. "Common Sense on 'Comparable Worth'" (editorial). 22A.

Los Angeles Times. 6/28/72. Note in "News Summary, State." 2.

———. 7/23/72. Note in "News Summary, State." A2.

———. 7/24/72. "Contra Costa County Strike Ends." 3.

Martinez Morning News-Gazette. 6/20/72. "CC Clerical Employees Vote Strike: County, Union, Still Continue Negotiations." 1.

———. 7/1/72. "Special Committee to Tackle Strike; Walkout Widens: 1,500 Employees on Picket Lines." 1.

———. 7/6/72. "Mediation of Strike Inches Near." 2.

———. 7/7/72. "State Conciliator to Tackle Dispute: Take Steps to Settle 11-Day County Strike." 1.

———. 7/19/72. "CCC Management's Offer before Strikers—Walkout May Not End; Unions Express Dismay." 1.

———. 7/20/72. "County Gets Court to Restrain Strikers." 1.

———. 7/22/72. "County Strike Ends as Workers Accept." 1.

———. 8/10/72. "To Probe CCC Hiring Policies: 2 Organizations Charge Discriminatory Practices." 1.

San Francisco Chronicle. 6/28/72. "A Strike by Clerical Workers." 21.

———. 7/19/72. "Contra Costa Workers Reject Pact." 2.

———. 7/22/72. "Tentative Pact OK in East Bay Strike." 3.

San Francisco Examiner. 6/29/72. "Contra Costa Unions May Join Strike." 11.

Bibliography

For references specific to the San Jose and Contra Costa County cases, see Appendices B and C, respectively.

Acker, Joan. 1987. "Sex Bias in Job Evaluation: A Comparable Worth Issue." In *Ingredients for Women's Employment Policy*, edited by C. Bose and G. Spitze. Albany: SUNY Press.

——. 1988. "Class, Gender, and the Relations of Distribution." *Signs* 13, no. 3: 473–497.

——. 1989. *Doing Comparable Worth: Gender, Class, and Pay Equity.* Philadelphia: Temple University Press.

AFSCME (American Federation of State, County, and Municipal Employees). 1983. "Breaking the Pattern of Injustice: AFSCME's Blueprint for Pay Equity." Washington, D.C., April.

Alcoff, Linda. 1988. "Cultural Feminism vs. Post-Structuralism: The Identity Crisis in Feminist Theory." *Signs* 13, no. 3: 405–436.

Aldrich, Mark, and Robert Buchele. 1986. *The Economics of Comparable Worth.* Cambridge, Mass.: Ballinger.

Alstott, Anne L. 1986. "Comparable Worth Is Unfair to Women." *New York Times*, May 24, 17.

Amott, Teresa, and Julie Matthaei. 1984. "Comparable Worth, Incomparable Pay: The Issue at Yale." *Radical America* 18, no. 5: 21–28.

——. 1988. "The Promise of Comparable Worth." *Socialist Review* 18, no. 2: 101–117.

Appelbaum, Eileen. 1987. "Restructuring Work: Temporary, Part-Time, and At-Home Employment." In *Computer Chips and Paper Clips: Technology and Women's Employment*, vol. 2, edited by H. I. Hartmann. Washington, D.C.: National Academy Press.

Arendell, Teresa. 1986. *Women and Divorce.* Berkeley and Los Angeles: University of California Press.

Aronowitz, Stanley. 1973. *False Promises*. New York: McGraw-Hill.

Attewell, Paul, and James Rule. 1987. "Computers and Post-industrial Society." Colloquium presentation at the Department of Sociology, New York University, April 10.

Baden, Naomi. 1986. "Developing An Agenda: Expanding the Role of Women in Unions." *Labor Studies Journal* 10, no. 3: 229–249.

Balser, Diane. 1987. *Sisterhood and Solidarity: Feminism and Labor in Modern Times*. Boston: South End Press.

Baran, Barbara. 1987. "The Technological Transformation of White-Collar Work: A Case Study of the Insurance Industry." In *Computer Chips and Paper Clips: Technology and Women's Employment*, vol. 2, edited by H. I. Hartmann. Washington, D.C.: National Academy Press.

Baran, Barbara, and Suzanne Teegarden. 1987. "Women's Labor in the Office of the Future: A Case Study of the Insurance Industry." In *Women, Households, and the Economy*, edited by L. Beneria and C. Stimpson. New Brunswick, N.J.: Rutgers University Press.

Bassnett, Susan. 1986. *Feminist Experiences*. London: Allen & Unwin.

Becalli, Bianca. 1984. "Italy: Working-Class Militancy, Feminism, and Trade Union Politics." *Radical America* 18, no. 5: 39–51.

Belkin, Lisa. 1989. "Bars to Equality of Sexes Seen as Eroding, Slowly." (First in the series "Women's Lives: A Scorecard of Change.") *New York Times*, August 20, 1.

Bell, Daniel. 1973. *The Coming of Post-industrial Society*. New York: Basic Books.

———. 1976. *The Cultural Contradictions of Capitalism*. New York: Basic Books.

Bell, Deborah E. 1985. "Unionized Women in State and Local Government." In *Women, Work, and Protest: A Century of U.S. Women's Labor History*, edited by R. Milkman. Boston: Routledge & Kegan Paul.

Beller, Andrea. 1984. "Trends in Occupational Segregation by Sex and Race, 1960–1981." In *Sex Segregation in the Workplace: Trends, Explanations, Remedies*, edited by B. F. Reskin. Washington, D.C.: National Academy Press.

Benokraitis, Nijole V., and Joe R. Feagin. 1978. *Affirmative Action and Equal Opportunity: Action, Inaction, Reaction*. Boulder, Colo.: Westview Press.

Benson, Susan Porter. 1978. "'The Clerking Sisterhood': Rationalization and the Work Culture of Saleswomen in American Department Stores, 1890–1960." *Radical America* 12, no. 2: 41–55.

Benston, Margaret. 1969. "The Political Economy of Women's Liberation." *Monthly Review* 21: 13–27.

Berg, Barbara. 1987. "The Guilt that Drives Working Mothers Crazy." *Ms.*, May, 56–59, 73–74.

Bergmann, Barbara R. 1985. "The Economic Case for Comparable Worth." In *Comparable Worth: New Directions for Research*, edited by H. I. Hartmann. Washington, D.C.: National Academy Press.

———. 1986. *The Economic Emergence of Women*. New York: Basic Books.

———. 1987. "Pay Equity—Surprising Answers to Hard Questions." *Challenge*, May/June 45–51.

Bianchi, Suzanne M., and Daphne Spain. 1983. "American Women: Three Decades of Change." U.S. Bureau of the Census, Special Demographic Analysis, August.

Bielby, William T., and James N. Baron. 1984. "A Woman's Place Is with Other Women: Sex Segregation within Organizations." In *Sex Segregation in the Workplace: Trends, Explanations, Remedies*, edited by B. F. Reskin. Washington, D.C.: National Academy Press.

———. 1986. "Men and Women at Work: Sex Segregation and Statistical Discrimination." *American Journal of Sociology* 91, no. 4: 759–799.

Blau, Francine D., and Wallace E. Hendricks. 1979. "Occupational Segregation by Sex: Trends and Prospects." *Journal of Human Resources* 14, no. 2: 197–210.

Bluestone, Barry, and Bennett Harrison. 1982. *The Deindustrialization of America*. New York: Basic Books.

Blum, Linda M. 1983. "Politics and Policy-Making: The Comparable Worth Debate." *Berkeley Journal of Sociology* 28: 39–67.

———. 1987. "Possibilities and Limits of the Comparable Worth Movement." *Gender & Society* 1, no. 4: 380–399.

———. Forthcoming. "Gender and Class in Comparable Worth." In *Comparable Worth/Equal Value in Britain and the United States*, edited by M. Kahn and E. Meehan. London: Macmillan.

Blum, Linda, and Vicki Smith. 1988. "Women's Mobility in the Corporation: A Critique of the Politics of Optimism." *Signs* 13, no. 3: 528–545.

Bohlen, Celestine. 1989. "Unions Say AT&T Pact Sets New Standard for Family Benefits." *New York Times*, May 30, 14.

Bolch, J. 1980. "How to Manage Stress." *Readers' Digest*, July, 81–85.

Braverman, Harry. 1974. *Labor and Monopoly Capital*. New York: Monthly Review Press.

Brenner, Johanna. 1987. "Feminist Political Discourses: Radical versus Liberal Approaches to the Feminization of Poverty and Comparable Worth." *Gender & Society* 1, no. 4: 447–465.

Brozan, Nadine. 1986. "NOW at 20: Reassessment in a New Era." *New York Times*, December 1, 18.

Bureau of Labor Statistics. 1989. *Handbook of Labor Statistics*, Bulletin 2340. Washington D.C.

Bureau of National Affairs. 1981. "The Comparable Worth Issue: A BNA Special Report." Washington D.C.

Burnham, Linda, 1985. "Has Poverty Been Feminized in Black America?" *Black Scholar*, March/April, 14–24.

Business Week. 1987. "Cover Story: Corporate Women." June 22, 72–78.

———. 1989. "The Mommy Track: Juggling Kids and Careers in Corporate America Takes a Controversial Turn." March 20, 126–134.

Buswell-Robinson, Cheryl, and Pete Kelly. 1982. "Viewpoint: Concessions Undermine Fight for Jobs and Equality." *Labor Notes*, no. 46 (November 23): 12.

Cady, Lois. 1980. "Comparable Worth for Nurses." In *Manual on Pay Equity*, edited by J. Grune. Washington, D.C.: Committee on Pay Equity, Conference on Alternative State and Local Policies.

Cain, Pamela Stone. 1985. "Prospects for Pay Equity in a Changing Economy." In *Comparable Worth: New Directions for Research*, edited by H. I. Hartmann. Washington, D.C.: National Academy Press.

California Comparable Worth Task Force. 1985. *Report to the Legislature*. Sacramento, August.

Cameron, Cindia. 1986. "Noon at 9 to 5: Reflections on a Decade of Organizing." *Labor Research Review* 8 (Spring): 103–109.

Carden, Maren Lockwood. 1974. *The New Feminist Movement*. New York: Russell Sage Foundation.

———. 1978. "The Proliferation of a Social Movement: Ideology and Individual Incentives in the Contemporary Feminist Movement." *Research in Social Movements, Conflict, and Change* 1: 179–196.

Carter, Michael J., and Susan B. Carter. 1981. "Women's Recent Progress in the Professions, or Women Get a Ticket to Ride after the Gravy Train Has Left the Station." *Feminist Studies* 7, no. 3: 477–514.

Cerullo, Margaret, and Roslyn Feldberg. 1984. "Introduction: Women Workers, Feminism, and the Unions." *Radical America* 18, no. 5: 2–5.

Chavez, Lydia. 1987. "Women's Movement, Its Ideals Accepted, Faces Subtler Issues." *New York Times*, July 17, 16.

Chodorow, Nancy. 1978. *The Reproduction of Mothering*. Berkeley and Los Angeles: University of California Press.

Collins, Sheila K. 1988. "Women at the Top of Women's Fields: Social Work, Nursing and Education." In *The Worth of Women's Work: A Qualitative Synthesis*, edited by A. Statham, E. M. Miller, and H. O. Mauksch. Albany: SUNY Press.

Cook, Alice. 1980. "Collective Bargaining as a Strategy for Achieving Equal Opportunity and Equal Pay: Sweden and West Germany." In *Equal Employment Policy for Women*, edited by R. Steinberg-Ratner. Philadelphia: Temple University Press.

———. 1985. *Comparable Worth: A Case Book of Experiences in States and Localities*. Manoa: University of Hawaii, Industrial Relations Center.

———. 1986. *Comparable Worth: A Case Book of Experiences in States and Localities—1986 Supplement*. Manoa: University of Hawaii, Industrial Relations Center.

Corley, Mary, and Hans O. Mauksch. 1988. "Registered Nurses, Gender, and Commitment." In *The Worth of Women's Work: A Qualitative Synthesis*, edited by A. Statham, E. M. Miller, and H. O. Mauksch. Albany: SUNY Press.

Coser, Rose Laub. 1982. "Women in the Occupational World: Social Disruption and Conflict." In *Women and Work: Problems and Perspectives*, edited by R. Kahn-Hut, A. K. Daniels, and R. Colvard. New York: Oxford University Press.

Costain, A. N., and W. D. Costain. 1987. "Strategy and Tactics of the Women's Movement in the United States: The Role of Political Parties." In *The Women's Movements of the United States and Western Europe*, edited by M. F. Katzenstein and C. M. Mueller. Philadelphia: Temple University Press.

Costello, Cynthia B. 1985. "'WEA're Worth It!' Work Culture and Conflict at the Wisconsin Education Association Insurance Trust." *Feminist Studies* 11, no. 3: 497–518.

Cowan, Alison Leigh. 1987. "The Plight of Female Miners." *New York Times*, August 10, IV, 3.

———. 1989. "Poll Finds Women's Gains Have Taken Personal Toll." (Second in the series "Women's Lives: A Scorecard of Change.") *New York Times*, August 21, 1.

Cox, Gail Diane. 1985. "Labor Attorneys Rephrase Terms of Pay Equity Battle." *Los Angeles Daily Journal*, April 30, 1.

Currie, Elliot, Robert Dunn, and David Fogarty. 1980. "The New Immiseration: Stagflation, Inequality, and the Working Class." *Socialist Review* 10, no. 6: 7–31.

Davies, Margery. 1982. *Women's Place Is at the Typewriter: Office Work and Office Workers, 1870–1930*. Philadelphia: Temple University Press.

Deaux, Kay K., and Joseph C. Ullman. 1983. *Women of Steel: Female Blue-Collar Workers in the Basic Steel Industry*. New York: Praeger.

Diamond, S. J. 1984. "Women on the Job: Surge Widely Felt." (First of a ten-part series, "Women's Work.") *Los Angeles Times*, September 9, 1.

di Leonardo, Micaela. 1985. "Women's Work, Work Culture, and Consciousness: An Introduction." *Feminist Studies* 11, no. 3: 491–495.

Dionne, E. J., Jr. 1987. "In a Changed Economy, Labor Tries New Tactics." *New York Times*, October 26, 15.
————. 1989. "Struggle for Work and Family Fueling Women's Movement." (Third and last in the series "Women's Lives: A Scorecard of Change.") *New York Times*, August 22, 1.
Donato, Katherine M. 1986. "Social and Economic Factors Governing the Changing Sex Composition of Systems Analysts." In B. Reskin et al. *Job Queues, Gender Queues: Women's Movement into Male Occupations*. Philadelphia: Temple University Press, 1990.
Edsall, Thomas B. 1984. *The New Politics of Inequality*. New York: Norton.
Edwards, Richard. 1979. *Contested Terrain*. New York: Basic Books.
Ehrenberg, Ronald, and Robert Smith. 1984. "Comparable Worth in the Public Sector." National Bureau of Economic Research, Working Paper no. 1471. Cambridge, Mass., September.
Ehrenreich, Barbara. 1987. "The Next Wave." *Ms.*, July/August, 166–168, 216–218.
Ehrenreich, Barbara, and Karin Stallard. 1982. "The Nouveau Poor." *Ms.*, August, 217–224.
Eisenstein, Zillah R. 1979. "Developing a Theory of Capitalist Patriarchy and Socialist Feminism." In *Capitalist Patriarchy and the Case for Socialist Feminism*, edited by Z. Eisenstein. New York: Monthly Review Press.
————. 1981. *The Radical Future of Liberal Feminism*. New York: Longman.
————. 1988. *The Female Body and the Law*. Berkeley and Los Angeles: University of California Press.
Engleberg, Stephen. 1985. "U.S. Drive to End Job Quotas Meets Broad Opposition." *New York Times*, May 4, 1.
Epstein, Cynthia Fuchs. 1981. *Women in Law*. New York: Basic Books.
Estabrook, Leigh S. 1984. "Women's Work in the Library/Information Sector." In *My Troubles Are Going to Have Trouble with Me*, edited by K. Sacks and D. Remy. New Brunswick, N.J.: Rutgers University Press.
Etzioni, Amitai, ed. 1969. *The Semi-Professions and Their Organization*. New York: Free Press.
Evans, Sara. 1979. *Personal Politics: The Roots of Women's Liberation in the Civil Rights Movement and the New Left*. New York: Knopf.
Evans, Sara M., and Barbara J. Nelson. 1989. *Wage Justice: Comparable Worth and the Paradox of Technocratic Reform*. Chicago: University of Chicago Press.
Feldberg, Roslyn. 1980. "'Union Fever': Organizing among Clerical Workers, 1900–1930." *Radical America* 14, no. 3: 53–67.

———. 1984. "Comparable Worth: Toward Theory and Practice in the United States." *Signs* 10, no. 2: 311–328.

———. 1987a. "Comparable Worth: The Relation of Method and Politics." In *Ingredients for Women's Employment Policy*, edited by C. Bose and G. Spitze. Albany: SUNY Press.

———. 1987b. "Women and Trade Unions: Are We Asking the Right Questions?" In *Hidden Aspects of Women's Work*, edited by C. Bose, R. Feldberg, N. Sokoloff, and Women and Work Research Group. New York: Praeger.

Fergusen, Ann. 1977. "Androgyny as an Ideal for Human Development." In *Feminism and Philosophy*, edited by M. Vetterling-Braggin, F. Elliston, and J. English. Totowa, N.J.: Littlefield, Adam.

Ferree, Myra Marx. 1985. "Between Two Worlds: German Feminist Approaches to Working-Class Women and Work." *Signs* 10, no. 3: 517–536.

———. 1987. "Equality and Autonomy: Feminist Politics in the United States and West Germany." In *The Women's Movements of the United States and Western Europe*, edited by M. F. Katzenstein and C. M. Mueller. Philadelphia: Temple University Press.

Ferree, Myra Marx, and Beth B. Hess. 1985. *Controversy and Coalition: The New Feminist Movement*. Boston: Twayne.

Firestone, Shulamith. 1970. *The Dialectic of Sex*. New York: Bantam Books.

Flexner, Eleanor. 1975. *Century of Struggle: The Women's Rights Movement in the United States*. Cambridge, Mass.: Harvard University Press.

Folbre, Nancy. 1987. "The Pauperization of Motherhood: Patriarchy and Public Policy in the United States." In *Families and Work*, edited by N. Gerstel and H. Gross. Philadelphia: Temple University Press.

Foner, Philip S. 1980. *Women and the American Labor Movement: From World War I to the Present*. New York: Free Press.

Form, W., and D. McMillan. 1983. "Women, Men, and Machines." *Work and Occupations* 10, no. 2: 147–178.

Foster, James C., and Mary C. Segers, eds. 1983. *Elusive Equality: Liberalism, Affirmative Action, and Social Change in America*. New York: Associated Faculty Press, National University Publications.

Frank, Miriam, 1986. "University Workers Inspired by Yale Strike: Columbia and NYU Unions Fight for Pay Equity." *Comparable Worth Project Newsletter* 6, no. 1: 6–7.

Freedman, Samuel G. 1986. "Of History and Politics: Bitter Feminist Debate about Advocacy." *New York Times*, June 6, II, 1.

Freeman, Jo. 1975. *The Politics of Women's Liberation*. Palo Alto, Calif.: Mayfield.

————. 1984. "Real, False Dilemmas." *Democratic Left* 12, no. 5: 15–18.

————. 1987. "Whom You Know versus Whom You Represent: Feminist Influence in the Democratic and Republican Parties." In *The Women's Movements of the United States and Western Europe*, edited by M. F. Katzenstein and C. M. Mueller. Philadelphia: Temple University Press.

Freeman, Richard B., and Jonathan S. Leonard. 1985. "Union Maids: Unions and the Female Workforce." National Bureau of Economic Research, Working Paper no. 1,652. Cambridge, Mass., June.

Fulenwider, Claire K. 1980. *Feminism in American Politics: A Study of Ideological Influence*. New York: Praeger.

Gallant, J. 1984. "Survey Reveals OA Accepted with Open Arms." *Computerworld*, March 5, 24.

Galloway, S., and A. Archuleta. 1980. "Sex and Salary: Equal Pay for Comparable Work." In *Manual on Pay Equity: Raising Wages for Women's Work*, edited by J. A. Grune. Washington, D.C.: Conference on Alternative State and Local Policies.

Gamarnikow, Eva. 1978. "Sexual Division of Labor: The Case of Nursing." In *Feminism and Materialism*, edited by A. Kuhn and A. Wolpe. London: Routledge & Kegan Paul.

Garrison, Dee. 1974. "The Tender Technicians: The Feminization of Public Librarianship, 1876–1905." In *Clio's Consciousness Raised*, edited by M. Hartman and L. Banner. New York: Harper & Row.

Gelb, Joyce. 1987. "Social Movement 'Success': A Comparative Analysis of Feminism in the United States and the United Kingdom." In *The Women's Movements of the United States and Western Europe*, edited by M. F. Katzenstein and C. M. Mueller. Philadelphia: Temple University Press.

Gelb, Joyce, and Marian L. Palley. 1987. *Women and Public Policies*. Princeton: Princeton University Press.

Gerson, Kathleen. 1985. *Hard Choices: How Women Decide about Work, Career, and Motherhood*. Berkeley and Los Angeles: University of California Press.

Gerth, H., and C. W. Mills. 1953. *Character and Social Structure*. New York: Harcourt, Brace.

Giddens, Anthony. 1973. *The Class Structure of the Advanced Societies*. London: Hutchinson.

Giddings, Paula. 1984. *When and Where I Enter: The Impact of Black Women on Race and Sex in America*. New York: Morrow.

Gilligan, Carol. 1982. *In a Different Voice*. Cambridge, Mass.: Harvard University Press.

Ginzburg, Eli. 1987. "Technology, Women, and Work: Policy Perspectives." In *Computer Chips and Paper Clips: Technology and Women's*

Employment, vol. 2, edited by H. I. Hartmann. Washington, D.C.: National Academy Press.

Glazer, Nathan. 1975. *Affirmative Discrimination*. New York: Basic Books.

Glenn, Evelyn N., and Roslyn Feldberg. 1977. "Degraded and Deskilled: The Proletarianization of Clerical Work." *Social Problems* 25: 52–64.

Greenberger, Marcia. 1980. "The Effectiveness of Federal Laws Prohibiting Sex Discrimination in Employment in the United States." In *Equal Employment Policy for Women*, edited by R. Steinberg-Ratner. Philadelphia: Temple University Press.

Greer, William. 1986. "Women Gain a Majority in Jobs." *New York Times*, March 19, 17.

Gregory, R. G., and R. C. Duncan. 1981. "Segmented Labor Market Theories and the Australian Experience of Equal Pay for Women." *Journal of Post-Keynesian Economics* 3, no. 3: 403–428.

Grimm, James W., and Robert N. Stern. 1974. "Sex Roles and Internal Labor Market Structures: The 'Female' Semi-Professions." *Social Forces* 21: 690–705.

Gross, Jane. 1985. "Columbia Workers Hail Union Pact." *New York Times*, October 23, II, 3.

Grune, Joy Ann. 1984. "Pay Equity Is a Necessary Remedy for Wage Discrimination." In *Comparable Worth: Issue for the '80's* (A Consultation of the U.S. Commission on Civil Rights), vol. 1. Washington, D.C.

———, ed. 1980. *Manual on Pay Equity: Raising Wages for Women's Work*. Washington, D.C.: Committee on Pay Equity, Conference on Alternative State and Local Policies.

Gurin, Patricia. 1982. "Group Consciousness." *ISR Newsletter* (Institute for Social Research, University of Michigan, Ann Arbor), Spring/Summer, 4–5.

———. 1985. "Women's Gender Consciousness." *Public Opinion Quarterly* 49, no. 2: 143–163.

Gutek, Barbara. 1988. "Women in Clerical Work." In *Women Working: Theories and Facts in Perspective*, 2d ed., edited by A. Stromberg and S. Harkess. Palo Alto, Calif.: Mayfield.

Habermas, Jürgen. 1971. "Science and Technology as Ideology." In *Towards a Rational Society*. Boston: Beacon Press.

———. 1975. *Legitimation Crisis*. Boston: Beacon Press.

Hacker, Andrew. 1985. "Women at Work." *San Francisco Examiner*. January 6, "This World," 15–16.

Hacker, Sally L. 1982. "Sex Stratification, Technological and Organizational Change: A Longitudinal Case Study of AT&T." In *Women and Work: Problems and Perspectives*, edited by R. Kahn-Hut, A. K. Daniels, and R. Colvard. New York: Oxford University Press.

Hamilton, Mildred. 1984. "Pay Equity—Most Explosive Job Issue of the '80's." (A three-part series.) *San Francisco Examiner*, April 22, 1; April 23, B10; April 24, B9.

Harrison, Cynthia. 1988. *On Account of Sex: The Politics of Women's Issues, 1945–1968*. Berkeley and Los Angeles: University of California Press.

Hartmann, Heidi I. 1979. "Capitalism, Patriarchy, and Job Segregation by Sex." In *Capitalist Patriarchy and the Case for Socialist Feminism*, edited by R. Eisenstein. New York: Monthly Review Press.

———. 1985. "The Political Economy of Comparable Worth." Paper presented at the Conference on Alternative Approaches to Labor Markets, University of Utah, Salt Lake City, October.

Hartmann, Heidi I., Rober E. Kraut, and Louise A. Tilly, eds. 1986. *Computer Chips and Paper Clips: Technology and Women's Employment*, vol. 1. Washington, D.C.: National Academy Press.

Heen, Mary. 1984. "A Review of Federal Court Decisions under Title VII of the Civil Rights Act of 1964." In *Comparable Worth and Wage Discrimination: Technical Possibilities and Political Realities*, edited by H. Remick. Philadelphia: Temple University Press.

Heilbrun, Carolyn. 1973. *Toward a Recognition of Androgyny*. New York: Knopf.

Hill, Herbert. 1987. "Race, Ethnicity, and Organized Labor: The Opposition to Affirmative Action." *New Politics* 1, no. 2: 31–82.

Hole, Judith, and Ellen Levine. 1971. *Rebirth of Feminism*. New York: Quadrangle/New York Times.

Humphries, Jane. 1977. "The Working Class Family, Women's Liberation, and Class Struggle: The Case of Nineteenth-Century British History." *Review of Radical Political Economics* 9: 25–42.

Hunt, H. A., and T. L. Hunt. 1987. "Recent Trends in Clerical Employment: The Impact of Technological Change." In *Computer Chips and Paper Clips: Technology and Women's Employment*, vol. 2, edited by H. I. Hartmann. Washington, D.C.: National Academy Press.

Hyman, Colette A. 1985. "Labor Organizing and Female Institution-Building: The Chicago Women's Trade Union League, 1904–1924." In *Women, Work, and Protest*, edited by R. Milkman. Boston: Routledge & Kegan Paul.

ILO (International Labor Office). 1986. *Job Evaluation*. Geneva: ILO.

Ireson, Carol, and Sandra Gill. 1988. "Girls' Socialization for Work." In *Women Working: Theories and Facts in Perspective*, 2d ed., edited by A. Stromberg and S. Harkess. Palo Alto, Calif.: Mayfield.

Jenkins, Craig. 1983. "Resource Mobilization Theory and the Study of Social Movements." *Annual Review of Sociology* 9: 527–553.

Johansen, Elaine. 1984. *Comparable Worth: The Myth and the Movement*. Boulder, Colo.: Westview Press.

Kahn, R. L. 1981. "Work, Stress, and Individual Well-Being." *Monthly Labor Review* 104 (May): 28–30.

Kanter, Rosabeth Moss. 1977. *Men and Women of the Corporation*. New York: Basic Books.

Katzenstein, Mary F. 1987. "Comparing the Feminist Movements of the United States and Western Europe: An Overview." In *The Women's Movements of the United States and Western Europe*, edited by M. F. Katzenstein and C. M. Mueller. Philadelphia: Temple University Press.

Kautzer, Kathleen. 1989. "Comparable Worth in the U.S. Private Sector: The Case of Yale University." Typescript, April 17. (Forthcoming in *Comparable Worth/Equal Value in the United States and Britain*, edited by M. Kahn and E. Meehan. London: Macmillan.)

Kelley, Maryellen R. 1982. "Discrimination in Seniority Systems: A Case Study." *Industrial and Labor Relations Review* 36, no. 1: 40–55.

Kelly, Rita M., and Jane Bayes. 1986. "Implementing Comparable Worth in the Public Sector: Theory and Practice at the State and Local Level." *Policy Studies Review* 5, no. 4: 769–775.

Kessler-Harris, Alice. 1982. *Out to Work: A History of Wage-earning Women in the United States*. New York: Oxford University Press.

———. 1986. "Equal Opportunity Commission v. Sears, Roebuck and Company: A Personal Account." *Radical History Review* 35: 57–79.

———. 1987. "The Debate over Equality for Women in the Workplace: Recognizing Differences." In *Families and Work*, edited by N. Gerstel and H. Gross. Philadelphia: Temple University Press.

———. 1988. "The Just Price, the Free Market, and the Value of Women." *Feminist Studies* 14, no. 2: 235–249.

Killingworth, Mark. 1985. "The Economics of Comparable Worth: Analytical, Empirical, and Policy Questions." In *Comparable Worth: New Directions for Research*, edited by H. I. Hartmann. Washington, D.C.: National Academy Press.

King, Wayne. 1989. "Strike Raises Issue of How Fair Is Pay." *New York Times*, October 17, 11.

Kirkby, Diane. 1987. "The Wage Earning Woman and the State: The National Women's Trade Union League and Protective Legislation, 1903–1923." *Labor History* 28, no. 1: 54–74.

Klein, Ethel. 1987. "The Diffusion of Consciousness in the United States and Western Europe." In *The Women's Movements of the United States and Western Europe*, edited by M. F. Katzenstein and C. M. Mueller. Philadelphia: Temple University Press.

Kort, Michele. 1987. "The Women of 'L.A. Law.'" *Ms.*, June, 38–44.

Kreiger, Linda J., and Patricia N. Cooney. 1983. "The Miller-Wohl Controversy: Equal Treatment, Positive Action, and the Meaning of Women's
Equality." *Golden Gate University Law Review* 13, no. 3: 513–572.

Kuhn, Annette, and AnnMarie Wolpe, eds. 1978. *Feminism and Materialism*. London: Routledge & Kegan Paul.

Kuhn, Sarah, and Barry Bluestone. 1987. "Economic Restructuring and
the Female Labor Market: The Impact of Industrial Change on
Women." In *Women, Households, and the Economy*, edited by L. Beneria and C. Stimpson. New Brunswick, N.J.: Rutgers University Press.

Ladd-Taylor, Molly. 1985. "Women Workers and the Yale Strike." *Feminist
Studies* 11, no. 3: 465–490.

Lamphere, Louise. 1985. "Bringing the Family to Work: Women's Culture
on the Shop Floor." *Feminist Studies* 11, no. 3: 519–540.

Lawrence, Jill. 1985. "Feminists Regroup, Return to Grass-Roots Politick-
ing." *San Francisco Examiner*, June 23, A13.

Lawson, Carol. 1985a. "NOW Focuses on Pay Equity for Women." *New
York Times*, April 29, 15.

———. 1985b. "Women in State Jobs Gain in Pay Equity." *New York
Times*, May 20, III, 12.

Lehrer, Susan. 1987. *Origins of Protective Legislation for Women:
1905–1925*. Albany: SUNY Press.

Leonard, Jonathan S. 1984a. "Employment and Occupational Advance
Under Affirmative Action." National Bureau of Economic Research,
Working Paper no. 1,270. Cambridge, Mass., February.

———. 1984b. "Unions and Equal Employment Opportunity." National
Bureau of Economic Research, Working Paper no. 1,311. Cambridge,
Mass., March.

———. 1984c. "What Are Promises Worth? The Impact of Affirmative
Action Goals." National Bureau of Economic Research, Working Paper
no. 1,346. Cambridge, Mass., May.

Lewin, Tamar. 1988. "For Feminist Scholars, Second Thoughts on Law and
Order." *New York Times*, September 30, 17.

———. 1989a. "Family or Career? Choose, Women Told." *New York
Times*, March 8, 17.

———. 1989b. "Pay Equity for Women's Jobs Finds Success Outside
Courts." *New York Times*, October 7, 1.

Livernash, Robert, E., ed. 1980. *Comparable Worth: Issues and Alternatives*. Washington, D.C.: Equal Employment Advisory Council.

Luker, Kristin. 1984. *Abortion and the Politics of Motherhood*. Berkeley
and Los Angeles: University of California Press.

Lynch, Roberta. 1986. "Organizing Clericals: Problems and Prospects."
Labor Research Review 8 (Spring): 91–101.

Lynch, Roberta, and Henry Bayer. 1986. "AFSCME's Success with Public Sector Clericals." *Labor Research Review* 8 (Spring): 98.

McGavin, P. A. 1983. "Equal Pay for Women: A Re-Assessment of the Australian Experience." *Australian Economic Papers* 22, no. 4: 48–67.

Machlowitz, Marilyn M. 1987. "Without the Playground, Mothers Meet at the Office." *New York Times,* July 19, F6.

MacKinnon, Catherine. 1979. *Sexual Harassment of Working Women.* New Haven: Yale University Press.

Malveaux, Julianne. 1982. "Moving Forward, Standing Still: Women in White-Collar Jobs." In *Women in the Workplace,* edited by P. Wallace. Boston: Auburn House.

———. 1985. "The Economic Interests of Black and White Women: Are They Similar?" *Review of Black Political Economy* 14, no. 1: 27.

———. 1985–1986. "Comparable Worth and Its Impact on Black Women." *Review of Black Political Economy* 14, nos. 2–3: 47–62.

Mansbridge, Jane J. 1986. *Why We Lost the ERA.* Chicago: University of Chicago Press.

Marable, Manning. 1986. "Twenty Years after Executive Order 11246, Where Are We?" Debate on Affirmative Action, University of California, Berkeley, Boalt Hall School of Law, February 4.

Marini, Margaret, and Mary Brinton. 1984. "Sex Typing in Occupational Socialization." In *Sex Segregation in the Workplace: Trends, Explanations, Remedies,* edited by B. F. Reskin. Washington, D.C.: National Academy Press.

Marschall, Daniel, and Judith Gregory, eds. 1983. *Office Automation: Jekyll or Hyde?* Cleveland: Working Women's Educational Fund.

Mason, Karen. 1984. "Commentary: Strober's Theory of Occupational Sex Segregation." In *Sex Segregation in the Workplace: Trends, Explanations, Remedies,* edited by B. F. Reskin. Washington, D.C.: National Academy Press.

Massachusetts History Workshop. 1985. *They Can't Run the Office without Us: Sixty Years of Clerical Work.* Cambridge: Book Committee of the Massachusetts History Workshop.

Matthaei, Julie. 1982. *An Economic History of Women in America: Women's Work, the Sexual Division of Labor, and the Development of Capitalism.* New York: Schocken Books.

May, Martha. 1982. "The Historical Problem of the Family Wage: The Ford Motor Company and the Five-Dollar Day." *Feminist Studies* 8, no. 2: 399–424.

———. 1985. "Bread before Roses: American Workingmen, Labor Unions, and the Family Wage." In *Women, Work, and Protest: A Cen-*

tury of U.S. Women's Labor History, edited by R. Milkman. Boston: Routledge & Kegan Paul.

Melosh, Barbara. 1982. *"The Physician's Hand": Work Culture and Conflict in American Nursing.* Philadelphia: Temple University Press.

Milkman, Ruth. 1976. "Women's Work and Economic Crisis: Some Lessons of the Great Depression." *Review of Radical Political Economics* 8, no. 1: 73–97.

———. 1984. "What's Your Job Worth?" *Redbook,* September, 206.

———. 1985. "Women Workers, Feminism, and the Labor Movement since the 1960's." *Women, Work, and Protest: A Century of U.S. Women's Labor History,* edited by R. Milkman. Boston: Routledge & Kegan Paul.

———. 1986. "Women's History and the Sears Case." *Feminist Studies* 12, no. 2: 375–400.

———. 1987a. *Gender at Work.* Urbana: University of Illinois Press.

———. 1987b. "Women Workers and the Labor Movement in Hard Times: Comparing the 1930s and 1980s." In *Women, Households, and the Economy,* edited by L. Beneria and C. Stimpson. New Brunswick, N.J.: Rutgers University Press.

Mill, John Stuart, and Harriet Taylor Mill. 1970. *Essays on Sex Equality.* Edited by A. Rossi. Chicago: University of Chicago Press.

Mitchell, Juliet. 1971. *Women's Estate.* New York: Pantheon Books.

Monthly Labor Review. 1985. "Changing Employment Patterns of Organized Workers." 108 (February): 29.

Moore, Richard, and Elizabeth Marsis. 1983a. "What's a Woman's Work Worth?" *Progressive* 47, no. 12: 20–22.

———. 1983b. "Will Unions Work for Women?" *Progressive* 47, no. 8: 28–30.

Ms. 1988. "For the Record: Pay Dirt." July, 69.

Mueller, Carol M. 1987. "Collective Consciousness, Identity Transformation, and the Rise of Women in Public Office in the United States." In *The Women's Movements of the United States and Western Europe,* edited by M. F. Katzenstein and C. M. Mueller. Philadelphia: Temple University Press.

Murphree, Mary C. 1987. "New Technology and Office Tradition: The Not-so-changing World of the Secretary." In *Computer Chips and Paper Clips: Technology and Women's Employment,* vol. 2, edited by H. I. Hartmann. Washington, D.C.: National Academy Press.

National NOW Times. 1986a. "Congress, Business Challenge Meese Attack on Affirmative Action." January, 5.

———. 1986b. "NOW Joins Flight Attendants on Picket Line against TWA Cuts." April, 3.

———. 1986c. "Pay Equity Gallops across America in 1985." January, 2.
National Organization for Women. 1985. Letter from President Judy
Goldsmith to launch the pay equity campaign.
NCPE (National Committee on Pay Equity). 1984. "The Cost of Pay Equity
in Public and Private Employment." Washington, D.C., December.
———. 1985a. "NCPE Poll." *Newsnotes*, May, 1.
———. 1985b. "Questions and Answers on Pay Equity." Washington,
D.C.
———. 1986. "AFSCME Wins $100 Million Settlement in Washington."
Newsnotes, April, 1.
———. 1987. "Pay Equity: An Issue of Race, Ethnicity, and Sex." Washington, D.C., February.
———. 1988a. "Closing the Wage Gap: An International Perspective."
Washington, D.C., October.
———. 1988b. "Future of Pay Equity at Federal Level Affected by New
Presidential Appointments." *Newsnotes* 9, no. 2: 4.
———. 1988c. "Survey of State-Government Level Pay Equity Activity,
1988." Washington, D.C.
———. 1989a. "Briefing Paper #1: The Wage Gap." Washington, D.C.,
September 22, 1987; updated April 1989.
———. 1989b. "Fact File." *Newsnotes* 10, no. 1: 10.
———. 1989c. "From the Courts." *Newsnotes* 10, no. 1: 3–5.
———. 1989d. "Pay Equity Activity in the Public Sector, 1979–1989:
Executive Summary." Washington, D.C., October.
Needleman, Ruth. 1986. "A World in Transition: Women and Economic
Change." *Labor Studies Journal* 10, no. 3: 207–228.
———. 1988. "Women Workers: A Force for Rebuilding Unionism." *La-
bor Research Review* 7, no. 1: 1–13.
Needleman, Ruth, and Anne Nelson. 1988. "Policy Implications: The
Worth of Women's Work." In *The Worth of Women's Work: A Quali-
tative Synthesis*, edited by A. Statham, E. M. Miller, and H. O.
Mauksch. Albany: SUNY Press.
New Politics. 1987. "Discussion: Race, Ethnicity, and Organized Labor."
Vol. 1, no. 3: 22–71.
New York Times. 1984a. "California Suit Charges Sex Discrimination." November 22, I, 21.
———. 1984b. "Concept of Pay Based on Worth Is 'Looniest,' Rights Chief
Says." November 17, 15.
———. 1985. "Clerical Workers Strike Columbia University." October 18,
16.
———. 1987a. "Business and the Law: States Leading on Pay Equity."
June 22, D2.

————. 1987b. "The Job Market Opens Up for the 68-Cent Woman." July 26, 6.

————. 1987c. "Prospects: The Price of Pay Equity." July 26, F1.

Noble, Kenneth B. 1985a. "Low-paying Jobs Foreseen for Most Working Women." *New York Times*, December 12, 12.

————. 1985b. "U.S. Action against Bias Seen as Already Weak." *New York Times*, September 2, 1.

————. 1986a. "Charles J. McDonald: Labor's New Chief Organizer." *New York Times*, October 21, II, 6.

————. 1986b. "Hiring Goals: A Big-vs.-Small-Business Split." *New York Times*, March 3, 1.

————. 1988. "Child Care: The Federal Role Grows in the 80s." *New York Times*, May 1, "Week in Review," 4.

Noyelle, Thierry. 1987. "The New Technology and the New Economy: Some Implications for Equal Employment Opportunity. In *Computer Chips and Paper Clips: Technology and Women's Employment*, vol. 2, edited by H. I. Hartmann. Washington, D.C.: National Academy Press.

Nussbaum, Karen. 1980. "Women Clerical Workers and Trade Union-ism." (Interview.) *Socialist Review* 10, no. 1: 151–159.

O'Farrell Brigid. 1988. "Women in Blue-Collar Occupations: Traditional and Non-traditional." In *Women Working: Theories and Facts in Per-spective*, 2d ed., edited by A. Stromberg and S. Harkess. Palo Alto, Calif.: Mayfield.

O'Farrell, Brigid, and Sharon L. Harlan. 1982. "Craftworkers and Clerks: The Effect of Male Coworker Hostility on Women's Satisfaction with Non-traditional Blue Collar Jobs." *Social Problems* 29 (February): 252–264.

————. 1984. "Job Integration Strategies: Today's Programs and Tomor-row's Needs." In *Sex Segregation in the Workplace: Trends, Explana-tions, Remedies*, edited by B. Reskin. Washington, D.C.: National Academy Press.

Oppenheimer, Martin. 1985. *White-Collar Politics*. New York: Monthly Review Press.

Padavic, Irene and Barbara Reskin. 1986. "Supervisors as Gatekeepers: Supervisors' Role in the Sex Segregation of Jobs." Paper presented at the annual meeting of the American Sociological Association, New York, August.

————. 1987. "Staying or Switching: Women's White-Collar Socialization and Organizational Rewards." Paper presented at the annual meeting of the American Sociological Association, Chicago, August.

Passell, Peter. 1988. "Economic Scene: On Guaranteeing Child Support." *New York Times*, July 6, 30.

Pear, Robert. 1985a. "Rights Unit Spurns Pay Equity Theory." *New York Times*, April 12, 1.

———. 1985b. "Equal Pay Is Not Needed for Jobs of Comparable Worth, U.S. Says." *New York Times*, June 18, 15.

———. 1986. "Justice Official Says Data Show Quotas for Jobs." *New York Times*, March 29, 1.

———. 1987. "Women Reduce Lag in Earnings, but Disparities with Men Remain." *New York Times*, September 4, 1.

Pearce, Diana. 1978. "The Feminization of Poverty." Department of Sociology, University of Illinois, Chicago Circle. Typescript.

Pearce, Diana, and McAdoo, Harriet. 1981. *Women and Children: Alone and in Poverty*. Washington, D.C.: National Advisory Council on Economic Opportunity, September.

Petersen, Iver. 1987. "Route 1's Missing Riders: Office Workers—Managers Abound, but the Clerical Shortage Is Critical." *New York Times*, March 22, Special Supplement: "Careers," 27.

Phillips, Anne, and Barbara Taylor. 1980. "Sex and Skill: Notes towards Feminist Economics." *Feminist Review* 6: 79–88.

Phipps, Polly A. 1986. "Occupational Resegregation: A Case Study of Insurance Examiners, Adjusters, and Investigators." In B. Reskin et al. *Job Queues, Gender Queues: Women's Movement into Male Occupations*. Philadelphia: Temple University Press, 1990.

Piven, Frances Fox. 1987. "Women and the State: Ideology, Power, and the Welfare State." In *Families and Work*, edited by N. Gerstel and H. E. Gross. Philadelphia: Temple University Press.

Piven, Frances Fox, and Richard Cloward. 1977. *Poor People's Movements*. New York: Pantheon Books.

Plotnick, R. D., and F. Skidmore. 1977. "Progress against Poverty: 1964–1974." In *American Society, Inc.*, edited by M. Zeitlin. Chicago: Rand McNally.

Portman, Lisa, Joy Ann Grune, and Eve Johnson. 1984. "The Role of Labor." In *Comparable Worth and Wage Discrimination: Technical Possibilities and Political Realities*, edited by H. Remick. Philadelphia: Temple University Press.

Poulantzas, Nicos. 1975. *Classes in Contemporary Capitalism*. London: New Left Books.

Prial, Frank J. 1987. "District 65 Becomes Unit of the U.A.W." *New York Times*, February 26, B3.

Quinn, Mickey. 1982. "Viewpoint: 'No Concessions' Stand Is Too Narrow." *Labor Notes* 45 (October 26): 12–13.

Remick, Helen. 1978. "Strategies for Creating Sound, Bias-Free Job Evaluation Plans." In *Job Evaluation and the EEO: The Emerging Issues*. New York: Industrial Relations Counselors.

————. 1980. "Beyond Equal Pay for Equal Work: Comparable Worth in the State of Washington." In *Equal Employment Policy for Women,* edited by R. Steinberg-Ratner. Philadelphia: Temple University Press.

————. 1981. Review of *Comparable Worth Compliance Handbook,* edited by Brady, Persson, and Thompson. In *Comparable Worth Project Newsletter* 2, no. 4: 8–9.

————. 1984. "Major Issues in *A Priori* Applications." In *Comparable Worth and Wage Discrimination: Technical Possibilities and Political Realities,* edited by H. Remick. Philadelphia: Temple University Press, 1984.

Remick, Helen, and Steinberg, Ronnie. 1984. "Technical Possibilities and Political Realities: Concluding Remarks." In *Comparable Worth and Wage Discrimination: Technical Possibilities and Political Realities,* edited by H. Remick. Philadelphia: Temple University Press.

Reskin, Barbara F. 1987. "Sex Differentiation and the Devaluation of Women's Work: Implications for Women's Occupational Progress and Comparable Worth." University of Illinois, Urbana-Champaign, June. Typescript. (Revised version of the Cheryl Allyn Miller Lecture on Women and Social Change, delivered May 1, 1987, at Loyola University.)

————. 1988. "Bringing the Men Back In: Sex Differentiation and the Devaluation of Women's Work." *Gender & Society* 2, no. 1: 58–81.

Reskin, Barbara F., and Heidi I. Hartmann. 1986. *Women's Work, Men's Work: Sex Segregation on the Job.* Washington, D.C.: National Academy Press.

Reskin, Barbara F., and Patricia A. Roos. 1987. "Status Hierarchies and Sex Segregation." In *Ingredients for Women's Employment Policy,* edited by C. Bose and G. Spitze. Albany: SUNY Press.

Reskin, Barbara F., and Patricia A. Roos, with Katherine Donato, Polly Phipps, Barbara Thomas, Chloe Bird, and Thomas Steiger. 1990. *Job Queues, Gender Queues: Women's Movement into Male Occupations.* Philadelphia: Temple University Press.

Rice, Barbara. 1983. "Minorities Bear the Brunt of Layoffs." *Labor Notes* 49 (February 24): 7.

Rimer, Sara. 1988. "Women, Jobs, and Children: A New Generation Worries." *New York Times,* November 27, 1.

Ritzer, George. 1972. *Man and His Work: Conflict and Change.* New York: Appleton-Century-Crofts.

Roback, Jennifer. 1986. *A Matter of Choice: A Critique of Comparable Worth by a Skeptical Feminist.* New York: Priority Press, Twentieth Century Fund.

Roberts, Patti. 1982. "An Introduction to Comparable Worth." *New Labor Review,* Fall, 1–18.

Roos, Patricia A. 1986. "Women in the Composing Room: Technology and Organization as Determinants of Change." In B. Reskin et al. *Job Queues, Gender Queues: Women's Movement into Male Occupations.* Philadelphia: Temple University Press, 1990.

Roos, Patricia A., and Barbara F. Reskin. 1984. "Institutional Factors Affecting Job Access and Mobility for Women." In *Sex Segregation in the Workplace: Trends, Explanations, Remedies,* edited by B. Reskin. Washington, D.C.: National Academy Press.

Rosenbaum, James E. 1984. *Career Mobility in a Corporate Hierarchy.* Orlando, Fla.: Academic Press.

———. 1985. "Jobs, Job Status, and Women's Gains from Affirmative Action: Implications for Comparable Worth." In *Comparable Worth: New Directions for Research,* edited by H. Hartmann. Washington, D.C.: National Academy Press.

Rosenberg, Jan. 1984. "Equal Pay Battles." *Democratic Left* 12, no. 5: 13–14.

Rosenberg, Rosalind. 1985. "Exchange: A Feminist for Sears." *Nation* 241, no. 13: 394.

———. 1986. "What Harms Women in the Workplace." *New York Times,* February 27, 23.

Rothschild, Emma. 1981. "Reagan and the Real American." *New York Review of Books,* February 5, 40–50.

Rozen, Miriam. 1987. "Is 'Flight Attendant' a Job or a Career?" *New York Times,* March 29, F14.

Rubin, Gayle. 1975. "The Traffic in Women: Notes on the 'Political Economy' of Sex." In *Toward an Anthropology of Women,* edited by R. Reiter. New York: Monthly Review Press.

Rupp, Leila J., and Verta Taylor. 1987. *Survival in the Doldrums: The American Women's Rights Movement, 1945 to 1960s.* New York: Oxford University Press.

Sacks, Karen B. 1986. "Women's Wages: Essential to Preserving Middle Income Jobs. The Telecommunications Industry Example." Oberlin College, August. Typescript.

Samuels, Catherine. 1975. *The Forgotten Five Million: Women in Public Employment.* New York: Women's Action Alliance.

San Francisco Examiner. 1986. "Pay Equity Breakthrough." February 2, S1.

Sape, George. 1985. "Coping with Comparable Worth." *Harvard Business Review* 85, no. 5: 145–152.

Schlafly, Phyllis, ed. 1984. *Equal Pay for UNequal Work.* Washington, D.C.: Eagle Forum.

Schneider, Beth. 1982. "Consciousness about Sexual Harassment among Heterosexual and Lesbian Workers." *Journal of Social Issues* 38, no. 4: 75–97.

Schreiber, Carol Tropp. 1979. *Changing Places: Men and Women in Transitional Occupations*. Cambridge, Mass.: MIT Press.

Schwartz, Felice. 1989. "Management Women and the New Facts of Life." *Harvard Business Review* 89, no. 1: 65–76.

Schwartz, Peter. 1982. "Women's Worth: Is Comparable Worth Good for Women?" *Reason*, July, 40–45.

Science News. 1981. "Stress: A Sign of the Times." 119, no. 21 (May 23): 328.

Segers, Mary C. 1983. "Problems of Implementing Affirmative Action II: *Weber* and Equal Employment Opportunity," "Justifying Affirmative Action," and "Evaluating Affirmative Action: The Limitations of Redistributional Politics in Achieving Equality." Chapters 5–7 in *Elusive Equality: Liberalism, Affirmative Action, and Social Change in America*, edited by J. Foster, and M. Segers. New York: Associated Faculty Press, National University Publications.

Selden, C., E. Mutari, M. Rubin, and K. Sacks. 1982. *Equal Pay for Work of Comparable Worth: An Annotated Bibliography*. Chicago: Business and Professional Women's Foundation.

Serrin, William. 1984a. "Strike at Yale Is Being Watched by Many. *New York Times*, October 11, 16.

———. 1984b. "U.A.W. Threatens Strike at Columbia." *New York Times*, December 31, 28.

———. 1984c. "Union's Success at Yale: New Focus on White-Collar Women." *New York Times*, April 10, II, 24.

———. 1985. "Yale Labor Pact Draws Other Schools' Attention." *New York Times*, January 24, II, 4.

———. 1986. "Union's Race with Change." *New York Times*, February 22, 1.

Sexton, Patricia Cayo. 1978. "Workers (Female) Arise!" In *Feminist Frameworks*, edited by A. M. Jaggar and P. Rothenberg-Struhl. New York: McGraw-Hill.

Shaeffer, Ruth Gilbert. 1980. "Improving Job Opportunities for Women from a U.S. Corporate Perspective." in *Equal Employment Policy for Women*, edited by R. Steinberg-Ratner. Philadelphia: Temple University Press.

Shinoff, Paul. 1985. "AFL-CIO's Bold Plan to Regain Its Power." *San Francisco Examiner*, March 31, A1.

Skerry, Perry. 1978. "The Class Conflict over Abortion." *Public Interest* 52: 69–84.

Skocpol, Theda, Kurt Back, Carole Joffee, Kathleen Gerson, and Robert Wuthnow. 1986–1987. "A 'Social Issue' in American Politics: Reflections on Kristin Luker's *Abortion and the Politics of Motherhood*." (A symposium.) *Politics & Society* 15, no. 2: 223–234.

Smith, Vicki. 1988. "Restructuring Management and Managing Restructuring: The Role of Managers in Corporate Change." In *Research in Politics and Society*, vol. 3, edited by J. Rothschild and M. Wallace. Greenwich: JAI Press.

Sorenson, Elaine. 1982. "An Economic Analysis of Comparable Worth." *New Labor Review*, Fall, 19–33.

———. 1987. "Effect of Comparable Worth Policies on Earnings." *Industrial Relations* 26, no. 3: 227–239.

Sparr, Pamela. 1984. "Re-evaluating Feminist Economics: 'Feminization of Poverty' Ignores Key Issues." *Dollars & Sense*, no. 99 (September): 12–14.

Spelfogel, Evan J. 1981. "Equal Pay for Work of Comparable Value: A New Concept." *Labor Law Journal* 32, no. 1: 31–39.

Spencer, Dee Ann. 1988. "Public Schoolteaching: A Suitable Job for Women." In *The Worth of Women's Work: A Qualitative Synthesis*, edited by A. Statham, E. M. Miller, and H. O. Mauksch. Albany: SUNY Press.

Stein, Eileen. 1988. "Perseverance, Growth, Cornerstones of Pay Equity Movement in 1988." *Newsnotes* (NCPE) 9, no. 2: 1.

Steinberg, Ronnie J. 1982. *Wages and Hours*. New Brunswick, N.J.: Rutgers University Press.

———. 1984a. "Identifying Wage Discrimination and Implementing Pay Equity Adjustments." In *Comparable Worth: Issue for the '80's* (A Consultation of the U.S. Commission on Civil Rights), vol. 1. Washington, D.C.

———. 1984b. "'A Want of Harmony': Perspectives on Wage Discrimination and Comparable Worth." In *Comparable Worth and Wage Discrimination: Technical Possibilities and Political Realities*, edited by H. Remick. Philadelphia: Temple University Press.

———. 1986. "The Debate over Comparable Worth." *New Politics* 1, no. 1: 108–126.

———. 1987a. "From Radical Vision to Minimalist Reform: Pay Equity in New York State, the Limits of Insider Reform Initiatives." Paper presented at the Department of Sociology, Pennsylvania State University, April 10.

———. 1987b. "Radical Challenges in a Liberal World: The Mixed Success of Comparable Worth." *Gender & Society* 1, no. 4: 466–475.

Steinberg, Ronnie, and Lois Haignere. 1987. "Equitable Compensation: Methodological Criteria for Comparable Worth." In *Ingredients for Women's Employment Policy*, edited by C. Bose and G. Spitze. Albany: SUNY Press.

Steinberg-Ratner, Ronnie. 1980. "The Policy and Problem." In *Equal*

Employment Policy for Women, edited by R. Steinberg-Ratner. Philadelphia: Temple University Press.

Strober, Myra, and Carolyn Arnold. 1987. "The Dynamics of Occupational Sex Segregation among Bank Tellers." In *Gender in the Workplace,* edited by C. Brown and J. Pechman. Washington, D.C.: Brookings Institution.

Strom, Sharon Hartman. 1983. "Challenging Women's Place: Feminism, the Left, and Industrial Unionism in the 1930's." *Feminist Studies* 9, no. 2: 359–386.

———. 1985. "'We're No Kitty Foyles': Organizing Office Workers for the Congress of Industrial Organizations, 1937–50." In *Women, Work, and Protest: A Century of U.S. Women's Labor History,* edited by R. Milkman. Boston: Routledge & Kegan Paul.

———. 1987. "'Machines Instead of Clerks': Technology and the Feminization of Bookkeeping, 1910–1950." In *Computer Chips and Paper Clips: Technology and Women's Employment,* vol. 2, edited by H. I. Hartmann. Washington, D.C.: National Academy Press.

Stromberg, Ann H. 1988. "Women in Female-dominated Professions." In *Women Working: Theories and Facts in Perspective,* edited by A. Stromberg and S. Harkess. Palo Alto, Calif.: Mayfield.

Taylor, Stuart, Jr. 1988. "Supreme Court Roundup: Procedure of Enforcing Child Support is Ratified." *New York Times,* April 28, 12.

Taylor, Verta. 1986. "The Continuity of the American Women's Movement: An Elite-sustained Stage." Paper presented at the annual meeting of the American Sociological Association, New York, August.

Thomas, Patricia. 1986. "Pay Equity: Educating for Union Action." *Labor Studies Journal* 10, no. 3: 278–289.

Thompson, E. P. 1963. *The Making of the English Working Class.* Harmondsworth, Eng.: Penguin Books.

Thornberry, Mary C. 1983. "Affirmative Action: History of an Attempt to Realize Greater Equality" and "Problems of Implementing Affirmative Action I: *Bakke* and Equal Educational Opportunity." Chapters 3 and 4 in *Elusive Equality: Liberalism, Affirmative Action, and Social Change in America,* edited by J. C. Foster and M. C. Segers. New York: Associated Faculty Press, National University Publications.

Tilly, Charles. 1978. *From Mobilization to Revolution.* Reading, Mass.: Addison-Wesley.

Tilly, Louise, and Joan Scott. 1978. *Women, Work, and Family.* New York: Holt, Reinhart & Winston.

Totten, Cosby, Goldie Totten, and June Rostan. 1988. "Women Miners Fight for Parental Leave." *Labor Research Review* 7, no. 1: 89–95.

Treiman, D. J. 1979. *Job Evaluation: An Analytic Review.* Interim report to the EEOC. Washington, D.C.: National Academy of Sciences.

———. 1984. "Effect of Choice of Factors and Factor Weights in Job Evaluation." In *Comparable Worth and Wage Discrimination: Technical Possibilities and Political Realities*, edited by H. Remick. Philadelphia: Temple University Press.

Treiman, D. J., and Heidi I. Hartmann. 1981. *Women, Work, and Wages: Equal Pay for Jobs of Equal Value*. Washington, D.C.: National Academy Press.

Turner, Wallace. 1984. "Pay Equity Issue Moving to Forefront." *New York Times*, December 14, 20.

———. 1986. "Drive Seen as Gaining Pay Equity for Women." *New York Times*, January 27, 22.

Tyack, David, and Myra Strober. 1981. "Jobs and Gender: A History of the Structuring of Educational Employment by Sex." In *Educational Policy and Management*, edited by P. Schmuck and W. Carters. New York: Academic Press.

U.S. Bureau of the Census. 1986. *Statistical Abstract of the United States: 1987* (107th ed.). Washington, D.C., December.

———. 1989. *Statistical Abstract of the United States: 1989* (109th ed.). Washington, D.C., January.

U.S. Commission on Civil Rights. 1985a. *Comparable Worth: An Analysis and Recommendations*. Washington, D.C., June.

———. 1985b. "Comparable Worth Doctrine Rejected." *Civil Rights Update*. Washington, D.C., June.

U.S. Department of Labor. Women's Bureau. 1983. *Time of Change: 1983 Handbook on Women Workers*, Bulletin no. 298.

Vogel, Lise. 1990. "Debating Difference: Feminism, Pregnancy, and the Workplace." *Feminist Studies* 16, no. 1: 9–32.

Walsh, Joan. 1987. "News Focus: Enterprising Women." *Ms.*, May, 69–72.

Wcislo, Celia. 1983. "Has Affirmative Action Been Sidelined?" *Labor Notes* 52 (May 26): 10.

———. 1985. "Service Employees Local Alters Seniority System to Keep Minorities in the Workforce." *Labor Notes* 77 (July 22): 1,6.

Weber, Max. 1975. "Bureaucracy"; "Politics as a Vocation"; "Science as a Vocation." In *From Max Weber*, edited by H. Gerth and C. W. Mills. New York: Oxford University Press.

Weitzman, Lenore. 1985. *The Divorce Revolution*. New York: Free Press.

West, Jackie. 1978. "Women, Sex, and Class." In *Feminism and Materialism*, edited by A. Kuhn and A. Wolpe. London: Routledge & Kegan Paul.

Wharton, Amy S., and James N. Baron. 1986. "The Impact of Gender Segregation on Men at Work." Paper presented at the annual meeting of the American Sociological Association, New York, August.

————. 1987. "So Happy Together? The Impact of Gender Segregation on Men at Work." *American Sociological Review* 52: 574–587.

Wiener, Jon. 1985a. "Exchange: A Feminist for Sears, Wiener Replies." *Nation* 241, no. 13 (October 26): 410–411.

————. 1985b. "The Sears Case: Women's History on Trial." *Nation* 241, no. 6 (September 7): 163, 176–180.

Williams, Wendy M. 1982. "The Equality Crisis: Some Reflections on Culture, Courts, and Feminism." *Women's Rights Law Reporter* 7, no. 3: 175–200.

Wilson, William J. 1978. *The Declining Significance of Race.* Chicago: University of Chicago Press.

Withorn, Ann. 1976. "Death of CLUW." *Radical America* 10, no. 2: 47–51.

Women's Labor Project (National Lawyers Guild). 1980. *Bargaining for Equality.* San Francisco: National Labor Law Center.

Woodworth, M., and W. Woodworth. 1979. "The Female Takeover: Threat or Opportunity?" *Personnel Administrator,* January, 46–52.

Wright, Erik Olin. 1982. "Class Boundaries and Contradictory Class Locations." In *Classes, Power, and Conflict,* edited by A. Giddens and D. Held. Berkeley and Los Angeles: University of California Press.

Zavella, Patricia. 1985. "'Abnormal Intimacy': The Varying Work Networks of Chicana Cannery Workers." *Feminist Studies* 11, no. 3: 541–558.

Zeitlin, Maurice, ed. 1977. *American Society, Inc.* Chicago: Rand McNally.

Index

Acker, Joan, 1n, 2, 3n, 7n, 13, 79n, 81n, 170n, 173, 174n, 176, 178n, 180n, 182, 183

Affirmative action, 4, 15, 19, 131, 201; benefits to white women, 33; business support for, 29–31; and class relations, 54; compared with comparable worth, 135; in Contra Costa County, 92, 94, 100, 102–3, 106, 109–11, 129; definition of, 20; and elimination of jobs, 141; employers' responses to, 28–34; enforcement of, 20, 23–24, 41n; and entry of men into women's jobs, 155, 157; under Executive Order 11246, 22; and federal government, 20–26, 32; and gender roles, 18; goals and timetables in, 33; and labor markets, 142; and low-paid women, 159; as management tool, 30; and organized labor, 26–28; in public sector, 25–26; and racial discrimination, 27; rhetoric of, 53, 59n; and San Jose movement, 90; and seniority, 26–27, 175; underlying principles of, 34; and women's economic status, 23

"Affirmative Action and City Women" (San Jose report), 61, 62

American Federation of Labor (AFL), 36; and "manly wage," 12

American Federation of Labor and Congress of Industrial Organizations (AFL-CIO), 7, 9, 105; and affirmative action, 26–28; in postwar era, 13. See also Congress of Industrial Organizations (CIO)

American Federation of State, County, and Municipal Employees (AFSCME), 11, 197; national activities of, 48, 103n; in Washington State, 47–49

American Federation of State, County, and Municipal Employees Local 101 (Santa Clara County), 55, 60–61, 67

American Federation of State, County, and Municipal Employees local 512 (Contra Costa County), 127n

Amercian Federation of State, County, and Municipal Employees Local 2700 (Contra Costa County), 100–103

American Library Association (ALA), 49

American Nursing Association (ANA), 105, 106

American Telephone and Telegraph, 30–31, 142; job integration at, 155

Automation, office, 148, 149

Banking industry, and affirmative action, 142

Baron, James N., 32–33, 153

Becalli, Bianca, 158–59

Bell, Daniel, 179

Beller, Andrea, 31–32

Benchmark Committee (Contra Costa County), 118–21

Benchmark jobs, 77, 120, 121

Benokraitis, Nijole V., 24

Bielby, William T., 32–33

Blue-collar workers, 8, 141–42; women, 138, 150, 196

"Bottlenecking," at job entry levels, 138, 139n, 150n

Bush administration, 11, 25, 196

"Business unionism," 11n; and AFL, 13

California Nurses Association (CNA), 104, 106

Callahan, Bill, 63n, 87, 88, 89, 190

Carter administration, 24–25, 44, 47

243

Cistermann, Harry, 115–16, 120, 164
City Women for Advancement (San Jose),
57–63, 69, 70, 184
Civil Rights Act (1964), 21–22
Civil Rights Commission, 27 n, 55; report
on comparable worth, 145 n
Civil rights movement, 21, 26, 40–41,
42, 191
Class antagonism, within women's movements, 34–46
Class differentiation, among working
women, 191–98
Class identification: in Contra Costa
County movement, 95–99, 163–66,
184–88; versus gender identification,
183–91; in San Jose movement, 63,
68–70, 88–90, 160–63, 184–88
Class politics, 2; in comparable worth,
169–75; discourse of, 12–14, 54,
183–89; in feminist discourse, 14–17,
197–98
Class structure, 7, 198
Clerical work, 7, 17; and changes in technology, 148, 149; growth of jobs in,
136–37
Clerical workers, 7, 8; in Contra Costa
County movement, 100–104, 128–29,
139, 212; job satisfaction among, 146–
49; participation in San Jose's Hay
study, 75–76, 77, 78; and San Jose
union, 68–72; unionization of, 10; at
Yale University, 53
Clerical workers, women, 8, 177; alliances with female professionals, 8 n,
166–67; in Contra Costa County
movement, 93, 95–100, 107; in San
Jose, 57–63; social relations among,
147 n, 188; value of comparable worth
for, 145. *See also* Women, low-paid
Coalition of Labor Union Women
(CLUW), 27, 43, 196
Collective bargaining, 2; by public-sector
employees, 10 n
Colorado Springs, Colorado, job evaluation studies in, 112
Commissions on the Status of Women,
41, 47, 48; in Santa Clara County, 58
Comparable worth (pay equity): advocacy
of librarians for, 48–49, 64–67; arguments for, 2, 4–6; during Bush administration, 25; during Carter administration, 24; as choice of San Jose workers,
62; and class conflict, 46, 175; and class
politics, 35; and class relations, 2,
169–75, 186; compared with affirmative action, 19, 135; definition of, 1;

economic consequences of, 198–202;
and entry of men into women's jobs,
154; and the family, 13, 14, 171; and
female professionals, 143, 145; and
feminism, 14–19, 131; gender-based
interest in, 160–68; and gender politics, 35, 46; and gender relations,
184–88; implementation in Contra
Costa County, 105, 111–14; implementation in San Jose, 86, 89–90; judi-
cial decisions concerning, 50–51; and
labor movement, 10, 11, 184; liberal
foundations of, 3–4, 16–17, 176; and
the marketplace, 16, 61, 96, 107, 116,
170, 172, 176, 198 n; and men's wages,
170; popularity of, among clerical
workers, 145; in private sector, 46–47,
149; in public sector, 46–47, 149; and
racial segregation, 5–6; radical elements of, 183, 191, 198, 202; during
Reagan administration, 25, 52, 128;
and sex stereotypes, 18, 132; among
white-collar workers, 8; in World
War II, 5
Comparable Worth Coalition (Contra
Costa County), 107, 109–11, 164, 176,
185; agitation tactics of, 122–24; collective bargaining efforts of, 114–18,
121, 124; constituency of, 126, 127 n;
formation of, 110; and job evaluation,
113–16; and San Jose strikers, 109–10
Comparable worth movement, 3, 4;
emergence of, 20, 46–53; limitations
of, 160–82; in San Jose, 139
Comparable Worth Project, 119 n
Comparable Worth Project Leadership
Training Conference (1986), 208
Concerned Library Active Workers
(CLAW) of San Jose, 64–65, 67, 184;
membership in MEF, 69
Concord, California, comparable worth
in, 128 n, 170
Congress of Industrial Organizations
(CIO), 9; organizing drives of, 11.
See also American Federation of Labor
and Congress of Industrial Organiza-
tions (AFL-CIO)
Consciousness-raising, 59, 174
Contra Costa Comparable Worth Task
Force, 140, 212
Contra Costa County, 3, 53; Board of Su-
pervisors, 95, 110–11, 114, 120, 122,
163; budget constraints in, 117–18,
130; career ladders in, 101; clerical activism in, 100–104, 184, 187; collective bargaining in, 114–18; comparable

Compositor:	G&S Typesetters
Text:	11/13 Caledonia
Display:	Caledonia
Printer:	Maple-Vail
Binder:	Maple-Vail